Checklist to Help You Manage Your Next Difficult Person

Awareness

- ❏ Do I understand the difference between annoying behavior and serious inappropriate behavior? (Ch2)
- ❏ Am I ready to focus on difficult behavior and NOT on personalities? (Ch2)
- ❏ Have I accidentally made myself a victim of the difficult person? (Ch1)
- ❏ Am I labeling this person and making it harder to deal with him or her? (Ch2)
- ❏ Do I understand what it means to make "difficult behavior" un-fun for the person doing it? (Ch5)
- ❏ Can I commit to a win/win attempt to solve the problem, or am I stuck trying to "get even"? (Ch12)
- ❏ Have I assessed the cost and impact of the difficult behavior for me, the work unit, and the company? (Ch1)
- ❏ Do I understand and accept the special responsibilities I have as a manager? (Ch4)

Ready for Action?

- ❏ Am I ready to listen more than talk when dealing with the difficult person? (Ch5)
- ❏ Am I working to change the language I use so it becomes more cooperative and less confrontational? (Ch25)
- ❏ Can I address the difficult person in a way that is non-blaming and aimed at problem-solving? (Ch5)
- ❏ Have I mastered the art of using empathy statements, and am I ready to use them? (Ch8)
- ❏ Have I resolved not to sink to the difficult person's level? (Ch5)
- ❏ Have I considered that the difficult person may lack the skills needed to behave more appropriately? (Ch3)
- ❏ Have I grasped the steps involved in progressive discipline before even starting to manage the difficult person? (Ch13)
- ❏ Do I understand the principles and parts of performance management? (Ch9)
- ❏ Do I understand the five different methods of managing conflict? (Ch20)
- ❏ Do I understand my legal obligations with respect to serious difficult behavior or illegal activities? (Ch13)
- ❏ Do I know the warning signs or general profiles of potentially violent people? (Ch14)

alph
boo

tear here

Agenda

- ❏ Am I using the best communication medium to get the message across? (Ch22)
- ❏ Have I prepared some positive self-talk phrases to help me keep my self-control? (Ch5)
- ❏ Before setting up a meeting with a difficult person, have I planned out how I need to approach the person so we appear to be "on the same side"? (Ch5)
- ❏ Am I prepared to set clear specific limits regarding what is acceptable or inappropriate difficult behavior? (Ch8)
- ❏ Do I ensure there is a clear agenda to try to prevent difficult people from disrupting the meeting? (Ch8)
- ❏ Am I prepared to give specific feedback, avoiding general personal comments or judgements? (Ch7)
- ❏ Am I ready to give the difficult person some control over the feedback I will be giving? (Ch7)
- ❏ If I need to mediate between two employees, do I have the necessary skills to do it well? If not, do I know where I can find a mediator to help? (Ch10)
- ❏ Have I assessed whether mediation is likely to succeed? (Ch10)

Colleagues and Bosses

- ❏ Have I done a reality check? Is my boss really impossible or just mildly annoying, and how does her behavior affect my life? (Ch16)
- ❏ When approaching the boss, am I ready to keep a positive focus and lay out the problem and its impact on things the boss thinks are important? (Ch15)
- ❏ Before addressing a problem with the boss, do I know enough about what she or he thinks is important so I can frame the issue effectively? (Ch15)
- ❏ If I choose to go to the boss's boss, have I considered carefully what can happen to me? (Ch16)
- ❏ If things go really bad with the boss, am I prepared for job searching, or am I going to be in big trouble? (Ch16)

All About Me

- ❏ Have I modeled appropriate behavior to my staff? (Ch8)
- ❏ Have I avoided the problem when it should have been addressed earlier? (Ch1)
- ❏ Have I become overly reactive to the difficult person, and are my emotional reactions interfering with managing the situation? (Ch5)
- ❏ Do I understand how to determine how difficult I am to others? (Ch23)
- ❏ Can I commit to becoming less and less difficult and work to that goal? (Ch25)

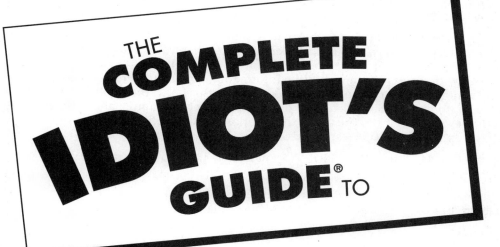

THE COMPLETE **IDIOT'S** GUIDE® TO

Dealing With Difficult Employees

Robert Bacal

alpha books

Macmillan USA, Inc.
201 West 103rd Street
Indianapolis, IN 46290

A Pearson Education Company

International Standard Book Number: 0-02-863370-9
Library of Congress Catalog Card Number: Available upon request

02 01 00   8 7 6 5 4 3 2 1

Interpretation of the printing code: The rightmost number of the first series of numbers is the year of the book's printing; the rightmost number of the second series of numbers is the number of the book's printing. For example, a printing code of 00-1 shows that the first printing occurred in 2000.

Printed in the United States of America

This is a *CWL Publishing Enterprises Book* developed for Alpha Books by CWL Publishing Enterprises, John A. Woods, President. For more information, contact CWL Publishing Enterprises, 3010 Irvington Way, Madison, WI 53713, 608-273-3710, www.cwlpub.com.

Publisher
Marie Butler-Knight

Product Manager
Phil Kitchel

Managing Editor
Cari Luna

Acquisitions Editor
Randy Ladenheim-Gil

Development Editor
Joan D. Paterson

Production Editor
Billy Fields

Copy Editor
Amy Borrelli

Illustrator
Jody P. Schaeffer

Cover Designers
Mike Freeland
Kevin Spear

Book Designers
Scott Cook and Amy Adams of DesignLab

Indexer
Tonya Heard

Layout/Proofreading
Steve Geiselman
Mary Hunt
Paula Lowell

Contents at a Glance

Part 1: You Can't Smack 'Em—Manage Them Instead   1

  1 Don't Just Sit and Suffer   3
*Recognizing that difficult people are costly in several ways
and learning to take action to manage difficult people to
reduce costs and increase benefits.*

  2 The Magical Manipulative Ways of the Difficult   17
*The importance of focusing on detecting and dealing with
difficult behavior, not on labeling people as difficult.*

  3 What Makes Difficult People Tick ... and Tick ...   31
*Understanding why people are difficult and how to use re-
inforcement to manage difficult behaviors.*

  4 Why Me, Lord, Why Me?—The Manager's Burden   43
*Realizing that difficult behavior may not be aimed at you,
recognizing how you might be contributing to behavior
problems, and reducing the damage by taking responsibility.*

  5 Keeping Your Feet on the Ground with Difficult People   53
*How to stay calm, think rationally, focus on positive out-
comes, change your self-talk, and avoid reacting in negative ways.*

Part 2: Managing Garden-Variety Employees   65

  6 Identifying the Garden-Variety Difficult Employee   67
*What you can do to manage common difficult behavior
through interpersonal skills, good communication, power
or authority, and establishing norms.*

  7 Providing Feedback to Difficult Employees   77
*How to help people understand that their behavior is diffi-
cult by letting them know, directly or indirectly, and by
giving positive feedback to reinforce good behavior.*

  8 Parrying the Difficult Thrusts   89
*Developing an approach to assess the damage caused by
difficult behavior, using empathy to better understand the
other person, and using returning responsibility and group
pressure to resolve problems.*

  9 Using Performance Management to Help   101
*How performance management, including performance
planning and ongoing communication, can be an effective
informal and formal tool for managing difficult people.*

  10 Monkey in the Middle: Mediation and Arbitration   115
*Intervening in conflicts: assessing the cost of inaction,
using mediation and arbitration.*

Part 3: Managing the Venomous Difficult Employees   **127**

11   Identifying the Venomous Difficult Employee   129
Identifying intentionally harmful behaviors and dealing with those employees to ensure a safe and healthy work environment.

12   Can You Create Win-Win with These Folks? And How!   143
How to achieve a win-win situation with difficult people: assessing your chances of success, using the right initial approach, working with skill and self-discipline, and keeping the focus on problems, not personalities.

13   I Fought the Law and ...?   155
Knowing the legalities of your situation and ensuring a safe and healthy work environment by establishing and maintaining policies, providing training, and using progressive discipline.

14   Worry About the Other Shoe Dropping—Violence   167
Ways to detect and deal with the potential for violence in the workplace.

Part 4: When the Difficult Person Is Your Boss   **181**

15   The Nutso Boss   183
How to recognize whether your boss is crazy, to understand why, and to decide whether to fight it, live with it, or get away from it.

16   Fighting Fire with Water—Your Difficult Boss Options   195
Your choices for dealing with a difficult boss, from best to worst, and ways to make your decision and go with it.

17   Silly Boss Behaviors—Specific Situations   209
Tactics for coping with bosses who steal credit for accomplishments or who make excessive demands—and realizing that sometimes you can't improve your situation.

18   Is Your Boss Doing Something Illegal?   221
What to do if your boss is breaking or bending laws or violating company policy and how to protect yourself.

Part 5: If It Wasn't for My Difficult Co-Workers   **231**

19   Difficult Colleagues   233
When the difficult people are your colleagues, ways to change your reactions and to deal with work killers, directly or indirectly, without getting personal or blaming.

20   Real Conflict and What to Do About It   249
Learn about two types of conflict, about good conflicts and conflicts that turn ugly, and five ways to address conflict.

21 Getting Help from Others, Including the Boss   263
How to build a good relationship with the boss, just in case you need some help from above, and how to involve other managers in dealing with difficult situations.

22 Knowing Your Communication Media   275
Understanding the advantages and disadvantages of the several means of communicating in the workplace, choosing the best medium for the situation, and then using it carefully for the best results.

Part 6: I Confess, I'm Difficult (Help for the Guilty)   287

23 We're All Difficult Sometimes—Are You Difficult Too Much?   289
Dealing with a harsh reality—even you can be a difficult person!—and using various means to understand how others perceive you and how you can become less difficult.

24 Getting Less Difficult—Words and Deeds   301
How to change your behavior and become less difficult and more trustworthy through greater consistency and congruence of words and actions.

25 Getting Less Difficult—The Words, Ma'am, Just the Words   311
The difference between confrontational and cooperative language—and ways to replace confrontational language with cooperative language.

Appendixes

A Glossary   325

B Additional Resources   331

Index   335

Contents

Part 1: You Can't Smack 'Em—Manage Them Instead 1

1 Don't Just Sit and Suffer 3

The Cost of Difficult People 4
 The Cost to You 4
 The Cost to Others—It's Not Just All About You 5
 Cost to the Organization 7
A Hundred and One Uses for Difficult People 8
 The Canary—Difficult but Handy 8
 Looking in the Mirror 10
Avoid Being a Victim...10
The Perils of Inaction 10
Leaping Before You Look...11
Four Reasons You Might Choose to Be a Victim 12
 Disbelief (This Can't Be Happening)......................13
 Desire to Avoid Confrontation 13
 Nobody Wants to Be the Bad Guy 14
 Fight or Flight 15
You Can Do Something—You Must Do Something 15

2 The Magical Manipulative Ways of the Difficult 17

It's Not the Difficult People, It's the Difficult Behavior 18
 How Labeling People as Difficult Causes Problems 18
 An Alternative—Focus on Behavior........................19
At Every Desk a Difficult Person (Sometimes) 21
It Takes Two 21
The Various Manipulative Techniques of the Difficult......23
 Direct Work-Related Difficult Behavior 24
 Attacks on You, the Manager 24
 Difficult Interpersonal Behavior 25
 Back-Channel Guerrilla Work.............................26
Chronic Versus Occasional Difficult Behavior 26
How Does Knowing All This Help?.............................28

3 What Makes Difficult People Tick ... and Tick ... 31

You Don't Need to Be a Shrink 31
Are They Just Screwed Up? *32*
It's About What People Have Learned..............................*33*
It's Also About Skill *34*
It's Also About Emotion *35*
What Are Difficult People After?..37
Sense of Control *37*
Straw That Stirs the Drink *38*
I'm Not Much So I Have a Lot to Prove....................*39*
A Reaction ... I Need A Reaction *39*
Weird Biology, Weird Science *39*
How Does Knowing All This Help? 40

4 Why Me, Lord, Why Me?—The Manager's Burden 43

It's Probably not Personal 43
... But It Might Be You..45
Identifying If It Is You *46*
It's Your Choice to Change *47*
The Manager's Extra Burden 48
Responsibility for Your Work Unit's Productivity *48*
Responsibility for Staff Welfare..............................*49*
Responsibility for Mediation *50*
It's in Your Self-Interest 50

5 Keeping Your Feet on the Ground with Difficult People 53

It Isn't Going to Work with Me...54
Blaming and Problem Solving—the Difference 55
Avoid the Lowest Common Denominator 57
Slow Down Your Talk and Responses *58*
Listen and Paraphrase *59*
Call Time-Out *59*
What You Focus on You Get More Of................................59
Think Big Picture—Think Long Term 60
Using Self-Talk to Stay Balanced 61
Negative, Nonconstructive Self-Talk *61*
Positive Constructive Self-Talk *62*

Part 2: Managing Garden–Variety Employees   65

6 Identifying the Garden–Variety Difficult Employee   67

Identifying the Difficult Employee 67
The Hidden Costs of the Garden-Variety
  Difficult Employee 69
Take Action to Prevent Worsening Behavior 70
  Your Interpersonal Tools 70
Formal Authority Tools 71
  So, You Think You Really Have Power? 72
  So When Is the Use of Authority Warranted? 73
Preventative Tools 74
  Creating Norms 74
  The Power of Norm Creation 75

7 Providing Feedback to Difficult Employees   77

Feedback—a Major Tool for Change 78
The Different Faces of Feedback 79
  Two Feedback Dimensions: Factual and Emotional 79
  Sources of Feedback 81
Feedback Strategies 81
  Direct Feedback 82
  Facilitating Feedback from Others 82
  Cueing Attention on Task Feedback 84
Giving Feedback That Gets Positive Results 85
  Feedback That's Somewhat Controlled by Recipient 85
  No Overload 86
  Feedback Should Be Specific and Refer to Behavior 86
  Balance Positive and Negative 86
  Frame the Feedback 87
  Recap Together 87

8 Parrying the Difficult Thrusts   89

Have Some Cheese with the Whine 89
  Beginning the Process 90
  Empathy Responses 91
  Returning Responsibility 91

Personal Attacks 92

Private Attacks *93*

Assertive Limit Setting *93*

Public Attacks *94*

Dealing With Minor Back-Channel Problems 94

Modeling Behavior *95*

Mobilizing Group Pressure *95*

Skill Building *96*

The Work and Responsibility Avoider.......................96

The Meeting Disrupter.......................................97

The Naysayer 98

9 Using Performance Management to Help   101

Performance Management Isn't What You Think 101

What Performance Management Isn't...................*103*

The Links Between Performance Management and

Managing Difficult People *103*

The Important Parts of Performance Management 104

Performance Planning *104*

Ongoing Performance Communication *106*

Documentation, Data Gathering, and Diagnosis................*107*

The Performance Review...................................*108*

Using Performance Management to Solve Performance
Difficulties and Soft Problems 109

Addressing the Productivity Issue *109*

Addressing the Softer Team Issues........................*110*

**10 Monkey in the Middle: Mediation
and Arbitration   115**

Deciding When to Step In—Whose Banana Is It? 116

Mediation—What Is It? When Does It Fit?....................117

When Is Mediation Likely to Work? *118*

Deciding to Mediate *118*

Hold Preliminary Meetings 120

Logistics and Establishing Context for
Three-Way Meetings 121

The Process..121

Working to the Breakthrough *122*

Tasks and Roles of the Manager-as-Mediator *122*

Framing Agreements and Following Up....................*124*

Arbitration, or When Someone Just Has to Decide 124
Arbitration Tips *125*
Mediation Versus Arbitration *126*

Part 3: Managing the Venomous Difficult Employee 127

11 Indentifying the Venomous Difficult Employee 129

What Separates Venomous from Garden Variety 130
Why the Venomous Employee Is So Dangerous.............131
Techniques of the Viper...133
Abuse and Personal Attacks *133*
Outright Sabotage *136*
Backroom Politicking and String Pulling *138*
The Pinocchio Problem.......................................*139*
Tying Up the Venomous Person in a Nice Pink Bow 141

12 Can You Create Win-Win with These Folks? And How! 143

Is Win-Win Possible with the Venomous? 144
Disadvantages of Win-Win Attempts *146*
So Is It Possible? Is It Worth It? *147*
Win-Win—Breaking Through with the Approach 147
Looking Under the Rock—Figuring Out What's
Going On 150
Your Turn—Presenting Where You Are 151
Collaborative Problem Solving 152
The End Game—Commitment and Follow-Up 152

13 I Fought The Law and ...? 155

The Legal Swamp...156
Layer upon Layer of Law *156*
How the Law Really Works *158*
Disciplinary Issues—Do You Have Protection? 158
The Disciplinary Prophylactic 160
Oral Warning..*160*
Formal Oral Warning with Documentation *161*
Written Warning *161*

Final Warning *162*
Termination *162*
Hey, You Have Another Legal Responsibility 163
Is There Any Good News Here? 165

**14 Worry About the Other Shoe Dropping—
Violence   167**

View from the Bridge—Some Background on Violence ..168
Violence, Disciplinary Action, and Dismissal 169
Preventive Measures and Dismissal *170*
Other Tips *172*
Is Workplace Violence Predictable? 174
Personal Indicators *175*
Workplace Behavior *176*
Obsessions *176*
Action Changes and Behavior *176*
Preventative Steps for All Workplace Violence 177
Corporate Initiatives *177*
Initiatives You Can Take *178*

Part 4: When the Difficult Person Is Your Boss   181

15 The Nutso Boss   183

Some Bosses Really Are Nuts 184
Jelly-Fished Out *184*
Egomaniac Puppeteer *185*
The Substance Abuser *185*
The Paranoid Empire Builder *185*
The Totally Incompetent Nice Addict *186*
Tricks to Survive a Nutty Boss 186
Get Connected *187*
Conduct Business Publicly *189*
The Written Word Is Gold *189*
Get Small, Get Invisible, Be Sneaky *189*
Developing a Productive Mind-set 190
Focus on the Work *190*
Don't Expect Squat *191*
Be Prepared for Surprises *191*
Explore Alternatives *191*

So You Want to Try Getting Through to Your Boss? 191

What Drives Your Boss?..*192*

Link Your Goals to the Boss's Problems...........................*192*

Do the Pitch...*193*

16 Fighting Fire with Water—Your Difficult-Boss Options 195

Consider the Consequences 195

Start with the Effects and Outcomes *196*

What's Your Personal Situation?......................................*198*

What Are Your Options? 199

Quitting Immediately 199

Laying Down the Groundwork for Leaving *200*

Laying Down an Ultimatum..*202*

Appeals *203*

Appeals to the Boss's Boss *203*

Appeals to the Human Resource Department....................*204*

Getting Sneaky *205*

Working It Out..206

Living With It 207

Wrapping It Up 208

17 Silly Boss Behaviors—Specific Situations 209

The Credit-Stealing Boss 209

Mary's First Step: Some Objective Thinking.....................*210*

Trying to Work It Out..*211*

Turning Up the Heat *213*

Last Resorts *213*

The Unreasonable-Demands Boss 214

Let's Put You in the Driver's Seat *214*

The Pitch *216*

Your Other "Working with" Options *217*

If None of That Works *217*

A Sobering Thought..218

18 Is Your Boss Doing Something Illegal? 221

Clearly Illegal Acts *221*

Rumor Versus Fact *222*

Three Options *223*

Ignoring It *223*

Try Company Channels 224
The Long Arm of the Law 226
How to Pass Along Information 226
Gray-Area Illegal Acts 227
When the Boss Violates Policy 229

Part 5: If It Wasn't for My Difficult Co-Workers   231

19 Difficult Colleagues   233

The Annoying and Frustrating 233
It's Your Annoyance.......................................234
OK, Wise Guy, How Do I Change My Perceptions? 236
The Work Killers 238
The Resource Hog 239
Just Insensitive..241
No-Fault Teflon Co-workers 243
Backstabbers and Gossips................................243
The Authority Underminers 245
The Turf Warriors 246

20 Real Conflict and What to Do About It   249

Two Kinds of Conflicts 249
Substantive Conflict..250
Personalized Conflict 250
Is Conflict Always Bad? 251
Conflict: The Good..251
Conflict: The Bad..252
Conflict: The Ugly 253
Five Different Ways to Manage Conflict............254
1: Avoidance and/or Denial 254
2: Giving In or Yielding 256
3: Compromise: Give a Little, Take a Little........257
4: Competition or Power-Based........................258
5: Collaborative Win-Win Method 259

21 Getting Help from Others, Including the Boss   263

Boss Cultivation—The Long Approach 263
Boss-Cultivation Principles 264

When to Involve the Boss 266
Approaching Smart—Involving Smart 267
   The Approach Process..267
   Smart Involvement 269
Help from Other Sources 270
Knowing When You Are in Big Trouble 271

22   Knowing Your Communication Media   275

How Communication Media Differ 276
   Speed of Communication 276
   Interactivity of Communication 277
   Spontaneity and Formality 278
Face-to-Face and Telephone Communication 278
Written Communication 280
E-mail Communication—A Brave New World 281
Things You Need to Know About E-mail 282
   The Paperless Message 282
   "I Really Didn't Mean It" 283
   "It's Lost in My To-Be-Read File" 283
   Not for Your Eyes Only..284
   Some E-mail Tips 284

Part 6: I Confess, I'm Difficult (Help for the Guilty)   287

23   We're All Difficult Sometimes—Are You Difficult Too Much?   289

Why It's So Hard to See Our Own Difficult Behavior......289
Why Looking at Yourself Is So Important.....................291
Some Difficulty Indicators..292
Sometimes You Just Have to Ask..................................294
   Informal Feedback 294
   More Formal Ways to Get Feedback 297

24   Getting Less Difficult—Words and Deeds   301

Getting Back to Behavior—the Starting Block 301
How People Come to See You as Difficult 302
   Are You Trustworthy?..303

Wanna Be More Consistent and Congruent? 306
Change How You Promise or Commit 306
Review Your Decision Making 307
What About Your Demeanor and Management
  Approach? 308
How to Become More Congruent 309

**25 Getting Less Difficult—The Words, Ma'am,
Just the Words   311**

What's Your Style? 311
Cooperative Language 312
Confrontational Language 312
What's Their Problem? 313
Lack of Listening/Understanding 313
"Less-than" Communication 314
Communicating Mistrust 315
Violation of Conversation Rules 316
Blatant Generalizations 316
Power/Status-Based Communication 317
Replacing Confrontational Language with
Cooperative Language 317
Move from Power to Cooperation 317
Get Rid of the Mistrust Stuff 319
Shed Blatant Generalizations 320
Lose Phrases that Cause Defensiveness 320
More Fixing Up 321
Infallibility Breeds Contempt 321
Hints for Improving at Cooperative Communication 322

Appendixes

A Glossary   325

B Additional Resources   331

Index   335

Foreword

No doubt about it. The ability to simplify is not only a wonderful talent of those who can do it, it's a precious gift for those who benefit. This book qualifies on both counts. Robert Bacal simplifies dealing with difficult employees and will help you do the same.

Bacal has taken a problem faced by every manager, separated it into its component parts, explained the consequences of bad decisions, and, best of all, given scores of real-life "What should I do now?" recommendations.

My favorite chapter focuses on performance management. The reason—performance management provides several tools managers can use to help people appreciate that their difficult behavior is causing problems and gives them ways to change that behavior.

To underscore the book's concentration on simplicity and practicality, each chapter ends with the bottom line summary, "The Least You Need to Know." I like that! Almost all business books could improve if they would encapsulate each chapter like that.

There are many ways to benefit, both directly and indirectly, from this book. First, readers will likely think of difficult people they must deal with immediately. My guess is that most readers will be tempted to actually write the names of those people in the margins as they read. That's not a bad idea because it will force a thought process that will help you apply the principles covered to the real-life situations you face as a manager. When the same name gets written in the margin several times, you know that's a person you really have to deal with. This book gives you the know-how to do just that.

When I think back on situations that required me to work with people who were making my life miserable, I wish I had had this book.

Ted, for example, tried his very best every day in every way to make me feel inferior. I tried my best to avoid a confrontation and usually did. But oh, how I wish I could have read Chapter 12, "Can You Create Win-Win with These Folks? And How!" at the time.

As a manager, when I got caught in the crossfire during a civil war between two or more employees, I usually tried to settle it myself. Looking back, my success record was mediocre at best. Why didn't I consider the benefits of a neutral mediator? Too proud? Afraid of admitting a weakness? Definitely! Now I can understand the value of such help, as explained in Chapter 10, "Monkey in the Middle: Mediation and Arbitration."

Be forewarned. This book is for those who are serious about managing more effectively. It is not light, puffy, cutesy stuff to read that may give you a laugh but not much help. Therein lies its value. It's easy to read, but it's real-world all the way. From learning how to handle manipulators to feedback strategies, to understanding personal attacks to sabotage, to backroom politicking to dealing with a nutso boss—it's all here! My conclusion—much good will come from this book.

Roger Fritz

Founder and President, Organization Development Consultants and best-selling author of 34 management and business books.

Web site: www.rogerfritz.com

Introduction

You can choose your spouse (but not your children). You can choose your friends. But you don't always have the option of choosing who you work with, your boss, or your employees.

We all find ourselves dealing with "difficult" people at work. And, boy, the versatility of difficult people is amazing. From foot-dragging, to whining and complaining, to sabotage and unreasonable bosses, difficult people seem to have an uncanny ability to make life miserable.

Mostly, they aren't bad people. In fact, they are probably more similar to you than you might imagine. Most difficult behavior is of the garden-variety type. Annoying, frustrating, and a nuisance, it's behavior that you and I and most people use at one time or another. We're all difficult sometimes.

Except, of course, for the more serious difficult people who ARE bad people. These folks seem to dedicate their lives to being consistent pains in the behind. I hope you don't have any of those!

I've worked in the field of verbal abuse and difficult people for over 10 years now, offering seminars and writing on the topic. I've had a chance to talk to thousands of people, just like you, who have to contend with people they find difficult. So this book, while containing many of my ideas, also contains the input of many of those thousands who have come up with good, practical ways of coping … no, that's not right … succeeding with difficult employees, coworkers, bosses, and customers.

In writing this book, I tried to do two things. First, I want to help you understand what difficult people are about and why they do what they do. That's important for creating a positive mind-set so you can manage difficult situations and not become a victim of them yourself. The second goal is to help you figure out what to do. Much of difficult behavior can be counterbalanced. In fact, by learning to manage it, you may very well be able to reduce or even eliminate it. When you refuse to play the difficult person's game, it becomes no fun anymore, and he or she will move on to find another victim or just give up the game completely.

How to Use This Book

We divided this book into six sections. Each has a slightly different focus, but I recommend that you read all the chapters. My suggestion is that you don't read too much at one sitting, since you can get overwhelmed. Read a few chapters at a time. Think about them for a day or two. Use some of the techniques to manage the difficult, then read a few more chapters.

Here's how the book is set up.

Part 1, "You Can't Smack 'Em—Manage Them Instead," helps you understand why difficult people seem so difficult, and what they are after. We'll outline some of the techniques of the difficult. And we'll explain why it's so important to manage them to minimize stress, misery, and loss of productivity.

Part 2, "Managing Garden-Variety Employees," helps you understand the minor forms of difficult behavior that employees use. We'll give you some techniques you can use to manage these situations—in fact, nip them in the bud. We'll talk about the naysayer, the work-avoider, and a few more common employee quirks.

Part 3, "Managing the Venomous Difficult Employees," looks at the more serious difficult behaviors that occur in the workplace. For example, how do you deal with verbal abuse, or outright sabotage? We'll talk about those.

Part 4, "When the Difficult Person Is Your Boss," addresses a different situation. What do you do if your boss is impossible, nasty, rude, or makes unreasonable demands on you and your staff? Clearly we have to tread more carefully here because, unlike situations with employees, your boss has more power than you.

Part 5, "If It Wasn't for My Difficult Co-Workers," shifts the focus to co-workers. They aren't below you in the hierarchy or above you, so they have about the same amount of formal power—but they can get in the way something terrible. We'll talk about different methods for managing co-worker conflict. We'll talk about more desperate techniques you can use. And we'll explain how some techniques (mostly sneaky ones) can backfire.

Part 6, "I Confess, I'm Difficult (Help for the Guilty)," addresses a fundamental issue: YOU and your own difficult behavior. Because it takes two to create difficult situations in the workplace, your behavior and your attitudes play critical roles in determining what happens to you. All of us can stand some work in this are, and here's a little secret. The less difficult you are, the less you will create difficult behavior in those around you. And the best bonus is that if you are perceived as not difficult, you are much more likely to advance your career!

Extras

We've tried to pull out the key ideas, hints, tips, and warnings so they are easy to find. Most pages will have little sidebars containing important information about the topic on that page. These are great for helping you figure out what's most important as you're reading, but they're also a big help after you've finished and want a little refresher.

Employee Handbook

This sidebar expands the definition of terms used in person-to-person interactions in the office environment.

From the Manager's Desk

Here you'll find useful tips to help your awareness of underlying causes of difficult situations.

This Won't Work!

This sidebar tells you how to avoid saying or doing something that might escalate conflict.

Insider Secrets

This sidebar gives the manager's viewpoint of why certain behaviors work—or why they don't.

Also, at the back of the book you'll find a listing of other resources related to difficult people. With increased accessibility to the Internet, you can research some really neat stuff. We've identified a number of free resources on related topics that you can visit on the Net. Perhaps most fun and useful of all, though, is the information about online e-mail discussion groups on conflict, communication, performance management and appraisal, and managing difficult people. All you need is a connection to the Internet and some way to send and receive e-mail. Then you can talk with thousands of other people interested in these topics, both experts and others struggling with the same problems you are. It's all free, and a great way to get advice. And, of course, that's the best way to contact me, because I'm there, too. Or you can write me at rbacal@escape.ca.

Acknowledgments

Special thanks to my wife, Nancy, for putting up with the grouchy, semi-crazed person I became during the grueling process of creating this book. And to the cats, Moondance, Tobin, and Griffey, who prevented me from overworking by sitting on my keyboard as required.

A special thanks goes to Dan Dana of Mediation Training Institute International, who was a gracious helper in assembling the material on mediation processes.

And a thank you to the thousands of people I have taught in seminars and who have also taught me. And thanks to the people on the Internet who have allowed me to bounce ideas around.

Also thanks to John Woods of CWL Publishing Enterprises, who suggested I write this and worked with me to complete it faster than he thought possible. Bob Magnan, also of CWL, worked with me to develop the glossary. Joan Paterson served as development editor, and copy editor Amy Borrelli helped us turn a manuscript into the polished final book you're now reading.

Trademarks

All terms mentioned in this book that are known to be or are suspected of being trademarks or service marks have been appropriately capitalized. Alpha Books and Macmillan USA, Inc., cannot attest to the accuracy of this information. Use of a term in this book should not be regarded as affecting the validity of any trademark or service mark.

Part 1

You Can't Smack 'Em—Manage Them Instead

Is there a manager alive who doesn't have to deal regularly with difficult people? Probably not. It goes with the territory, and as the saying goes, "That's why they pay you the big bucks. "Difficult people eat up your time, slow down work, and erode productivity. But perhaps as important, they create huge amounts of stress for you and other people in the workplace.

You aren't helpless though, unless you allow yourself to be. You may not be able to smack them or get rid of them, but you can indeed manage difficult people and ensure you don't become a victim. We'll begin by looking at the cost of difficult people, what makes them tick, and the importance of accepting your responsibility to address difficult people in your workplace.

Chapter 1

Don't Just Sit and Suffer

> ## In This Chapter
>
> ➤ How difficult people cost sanity and productivity
>
> ➤ Difficult people can be useful, too
>
> ➤ Avoid becoming a victim of difficult people
>
> ➤ Why you can't just do nothing

Let's do a little head count. Think of all the people you work with. How many of them do you consider "difficult"? If you are like most people, there's at least one particular person that comes to mind: "Yes, John, definitely John is a pain in the neck." If you've been well cursed, maybe Mary is difficult, too. Working with one or even two difficult people is bad enough. But it gets even worse. Now think. How many people around you are difficult *sometimes*? What? Is your answer most of them? If so, you're normal, completely normal. Difficult people and the sometimes difficult are all over the place. None of us is perfect, and all of us are difficult at times to someone. Psst! That means even you.

Unfortunately, difficult people cost us a lot. Yes, they cost money in terms of lost time and productivity. But perhaps more importantly, they cause you to lose your mind … or feel like it, anyway. It's easy to become a victim of difficult people, and even to become difficult oneself as a result. It's easy to fall into victimhood, to suffer the slings and arrows of the difficult, but you can do something. You can keep your sanity and increase productivity by managing difficult people so the damage they cause is reduced. And when the stars are in proper alignment, you may even be able to turn their negative behavior into constructive, useful behavior.

In this chapter we'll look at the costs of difficult people and explain what you can do so you don't become a victim. You need not end up in a fetal position muttering to yourself at the end of the working day!

The Cost of Difficult People

Let's face it. Most of us try very hard to avoid managing *difficult people.* Somehow we believe that, left to their own devices, they will "smarten up" or "grow up," or if we're really lucky, simply quit or go away. It rarely works that way. Still, if you want to be able to work with the difficult folks, you need to know *why* you must manage their behavior. And that means understanding the toll difficult people exact from everyone around them. Let's start with the most important person here: you. After all, if you don't see a personal benefit to being proactive in dealing with that difficult person, why would you put the time and energy into trying to turn around a difficult situation?

Employee Handbook

A **difficult person** is someone whom you or others do not like to interact with, due to his or her stubbornness, abusiveness, or other irksome behavior. Difficult people get in your way.

The Cost to You

Since you are reading this book, you obviously have a very personal interest in managing difficult people. So, let's start by talking about how a difficult person affects you.

First, let's talk about your mental and physical health. OK, you aren't likely to go loony on us because of a difficult person (although it has been known to happen). Unfortunately, it only takes one very difficult person to affect your enjoyment of your job, your stress level, and your ability to do your work.

That's serious. If you have an extremely difficult employee, co-worker, or boss, each time you deal with his or her difficult actions, your heart rate goes up, your blood pressure escalates, and all manner of other unpleasant things happen inside your body. That's not healthy. Difficult people can make you feel like crap.

Do you leave work muttering to yourself about what John the Difficult or Mary the Naysayer did today? How about Bob the Backroom Politicker? Difficult people not only intrude upon your workday, but can also follow you to your car, get in the passenger side, and drive home with you. If they are really bad, they can even climb into bed with you, snoring their difficult snores, keeping you up all night.

Not only do difficult people have a nasty effect on your physical and mental health, but they also cost you in terms of being able to do your own job properly. If you spend time everyday fixing the damage done by a difficult person, you are not doing the other things you need to do as part of your job. That can make you look bad to your boss. At minimum, losing time to difficult people is frustrating.

Insider Secrets

According to the U.S. Bureau of Labor Statistics, in 1997 about two-thirds of stress-related work absences occurred in white-collar occupations (for example, management, technical, or sales positions). Of course, other employees also can suffer stress reactions, too. While stress is caused by a number of factors like overwork, tight deadlines, and personal/family problems, underlying most workplace stress you will find a common thread—difficult people. By building good relationships with people who seem difficult, you can reduce your own work stress and the symptoms associated with it. And, you become more effective in addressing problems like unreasonable deadlines, or impossible expectations.

Convinced yet that you need to reduce the costs of difficult people? Here's a list of costs you pay personally to the difficult person. Difficult people often …

➤ adversely affect your mental health.

➤ adversely affect your physical health.

➤ reduce your enjoyment of your job.

➤ make you look bad as a manager or employee.

➤ suck time out of your busy day.

➤ interfere with promotions or pay increases.

As someone once said, "It ain't pretty."

The Cost to Others—It's Not Just All About You

Some people are extraordinarily tolerant of the pain and suffering difficult people can inflict on them personally. These amazing folks are able to shrug off the stress of difficult people without experiencing physical or mental damage. If you are one of these, I congratulate you, but that doesn't absolve you from managing difficult people.

That's because it isn't just about you. Imagine what happens when you throw a rock into a quiet lake. When the rock hits, it creates a set of circles or ripples in the water that move farther and farther out. As a manager or supervisor, you are at the center of the disruption. But the ripples go beyond you. They carry out further and further in the water. That's how difficult people affect not just you as a manager, but many others in the organization. In severe cases, those ripples hit other employees with whom the difficult person comes in contact. Not only does a difficult person affect those in immediate contact, but the more difficult a person, the more those ripples affect others—customers, people in the human resources department, and even other department staff members who don't have immediate contact with the difficult person.

What's the worst part? Those little ripples aren't really little. They can hit people like huge tsunami ... even people who don't have to deal with the difficult person directly.

This Won't Work!

A common mistake made by managers is to ignore how a difficult person affects others. A difficult person might get along fine with the boss, but not fine with co-workers or customers.

Let's make this more concrete. Noah, the Prophet of Doom, works for you. At meetings, whenever an idea is suggested, Noah is the first to tell everyone why it won't work, and why he knows best. If left unchecked, what do you think will happen? Well, people aren't stupid. Eventually, they tire of having their ideas and their heads bashed with a two-by-four and stop suggesting ideas. The source of new ideas dries up. No new products. No new services. No new improvements. No business!

Apart from the business side, Noah and his dire predictions depress co-workers and others around him.

Regardless of the difficult person's particular style of being difficult, he or she can have a profound effect on others. For example, difficult people affect others by ...

➤ reducing enjoyment of their work.

➤ wasting large amounts of their time.

➤ reducing their productivity and job satisfaction.

➤ causing them to consider resigning and moving on.

➤ eating up huge amounts of time in meetings.

➤ damaging relationships with customers.

➤ turning other people into difficult people.

The last point deserves a bit more discussion. If you have a single difficult employee, don't believe that only that person's behavior is at stake here. A difficult person is contagious. Yes, being difficult is catchy.

I once worked with a person who was extremely difficult. Let's call her Donna to protect the guilty. While very smart, she had little ability to work with people, and wherever she went she was followed by a little black cloud. Her blunt rudeness, tendency to interrupt, and general "Queen-of-the-Empire" attitude made people mad or just drove them nuts. Her manager probably spent literally hundreds of hours fixing up things that went sour due to Donna's attitude.

The people around her were generally easygoing and interacted well with each other. However, after years of dealing with her behavior, even the easygoing employees started acting difficult, both to Donna and even to each other. That happened for two reasons. First, Donna set a tone of incivility in the workplace. People felt they must eat or be eaten, and adjusted their actions accordingly. Secondly, Donna affected almost everyone everyday, and people just got frustrated. That frustration spilled over into their interactions with others. In the end, the office was overflowing with difficult people.

From the Manager's Desk

No single thing makes a difficult person "difficult." To red flag a difficult person so you can take action, look at the pattern of behavior the person shows and look at how they affect you, co-workers, customers, and others.

So, Donna—and difficult people in general—don't just affect their bosses or one or two people. They affect many, many people around them. Left to their own devices, they can bring real work to a virtual halt, cause good employees to quit and generally make the office a lousy place to be.

Cost to the Organization

By now you've probably realized that when a difficult person is making your life miserable and making the lives of other employees miserable, that person is also costing the company a lot of time, energy, and money.

The truth is that companies damaged heavily by difficult people are operating on one or two cylinders. In today's competitive marketplace, that can be serious indeed. Companies need to innovate, need to have their employees work together, and need to maximize the resources they have, not have people milling around at the watercooler cursing each other out. Difficult employees can affect companies by ...

This Won't Work!

When difficult people are allowed to run amok, without management intervention, other employees lose faith in management and the company.

➤ causing good employees to leave.

➤ reducing productivity.

➤ reducing the generation of good ideas.

➤ reducing morale and commitment.

➤ making management look stupid or neglectful.

All of these impact the bottom line. So at this point, let's take a moment to remember that our own jobs depend on the continued existence of our companies. A company crippled by difficult people may not be long for this world. And as our company goes, so go our own jobs.

Now, here's the kicker. While difficult people often cost the manager, co-workers, and the company in terms of mental health, productivity, and so on, it doesn't have to be that way. The key here is that difficult people must be managed, not ignored. That's the only way to avoid or prevent incurring the costs I've outlined.

A Hundred and One Uses for Difficult People

I've explained the costs associated with difficult people at work, but there's a tiny spot of sunlight we don't want to miss. Difficult people can be valuable. There may not be exactly 101 uses for them, but there are at least two.

The Canary—Difficult but Handy

Difficult people can serve as canaries in a mine. In the old days, miners used to bring birds down in the mines with them because they were more sensitive to poisonous gases than human beings. The birds would … well … die before the level of the gases killed all the miners. When the birds either started squawking or keeled over, it was time to fix the problem, and fast!

Difficult people, amidst all the muck they stir up, may be a bit more sensitive (usually overly so) to important things occurring in the workplace that need to be addressed. While the way they say things may be a pain, what they have to say may be helpful and even important.

Remind yourself that difficult people are not necessarily stupid or incompetent. Sometimes they may appear so, but many difficult people are highly educated and quite talented. It's just that their interpersonal skills are impaired.

From the Manager's Desk

The key to getting something positive from a difficult person is to learn how to separate what they have to say from the way they say it. Even difficult people have insight. Learn to listen to the words first, not the tone.

Insider Secrets

I often do straw polls and ask people which professionals are the "most difficult" to deal with. The results are in. Survey says: Number 1 most difficult group—teachers. Number 2—lawyers. Third on the list of infamy—doctors. All are highly educated, often talented, and bright individuals. Why are they perceived as the most difficult? Two reasons. First, both teachers and lawyers (less so doctors) make a living based on their communication abilities. So they have developed ways of pressuring or manipulating people that others have not. They have more ways of being difficult. Second, all three groups are used to having people obey their wishes. Sometimes they carry that expectation into non-professional situations.

Here's an example.

> Sam, an engineer, lacks tact and is prone to rather intense ways of communicating. You know the type. Dramatic, even melodramatic, Sam doesn't pull his punches (or kicks, gouges, and other illegal moves). At a meeting where building construction is being discussed, Sam gets up, ranting and raving about the instability of the structure and the dangers and how the company is going to heck in a handbasket, and on and on.

What if he's right? Sam is a good engineer—in fact, one of the best. His approach, difficult and perhaps abusive, makes it hard for others to hear. But the company and those at the meeting better hear it.

Being difficult doesn't mean the person is useless. It means that it's harder to hear the content of what is said.

Managing the difficult person means getting the best out of them despite their flaws. That's important. If we ignored or fired people whenever they became difficult, we would have a whole lot of empty office buildings.

Getting the best from difficult people involves managing them, not ignoring them. It means separating the content from their tone and difficult ways.

Looking in the Mirror

There's a second use for difficult people. Because difficult people lack some or many of the social graces and courtesies the rest of us have, they say things that have the power to provoke us to look in the mirror and see ourselves in different ways. That allows us to change and improve.

In other words, they say things others won't. They provide a mirror to look at ourselves in ways we might otherwise miss. Of course, that's only if they have some useful insights and if we can stand to be around them long enough to actually listen.

Still, though, a difficult person can be of value provided the costs associated aren't too high and we are prepared to listen and filter through the static.

Again, we come back to the importance of managing difficult people to enhance their value and reduce their destructiveness.

Avoid Being a Victim

Here's a circle for you. To manage a difficult person, it is absolutely essential that you avoid becoming a victim of that person. However, to avoid becoming a victim, guess what you need to do? Manage the situation and the person.

Employee Handbook

Victim mentality refers to a state of mind, often a feeling of helplessness, that ends up attracting difficult people and behaviors.

True victimhood comes from adopting a *victim mentality*. That means allowing the difficult person to push you and pull you emotionally. It may also mean that the true victim becomes an unwitting accomplice to the difficult person by encouraging the difficult person to open up with guns blazing.

It's really simple. The more you permit a person to get under your skin, the more you get stuck in the victim role. The more you get stuck, the less able you are to fix the problem. And so you become more and more of a victim.

How, exactly, do people end up trapped in a victim mentality? There are two ways. One is to avoid dealing with a difficult person, to gut it out without being proactive. The second is to act too quickly, the leap-before-you-look syndrome.

The Perils of Inaction

Don't feel bad about yourself if you are prone to inaction when faced with difficult people. You are like the rest of us. We all avoid dealing with difficult situations and difficult people at one time or another.

While it may be perfectly normal to choose inaction over taking control of the situation, it isn't useful to you or other people who interact with the difficult person. Here's why.

Difficult people thrive when others tolerate their difficult behavior. That's because somehow or other, the difficult person feels rewarded in some odd ways; in fact, that's one reason why they are difficult. They haven't caught on that it's more re-warding to behave nicely than to be difficult. And they aren't going to catch on unless they get some help.

This Won't Work!

Most of us wait too long to deal with a difficult person. It's normal, but delaying allows a conflict situation to escalate, sometimes beyond the point of repair.

Doing nothing isn't going to change anything. In fact, one of the major issues with difficult people is that doing nothing makes them more difficult over time.

The more you do nothing, the worse they get. The worse they get, the bigger the problem and the more likely you will try to avoid facing the problem. There are those circles again!

Where does all this lead? If you do nothing long enough, you can enter the chronic "Kick Me, I'm Easy" Club. If that doesn't suit you, you can join the "Hello, I'm a Perpetual Victim" Fraternal Association. While you are attending meetings of those organizations, the difficult person is wreaking havoc, not only with your life, but the lives of everyone around them.

Inaction isn't the solution. Just taking action isn't enough, either. It has to be the right action.

Leaping Before You Look

Inaction isn't the only fast track to victimhood. There is another risk. Most of us, when faced with a difficult person, get frustrated at their antics, even angry. After all, who likes to feel manipulated, bullied, pushed, and pulled? Nobody.

I certainly understand if your first reaction or desire with respect to difficult people is to put them in their place or to do anything just to beat them. Again, that's normal. But while it may be normal, it can put you in a worse position in terms of dealing with that difficult person. In fact, it may actually invite the difficult person to become more difficult.

Let's say you're at a meeting having a heated discussion with Marianne, who is being completely unreasonable and rude in her remarks. She comments in a sneaky way about "how some people at the meeting behave like hypocrites." That's nasty. You leap in with your own tirade to let her know that you won't stand for such comments, and that she should have the guts to be specific if she is going to make accusations.

What do you think will happen? Do you think Marianne will tender a public apology and behave more appropriately? Or is it more likely she will turn up the heat on the burner, with you firmly placed in the center? If you chose the latter, you are correct.

Few difficult people react well to this form of outright confrontation. As a result of your immediate leap into the fray, you are almost guaranteed to receive more abuse.

That's the core of victimhood. When we add fuel to a fire, we make a bigger fire.

Almost always our first gut response to difficult people is one that is going to increase the likelihood we will be victimized again, perhaps to a greater degree than before.

It's really important that you understand that both in-action and overly quick action contribute to the increase of abuse from difficult people.

Here are a few of the kinds of things you must avoid if you want to succeed in managing difficult people:

> **From the Manager's Desk**
>
> Acting without thinking, the old knee-jerk reaction, is the other fast track to victimhood. Apply Grandma's rule: When you feel a nasty or aggressive response coming from your gut, count to 10 before saying anything.

➤ Responding to personal attacks with personal attacks

➤ Trying to win rather than addressing the issue

➤ Trying to shut down discussion too fast

➤ Becoming difficult yourself

> **This Won't Work!**
>
> If you lack self-awareness of your own reactions and why they occur, you are not likely to be able to deal well with difficult people. Oddly, the first step in learning to deal with the difficult is to examine yourself.

Four Reasons You Might Choose to Be a Victim

OK, hands up out there. How many of you have chosen not to take action with a difficult person when you should have? How many of you have reacted to a difficult person in an angry or nonconstructive way? You with the book in your hand—why isn't your hand up?

Everyone has done both of these things at some point or another. There's no shame in that. However if you consistently repeat the same mistakes over and over and end up paying the cost by becoming a victim, that's not a good thing.

So, why do you do it? And why is it important to know the reason? Because if you don't know what it is about difficult people that causes you to make poor decisions, it isn't likely you will be able to change. If you don't change, you are going to be a consistent victim.

There are four main reasons that people make bad decisions, avoid taking action, or take the wrong actions. The first three have to do with avoidance, while the final one is a biological reason that has to do with our initial gut reactions to difficult people and our feelings of threat. Let's look at these one by one.

It's important that you look at yourself to identify which of the four (or perhaps all four) reasons are relevant to you. If you become more aware of the reasons why you sometimes choose victimhood, you will be better prepared to make better, more rational decisions.

Disbelief (This Can't Be Happening)

Ever been in a situation where you've said to yourself, "I can't believe she said that"? Probably. One reason we fail to take action with difficult people is we don't expect them to be difficult. Most normal people don't go through life looking for trouble from others. When trouble arises unexpectedly, or someone's behavior is simply outrageous, we have a tendency to freeze, like a deer caught in the headlights—stunned. We are at a loss for words, almost disbelieving what is right in front of us.

Not only can we freeze up in the immediate moment, but sometimes difficult behavior is so weird that even after the fact we don't believe it really happened. Or we deny it or excuse it as a one-time aberration.

Do you do this? If so, you need to realize that people do hurtful, difficult things and that they are indeed real. To deny what is happening is only going to make the situation worse.

From the Manager's Desk

Believe it! Even the best of people do difficult, hurtful, and unpleasant things. Don't pretend it isn't happening. If you do, it may just get worse.

Desire to Avoid Confrontation

Even if you recognize that someone is being nasty, difficult, or unpleasant, you may hesitate to act because you think this way: If I say something, it's just going to make the situation worse.

Sometimes that will be true. There are cases where making a big deal of something that is, in the grand scheme of things, rather trivial, will have you come off as a difficult pain in the butt yourself.

Or perhaps you know that the difficult person argues about everything, and you are tired of it.

There has to be a happy medium here. I don't suggest that you jump on every little thing. However, if you ignore and ignore, all you end up doing is hanging a "kick me" sign on your rear end.

Recognize that dealing with a difficult person in a constructive way doesn't have to mean getting into an argument or a confrontation. In Chapter 5, "Keeping Your Feet on the Ground with Difficult People," I'll talk about techniques you can use to approach difficult people with the right mind-set and a non-confrontational approach. Try not to let your dread of confrontation interfere with taking control of difficult situations, because it doesn't have to be horrible.

Nobody Wants to Be the Bad Guy

The third reason people tend to wait too long to intervene with difficult people has to do with not wanting to come across as the heavy. This is particularly true of managers who are sensitive to the need to use power sparingly in today's workplace.

Get over it! You get paid to manage, so manage. Whether it's someone not doing a good job, someone interfering with the work of others, or someone polluting the work environment, you as a manager have a responsibility above and beyond those who are not managers. You are, in effect, charged with ensuring the welfare of those in your care.

Insider Secrets

Employees look to managers and expect them to take action to correct difficult situations. For example, if you allow one employee to make life difficult for another, there's a fair chance that the victim will come to blame you, even though you aren't directly involved. And in a sense the victim would be right to place at least some blame on your shoulders. Not only do employees expect managers to "protect" them from difficult or abusive people, but in some cases, managers may have a legal obligation to provide that protection and provide a safe environment in which to work. Beyond that, though, if you don't take action regarding difficult situations, employees will lose respect for you and your position. And that, in turn makes THEM more difficult to manage.

Besides, just as intervening need not bring about a confrontation, stepping in need not make you the bad guy.

Fight or Flight

The final underlying reason for mishandling difficult situations is the "fight or flight" phenomenon. It's biological; all animals have it. It works this way; when you believe you are under some threat, your body reacts by sending hormones and doing a bunch of other things to prepare to either run away, or to stand and fight.

It's those chemical changes in your body that cause things like sweating, higher pulse rate, and even shaking during or after perceived danger.

Unfortunately, those chemical changes, while allowing you to make a quick escape or engage in a quick fight, also cause those quick, destructive verbal responses. So, if it's any solace, there is actually a biological reason why you might speak or react too quickly when dealing with a difficult person.

Fortunately, we aren't slaves to the flight or flight thing. We can learn to control ourselves, and even to react less aggressively when we are in difficult situations. Later on in the book, I will help you with some techniques for slowing down reactions, and avoiding the fuel-on-the-fire syndrome.

You Can Do Something—You Must Do Something

As we wrap up this starting chapter, let's focus on the major theme. While it may seem like you are helpless to deal with difficult people, it ain't so. I'm not saying it's easy, but here's the bottom line: If you adopt a victim attitude, you are sure to attract difficult people and create more difficult situations.

If you avoid dealing with situations, most of the time they will get worse. Also, if you react without thinking, then you are likely to increase the chances that you will be chosen as a future victim.

Your responsibilities as a manager are important, too. Not only must you act to save yourself from victimhood, but you must act when people in your charge are being damaged, or the capabilities of your organization are reduced because of one or more difficult people.

The Least You Need to Know

➤ Recognize that difficult people are costly.

➤ Don't adopt a victim mentality.

➤ Manage difficult people to reduce cost and increase benefit.

➤ Separate the content from the tone.

➤ Identify the reasons you delay or act without thought.

Chapter 2

The Magical Manipulative Ways of the Difficult

In This Chapter

➤ How you benefit by focusing on difficult behavior, not on difficult people

➤ How your expectations help or hinder

➤ Everyone's difficult—sometimes

➤ Identifying difficult behavior

You can't succeed at dealing with difficult people unless and until you understand what they are about, how they behave, and the techniques they use to get to you and affect your life. That's because there isn't a single mold out of which difficult people are formed. It would be nice if there was only one kind of difficult person. Then we could simply apply some kind of anti-difficult people prescription. We can't.

One of the keys to managing difficult people is recognizing when and how they are being difficult, because some of their ways are sneaky. Then it's possible for you to take early action before the difficult person in training becomes the professional difficult person.

In this chapter we're going to outline how difficult people manipulate, control, and generally make life miserable for others. We will also focus on the idea that while we often talk about difficult people, we really should talk about difficult behavior, because it is the behavior that affects us. As you will see later in this chapter, our major strategy for managing difficult people is to deal with the behavior, rather than focus on trying to change the person's personality. By learning to recognize difficult people early, you can respond specifically to the difficult behavior in a proactive, take-charge manner.

It's Not the Difficult People, It's the Difficult Behavior

It's a human tendency to identify people as being difficult or easy to get along with, and that affects how we interact with them. But the question is, is it that some people are difficult, or is it their behavior that bothers us?

How Labeling People as Difficult Causes Problems

Most—if not all—of us talk about difficult people. We think,

"Oh, that's John again, why is he always a pain in the posterior,"

or,

"Why is Mary so darned stubborn and difficult all the time?"

We tend to characterize (or label) people and put them into boxes or categories.

If you do that, it's not a character flaw on your part, but a way of trying to simplify the world. In fact, our brains are wired to do this automatically. Brains are wonderful information reduction and labeling machines. They classify, label, and organize information to make our lives easier.

Unfortunately, while our brains do this labeling almost automatically, the process makes dealing with difficult people … well … more difficult. Here's why.

When you label a person as difficult (or stubborn, boring, or untrustworthy), you use that label to predict their behavior and actions in the immediate and long-term future. In other words, you use the labels to create expectations *on your part* about how the person will behave. In one sense, that's not necessarily bad. Predicting difficulties can help us prepare.

In another way, it *is* really bad. When we have negative expectations about someone based on a label, we act differently than we would with someone about whom we have positive expectations.

This Won't Work!

Although our brains tend to label people as difficult, that's not the best way to address difficult situations. If you label a person as difficult, you are likely to create more troublesome situations with that person, because you will be expecting bad things to happen.

When we label a person difficult and have poor expectations about the person, we are more likely to …

➤ interpret their actions as negative.

➤ have strong emotional reactions to them.

➤ treat them abruptly.

➤ expect less from them.

All of these factors can create difficult situations with someone when no difficult situation was actually present in the first place.

In other words, your expectations and labels of people can cause you to create the exact behavior you believe will happen—a self-fulfilling prophecy situation.

Insider Secrets

Some time ago, researchers looked at the power of expectations in classrooms. They assigned children to classrooms randomly, so no class was smarter or dumber than the others. They told half the teachers their kids were "smart" and the other half that their kids were "less smart." Then they measured how well the kids did.

Although the kids in each class were equally smart, the kids labeled "less smart" did significantly worse than the kids teachers believed were "smart." In other words, our expectations affect how we behave and interact with others, and those others react to our behavior in ways that usually reinforce our expectations.

The power of expectations was labeled the "Pygmalion effect."

An Alternative—Focus on Behavior

If labeling people as difficult is likely to create more difficulty, what exactly is the alternative? Good question.

The answer is pretty straightforward. We can adopt a mind-set that doesn't focus on labeling people, but on identifying when difficult, manipulative, or hostile behaviors occur. We focus on *behavior*.

To show you the difference, let's look at two different ways you might look at a person. Rather than thinking:

"Oh, Mary's always so darn difficult,"

you might think to yourself:

"Mary is being difficult by not listening to me right now."

Can you see the difference? It's a bit subtle. In the first phrase, you classify Mary as a difficult person (always difficult, always a problem). That predisposes you to treat Mary in a way that may actually push her into being more difficult.

The second phrasing identifies that, at that moment, Mary is using a particular technique (not listening) that is creating difficulty for you. By thinking this way, you are more likely to deal with the specific behavior in a constructive way.

There are a few other reasons for thinking about difficult behaviors, rather than labeling people as difficult. First, most people aren't difficult all the time. People behave in what we call situation-specific ways. Generally people are quite smart. They vary what they do depending on the context.

From the Manager's Desk

Think in terms of difficult behaviors, not difficult people. When you catch yourself labeling people as difficult, focus on the present, identify the specific things they are doing that are difficult, and go from there. Get the behavior-focus mind-set.

For example, a person may act difficult with you, but be all smiles, pleasantness, and cooperation with the CEO of the company. Or vice versa. A person may behave nicely with his or her spouse but treat you badly. Or an employee may treat his or her co-workers in ways that are offensive but treat you, a manager, quite nicely, thank you!

People just aren't very consistent. They operate differently depending on the situation.

So labeling a person as difficult doesn't help us solve the difficultness, because it's inaccurate. It doesn't help us figure out why someone is difficult on occasion, or when or under what circumstances. And, if you are to make headway dealing with difficult people, you may need to know those things.

Another reason it's important to focus on behavior is that the behavior is what we need to deal with.

Dealing with difficult behavior requires keying our responses to what the person is doing at the moment, and our responses may vary depending on the nature of the behavior. Consider the following:

➤ If we can eliminate the difficult behavior, we no longer have a problem.

➤ The only way we know someone is difficult is through his or her behavior.

➤ The negative impact of difficult people comes from the way they behave. We get angry, frustrated, and stressed out because of *what difficult people do,* not who they are or what they are.

Focus on what people do, not who you think they are or how you label them. That will prepare you to deal more constructively with difficult behavior.

At Every Desk a Difficult Person (Sometimes)

Because it's true that almost no one is difficult all the time, we need to examine the flip side of the equation. Are there people who are never difficult, and who are always easy to get along with? Before we answer the question, let's identify why it is important.

One of the keys to managing difficult people and awkward situations involves being prepared. That means when we are faced with difficult behavior, we respond quickly and effectively (based on the specific behavior) in a way that will reduce the impact of the difficult behavior. In other words, when we are prepared, we are less likely to act badly. We are less likely to make a mountain out of the molehill. We are less likely to escalate a difficult situation.

When difficult behavior comes from someone who doesn't usually act that way, it can catch us unawares. That's when we make mistakes.

Back to the question. As we said earlier, people act in situation-specific ways. Also, everyone is capable of acting in difficult ways. True, some do it more often than others, but everyone, let's repeat, *everyone* is difficult sometimes, even the most mild-mannered individual.

This Won't Work!

Don't assume that because a person is normally not difficult that they can't be difficult in some situations. By realizing everyone is difficult sometimes, you are less likely to be shocked or surprised, or to respond in ways that make situations worse.

To be prepared to deal with difficult behavior, recognize that it can come from anyone. After you get that mind-set, you are less likely to be surprised or stunned and handle the situation badly.

It Takes Two

They say it takes two to tango. It takes two to make a baby. It also takes two to make an argument and to make a difficult situation worse. Why am I telling you this?

It's simple. We live in a blaming culture. When something unpleasant happens, the first thing people do is to pick someone to blame, someone to hold at fault. Unfortunately, that approach doesn't work very well in solving problems, and it certainly doesn't work very well in dealing with difficult people.

A very important step in becoming better at dealing with difficult people and situations is to put the blaming aside. There's a very simple reason. When you blame someone you tend to get angry and act angry. When you are angry you are less able to deal with the difficult situation in a constructive way. You lose control. You say things you regret. You do all the things human beings do when they get angry, and unfortunately most of those things make it worse.

This Won't Work!

People habitually involved in conflict tend to make a simple error. They blame the other person for the whole problem, not realizing it takes two to make a difficult situation into a major problem. Never assume that the other person is the sole source of the problem or difficulty.

So, consider this situation. An employee approaches you and makes an unpleasant remark about your management ability. I think we'd both consider that a difficult behavior. Is there a problem? Well, that depends on you.

If you react badly, you will create a much worse situation than existed in the first place. If, for example, you reply in some nasty way, then the situation is likely to escalate, becoming an argument. Even worse, your reaction may create problems, not only in the present but in the future as well.

So, while difficult behavior is, for lack of a better word, difficult, how you handle it will determine whether you create a permanent problem and a big blowup, or reduce or eliminate the fallout from the difficult behavior.

It's up to you. It does take two to argue. It almost always takes two to poison relationships. It takes two to escalate a small 10-second piece of difficult behavior into an all-out war.

That's a good thing. It means you—again, let's repeat, you—as recipient of the difficult behavior often get to determine what happens, provided you keep your wits about you, stay away from blaming, and stay constructive.

If you stay away from blaming the person being difficult, recognize that you can take control of the situation, and understand that what happens after the "first shot" will be determined by *your* reaction, you will be in a better position to deal with those unpleasant situations.

The Various Manipulative Techniques of the Difficult

Believe it or not, the first step in dealing effectively with difficult people and situations is identifying that you are, in fact, being manipulated, attacked, or faced with difficult behavior. To do that, you need a sense of the kinds of tactics used when people are being difficult.

Think of it this way. The earlier you recognize something difficult is going on, the more quickly you can react. That's important because the longer the behavior continues without you talking the initiative, the harder it is to stop or turn the person away from that difficult tactic.

Think of it as a kind of early warning system. The earlier you detect it, the better your chances of ending the behavior.

Before we look at the common difficult tactics, we need to consider a question. Is there some universal standard for defining difficult behavior? The answer is no. What you consider difficult may be quite different from your boss' definition. One employee may consider use of swear words out of bounds, while another may not. It's rather subjective.

So, ultimately you have to decide for yourself what constitutes difficult behavior. Part of that is a personal process. Luckily, it's not all a personal, subjective process. It's possible to identify a number of situations, actions, and behaviors that most people will consider problematic or difficult.

From the Manager's Desk

It's important to apply the reality check principle. It goes like this. Because our initial reaction to what we see as difficult behavior tends to be emotional, before we take action, we need to assess whether the "difficult behavior" is really causing concrete problems. So, always start by looking at the effects or result of what they are doing. Is it causing problems for others? Is it making it more difficult to get things done? By looking at the effects, you are less likely to get overly subjective.

I've divided the manipulative difficult techniques into a number of categories. No doubt you'll be familiar with some or most of the techniques, but you may also find some you hadn't really thought of before.

The point in describing these behaviors is so you will be less likely to ignore difficult behavior when it starts. You'll be able to identify and manage the behavior before it becomes a bigger and more difficult problem.

Direct Work-Related Difficult Behavior

This category includes difficult behaviors that are directly related to getting work done (or not done). Here are some examples:

➤ Directly refusing work assignments

➤ Indirect or covert sabotage of work assignments

➤ Unwillingness to take direction or suggestions

➤ Poor performance, defensiveness

➤ Hoarding of resources or competition for resources

Employee Handbook

Because **guerrilla attacks** occur behind your back, they are more dangerous because you may not be aware of them. One person bad-mouthing you in private can, over time, create splits among the employees of your organization. You need to be particularly alert to these tactics. This attack often occurs back-channel—that is, through rumors and private comments made behind your back.

As a manager, you have a responsibility to deal with problems as they occur, because to not do so may result in lower productivity. As a manager, you are accountable for that productivity.

Attacks on You, the Manager

Attacks on you, the manager, take two forms. One is "in your face," where the person is both vocal and public about his or her opinion about you personally or about your competence and decisions. The other form, a *guerrilla attack,* is more insidious because it occurs behind your back, often with other employees.

While some people may be fairly tolerant of such attacks (and that's admirable), we need to apply the reality check principle here. What are the effects? While you may believe that people should be entitled to their say, constant attacks, both public and private, tend to undermine your authority and credibility to other employees. That's a major reason why these kinds of difficult behaviors need to be addressed proactively.

Further, they have the potential for causing splits or camps among your employees, with people taking sides. Side-taking can be fatal to effective teamwork.

Specific attacks include ...

➤ sustained public argument with you.

➤ public airing of differences when not appropriate.

➤ personal outbursts and attacks in private with you.

24

➤ back-channel (behind-the-back) criticism.

➤ critical comments about you made to outsiders (for example, customers).

➤ gossip about your personal life.

These behaviors are fairly serious and warrant quick intervention.

Difficult Interpersonal Behavior

The most common difficult behaviors managers face center around interpersonal behavior that is either disruptive, rude, inconsiderate, or self-centered. Often people incorrectly call these behaviors evidence of a personality conflict. Rather than thinking of it that way, it's better to address the behavior, because it isn't likely that anyone's personality will change.

The examples we've included can occur in any context—publicly in meetings, privately in one-on-one discussions, or with other employees.

Here are some examples:

➤ Interrupting others

➤ Constant negative comments or body language

➤ Refusal to take other people into account

➤ Obnoxious tone towards others

➤ General rudeness

➤ Harassing behavior (either sexual or personal)

➤ Unnecessary personal comments and attacks

➤ Blaming others

➤ Intimidation tactics

➤ Aggressive behavior (yelling, shouting)

In any workplace we find people who use some of these tactics sometimes, and unfortunately, there needs to be at least some room for people to be interpersonally human. That's the term we use for the "someone's-having-a-bad-day" thing.

When determining how difficult these behaviors are for you in your workplace, again apply the reality check principle. Regardless of whether the person and the behavior aggravate you personally, ask yourself the question: "How is this behavior likely to affect our workplace if it is allowed to continue?" Answer this objectively as possible. The answer will help you decide whether action is called for.

Back-Channel Guerrilla Work

We mentioned guerrilla difficult behaviors in the section about attacks on the manager, but it shows up in other forms, just as insidious and tricky.

Apart from difficult behavior which has a violent component to it (for example, shouting, yelling, threats), back-channel difficult behavior is the most difficult to address—and the most important. It's like dry rot in a house or having termites quietly destroy the foundation of your house without your knowledge.

Here are some of the specific examples:

From the Manager's Desk

Be alert to back-channel guerrilla work. Back-channel behavior can poison a work environment over time. It's like death by a thousand mosquito bites.

➤ Gossiping (about anyone)

➤ Critical comments about co-workers

➤ Unnecessary foot-dragging on job tasks

➤ Back-room lobbying to get decisions changed

➤ Going over your head without first discussing an issue

➤ Refusal to communicate important information

➤ Ignoring of management or company directives

➤ Mistreatment or harassment of co-workers

➤ Bad-mouthing of you, the work unit, or staff to outsiders

You need to be on alert for these kinds of behaviors.

Chronic Versus Occasional Difficult Behavior

We've suggested it is important to avoid labeling people as difficult and to focus on the here-and-now difficult behavior that you come across. You're probably sitting there thinking you know of one or more truly difficult people who are almost *always* difficult. Where do they fit into all this?

First, reconsider your thinking on this. Is that person you are thinking of really difficult all or most of the time? Or does it just seem so because they frustrate you so much? To help you think that through, you can count the times in the last week the person in question has caused difficulties.

Still think the person is consistently difficult? Well, that's possible. There are some people who seem to walk around with a black cloud over their heads that rains on everyone else. Maybe you have got one of those.

What distinguishes the chronic difficult person from the person who is occasionally difficult is that the former shows a pattern of difficult behavior over time. The chronically difficult tend to repeat the same difficult behaviors over and over again, sometimes even when they've been told that the behavior is driving people nuts. Occasionally difficult people tend to be easier to deal with, because you can focus on a single event and deal with it quickly.

We'll return to this idea of patterns of difficult behavior in Chapters 11, "Indentifying the Venomous Difficult Employee," and 12, "Can You Create Win-Win With These Folks? And How!," when we discuss how you can approach a more destructive difficult person and communicate with him or her. In Chapters 12, and 13, "I Fought the Law and … ?" we'll talk about management sanctions or disciplinary action that you can use to address chronic difficult behavior.

For now, though, keep this in mind. It's very important that you don't allow chronically difficult people to cause you to do things that will make them more difficult. For example, if you blow up at someone, that's not going to help. If you show your exasperation, that's not going to help, either. If you drop the disciplinary hammer too early or do it improperly because you've allowed it to get personal, you are going to have a mess you will regret for a long time.

Insider Secrets

At a seminar, one of the supervisors attending wanted help dealing with a difficult employee who had bedeviled her for seven years. She told a rather one-sided story of how the difficult employee had made her miserable, almost driving her to commit violence. While the group tried to help her she pooh-poohed every suggestion. It became clear that the supervisor had been a major contributor to the problem. The moral: Look at your own behavior and not just that of the difficult person.

Try to keep an objective view and realize that the person is probably not evil, and may have some reasons for his or her behavior that can be used to solve the problem, after you know what the reasons are. You will need to explore those reasons before taking extreme actions.

How Does Knowing All This Help?

It's probably a good time to summarize where we've been so far. We've suggested that:

➤ it's better to focus on behavior, not labels.

➤ it takes two people to make a difficult situation worse.

➤ difficult behavior is defined somewhat subjectively.

➤ we can apply a reality check to determine whether something is difficult by evaluating the results or consequences.

➤ the term "difficult behavior" takes many forms, some obvious, some less so.

➤ some people are consistently difficult and we may have to deal with them differently than the occasionally difficult.

While these points may seem unimportant now, you will see as we go along that they are extremely important in developing an effective mind-set for dealing with difficult behavior and situations.

When you understand that it's better to focus on behavior and get good at thinking that way, you are less likely to take things personally. You won't demonize a person who is acting in a difficult way. Focusing on behavior also helps you step back that extra few feet so you can gain some perspective on things.

When you understand that what constitutes difficult behavior is a somewhat subjective call, you realize that some of the difficult behavior you encounter is specific to you personally. That's important, because some things that you may find annoying or aggravating may not have any real negative effect on your workplace. Sure, it may drive you nuts, but we need to step back. Sometimes the problem may lie with you, not the other person.

It's the same reasoning for applying a reality check. Determine whether the behavior is really having a negative effect. If not, it may be too trivial to address, or just something you need to become desensitized to.

By understanding that difficult behavior comes in many forms and ranges from the in-your-face stuff to the covert guerrilla actions people take, you are better able to address the sneaky difficult tactics people use. That's really important, because it is often what you don't see, the more subtle techniques, that are most damaging. You need to know they exist so you can act accordingly.

So, that's how the information contained in this chapter is going to help you. Not only is it important in its own right, but we are preparing you for the more specific techniques we will be covering in the next section of the book.

The Least You Need to Know

➤ Focus on difficult behavior, not labels for people.

➤ Be alert to all forms of difficult behavior—the obvious and the not so obvious.

➤ Remember that difficult behavior is often in the eyes of the beholder. Sometimes what you may think is difficult is simply something that bugs you.

➤ If you deal with a chronically difficult person, you need to look at the patterns of their behavior.

Chapter 3

What Makes Difficult People Tick ... and Tick ...

> **In This Chapter**
>
> ➤ Why people behave in difficult ways
>
> ➤ What difficult people are after
>
> ➤ Why me, Lord, why me?
>
> ➤ Applying your understanding of difficult people

As you go through the rest of this book, you're going to find lots of tips to help you deal with difficult people and situations. You'll save yourself time, money, and frustration by remembering that there isn't a single magical prescription for dealing with every difficult person and every difficult situation.

You need to know what strategies to use in which situation and when to use them. To make that decision properly, you need to understand what makes difficult people tick—what drives their behavior. What are they trying to obtain by behaving in ways you think are difficult?

That knowledge will help you determine how to respond more effectively and tailor your actions to the situation. In this chapter we focus on the reasons why people behave in difficult ways.

You Don't Need to Be a Shrink

There's a trick to understanding difficult behavior. If you'll remember, in the last chapter we talked about how important it is to avoid labeling people as difficult, and to look at the difficult behaviors. In that discussion we suggested that labeling people makes you less able to deal with difficult situations, because it can create a self-fulfilling prophecy; you believe a person is difficult and in doing so treat them in ways that tend to encourage them to be difficult.

When you focus on the person and his or her personality or character rather than behavior, you tend to try to analyze the person into the ground. In a way, you play amateur psychologist. You sit there, ruminating and mumbling; did the person have a tough childhood? Does he have some strange psychological malady? Is she some strange psychological type that just doesn't fit in?

This Won't Work!

Becoming too involved in figuring out why people do what they do is usually a bad idea. It takes time; you'll often reach in incorrect conclusion; and it keeps you from dealing with behavior.

You don't want to do that. First, you're not a psychologist, so all this thinking and analyzing is bound to increase your stress levels and consume time, giving the difficult person more opportunities to be difficult. Second, even if you knew that a person, let's say, had a rough childhood, how would that help you deal with him or her more effectively? You can't change the past. You can only deal with the present.

In fact, you can't change the person's personality or character or much to do with who a person is. What you can do is react in ways that will reduce the difficult behavior, and perhaps help the person change the behavior over time. But changing the *person*—uh uh!

Third, you don't need every bit of information about why a person acts in difficult ways, or what in a person's past is causing it. You can deal effectively with difficult behavior with a minimum of psychological knowledge. How can that be?

Because the huge majority of difficult situations involve people who are "normal," you don't need to know more than the common motivations behind garden-variety difficult behavior. Keep in mind that difficult people aren't usually nuts, crazy, or mentally ill. They are just being difficult from where you sit. They may seem unbelievably inconsiderate, weird, or rude, but they are not often in need of psychological counseling—at least, they are in no more need than you or I.

Are They Just Screwed Up?

For the most part, when a person acts in difficult ways, it is within what might be called the normal range of human behavior. Think of yourself. If we asked 10 people who know you whether you are ever difficult, would you get a perfect score? Of course not. You have people who think you are difficult, and no doubt, on occasion, you are. It's the same for the people around you. You aren't crazy, right? Neither are they.

It's About What People Have Learned

If difficult people aren't screwed up, how can you begin to understand why they do what they do? It's all about learning. People tend to repeat behaviors that have gotten them what they wanted in the past and seem to be getting them what they want in the present.

That's such a simple principle, but it is essential to understand. Read it again. Think about it for a minute.

People behaving in difficult ways are doing so because they have received some *reinforcement* for behaving that way; in nonpsychological terms, they have been rewarded (or believe they have been) for behaving that way.

Insider Secrets

Non-psychologists usually equate reinforcement with reward. Technically, rewards and reinforcements aren't exactly the same thing but the differences are unimportant for our purposes here. Reinforcement refers to an event that follows after a behavior, one that increases the probability that the behavior will be repeated. For example, the person who interrupts others may end up encouraged to interrupt again because his behavior is being rewarded or reinforced. How? By the attention he receives after the interruption. Even if the reaction is negative, but shines the spotlight on the person, it may reinforce the behavior we don't want. And, what one person finds rewarding or reinforcing may be quite unrewarding for someone else.

Perhaps more importantly, they continue to behave in difficult ways because in many situations, they *are* receiving some reward or reinforcement for doing so. Here's the kicker. If you are the target of difficult behavior from someone, often it is because you have reacted in ways that allow the difficult person to get what they want, either in real terms, or more often, in psychological terms. In other words, you may very well be part of the problem, contributing to its continuance.

You can't change what the person has learned in the past, although you may help them relearn better behaviors. What you can do is act in ways that do not encourage the person to continue the difficult behavior. And that's our focus—to deal with difficult behavior so that it isn't rewarding for the person to continue.

It's Also About Skill

It's natural to label people as difficult or even unbalanced when we perceive their behavior to be difficult, particularly when it seems to be chronic. But there's another consideration.

Often, the people we label as difficult just don't know any better. Think about these folks as not knowing how to deal successfully with a situation they face. They are not bad people, any more than a bad baseball player is a bad person or a poor writer is a bad person. They may not know how to act differently, or how to deal with a specific situation that is causing them discomfort.

This Won't Work!

It's easy to mistake a lack of social skills or communications skills for something that is intentionally hurtful or damaging. Be alert to the fact that some people just don't know how to act more appropriately.

Let's use an example.

You have just told John that one or two aspects of his work performance need some improvement (heck, nobody is perfect, right?). You explain—gently—what could be improved, and tell John that you will help him in the improvement process. You think you've handled the situation really, really well.

John becomes sullen and clams up in front of you. At the staff meeting held a week later, John, normally a productive team member, doesn't say a word and sits, looking bored (obviously intentionally). Later you also hear that John has made some comments about you to other employees.

There's a lot of ways you could interpret this. John could be some psychotic nut case in development, waiting to explode. John could be just plain angry and out to get you (so it seems). Maybe John has trouble with authority figures because they remind him of his abusive father.

Speculating in this way, however, is not going to help you deal with John's behavior. In fact, doing this might very well interfere with handling this situation well. Here's another more constructive way to think about this.

Is it possible that John is upset about the critical (but well-intended) comments? Perhaps his feelings are hurt? Of course that's possible. Does that solve the problem? No. But what does help is to realize that John may be upset and not know how to deal with it constructively. John may not know how to express that feeling constructively, or how to approach you to talk about his reaction and what should be done next.

Simply, John may be like a baseball pitcher who doesn't know how to throw a curveball. He still has to throw something, so he continues to go with what he does know how to do, which is to sulk and express his feelings in destructive ways. He *is* going to get his message of being upset out. He *is* going to communicate his unhappiness. He's just going about it the only way he knows how, which isn't a very constructive or useful way.

Also, while it may seem that that John isn't getting rewarded for his behavior, think again. By acting in his own difficult way, he is likely focusing attention on himself (usually a reinforcing thing), and most importantly, he feels he is expressing his feelings in the way that makes the most sense to him. And that's definitely reinforcing, at least psychologically.

Where does all this leave you, the person having to experience all this? First, if you think of John as confused or not knowing what to do, you can be more positive and helpful than if you view John's behavior as evil, intentional behavior. Secondly, it helps you address part of the problem here; John just may need to learn more effective ways of expressing his concerns.

From the Manager's Desk

Be alert to rewards or reinforcements a person might receive for bad behavior. People sometimes find odd things rewarding—for example, any attention (even negative attention) or getting easier assignments due to poor performance. Make sure your reaction doesn't turn out to reward the behavior you want to stop.

It's Also About Emotion

Difficult behavior is about learning and how people have been and are rewarded. It's about skill or the lack of it. But we can't complete the picture without talking about emotions. We are dealing with people here. Real people. And often the driving force behind difficult behavior is some sort of *emotional* state, usually one of anger or frustration, coupled with the other two elements.

A number of times we've stated that most people aren't difficult all the time. Again, think of yourself. You have good and bad days, patient and impatient days. Most of the time you behave constructively, but not always, right?

Think of the last time you can remember behaving in a difficult way, or in a way that you later regretted. In all probability, you were angry or frustrated. Remember? There is clearly an important link between our emotional states and our difficult behavior. This applies not only to ourselves, but also to the difficult people we deal with.

Here's how it works.

Most people are able to go through their days behaving cooperatively and helpfully. They have sufficient skills to do so, and generally are rewarded for doing so. So, why do people sometimes do dumb things to others?

As a person's emotional state increases in intensity (for example, higher frustration and anger), the person tends to return to the ways used to deal with frustration and anger when he or she was much younger. In fact, the person returns to a much more childlike or childish way of dealing with his or her emotions. This applies to almost everyone. If you look at how an angry child behaves and how an angry adult behaves, you might be surprised to see just how similar the two are.

Insider Secrets

As people become more emotionally activated, they show less control over their emotions and do things they wouldn't normally do if they weren't so emotional. They revert back to the skills they have used longest. Unfortunately, those are the skills of the young child, which is why the difficult behavior of adults can resemble the difficult behavior of children. What's interesting is that this childish behavior often draws an equally childish response from the other person as he or she gets angry. Or, the person facing the childish behavior acts in a parental, superior way. Both of these responses tend to make emotional situations worse.

That explains why people who normally behave pretty well suddenly start behaving badly. It's because their level of anger has reached a point where their skills don't function well enough to deal with situations constructively. They go back to the behaviors that *did* work (and were reinforced) when they were children.

So, again, how does this knowledge help you deal more effectively with difficult behavior? It's the mind-set thing. You have a choice. You can look at people behaving in difficult ways as evil, out to get you, or as disturbed, and that's not going to help you be constructive. Or, you can consider that people behaving badly are doing so as a result of …

➤ being rewarded for it in the past or the present.

➤ an inability to do things in a more constructive way.

➤ an emotional intensity that they can't handle well.

Taken together, these things tell you something. The difficult person is often someone who needs help. You have the option of providing that help and being constructive and compassionate, or coming down hard on the person. Which of these do you think is going to be more likely to succeed?

Right! While sometimes it is necessary to be firm, looking at difficult people as people who need our help is a much more effective starting point for improving things.

What Are Difficult People After?

We've explained part of the "why" of difficult behavior, but there's still more to the picture. Apart from having learned that difficult behavior is rewarding or lacking the skills to handle a situation better or even being upset, what is it that those darn people want?

Another way of putting it is: If people are difficult because they tend to be rewarded for it, what are the rewards?

On the surface of it, the whole thing is very puzzling. People who act difficult don't appear to get what they want. They create grief, not only for others but for themselves, as their audience gets tired of their acts or reacts negatively to them. Aside from the old saying that squeaky wheels often get greased, are there some forms of psychological reward that are attached to difficult behavior? Yes, there are, and you need to understand them so you can make sure that these rewards don't encourage more difficult behavior.

From the Manager's Desk

Some people will respond positively to the things that give them a sense of control. You might try giving difficult people more responsibility, or soliciting their input more often to see whether that has a positive effect.

We're going to look at the most common rewards in a psychological sense. Again, we need to caution you that many of us, at one time or another, allow these rewards to drive our behavior.

Sense of Control

Perhaps many, if not all, individuals have a need to feel in control of their lives and what's going on around them. Very few people feel comfortable with the idea that their lives and welfare—present and future—are totally beyond their own control. For many, the feeling of helplessness associated with not being able to control things is scary. That's pretty normal. Most people aren't control freaks, but they do want some feeling of control over what happens to them.

How does this link up with being rewarded for bad behavior? Simple. Many of the behaviors exhibited by difficult people have, at their core, the outcome of controlling the situation or other people's reactions. A person being difficult and creating problems is, in a sense, controlling those around him or her. People react to a difficult person. That allows a difficult person to manipulate, control, and influence, even if the reactions are negative. In a sense, the difficult person is creating those reactions, and therein lies the reinforcement. It's kind of like parents and children. After children know what the parents don't want them to do, they have the exact information they need to get the parents' attention.

Insider Secrets

Some people really are control freaks and want power over others. Most people want something that's less problematic—a sense that they have a hand in their own destiny and are not hurtling out of control. Interestingly, there are also some people who are comfortable not being in control because they believe that no matter what they do, others are going to determine what happens to them.

It's a psychological reward. Even if bad things happen to people who are difficult, they have created the situation, and that gives them a sense of control.

Straw That Stirs the Drink

If you are an old baseball fan, you might recall that Reggie Jackson, who played for the Oakland Athletics and the New York Yankees, described himself as the "straw that stirs the drink." What Reggie meant by this was that, among the 25 players on the team, it was he who was at the center—the player who made things happen. (As an aside, he may have been right.)

It's about ego, really. Some people need to feel they are the central attraction, the star performer, the wonderboy, and that can create problems for others. This particular motivation, of course, causes problems in and of itself, because the attitude is really annoying. But more than that, it explains what some difficult people are after with their difficult behavior.

For example, let's consider Marie. She's bright and a good performer but is seen as difficult and hard to deal with by those around her. Why? Because she acts as if she's perfect. She knows it all, doesn't listen to others, interrupts, and doesn't take management guidance (she actually ignores it). What does she get out of those behaviors?

First, she gets away with it. People often defer to her because she is often (but not always) right. Or they defer because it's easier than trying to have an intelligent dialogue with her.

Second, she's acting like she's the star performer. She's reinforcing that she is special or better than others; she's the straw that stirs the drink every time she behaves this way. She is a legend in her own mind and becomes the star everytime she acts like the star.

I'm Not Much So I Have a Lot to Prove

While the person who wants to be the straw that stirs the drink really does think he or she is special and worthy of star status, the "I'm not much so I have a lot to prove" person comes from a different place. The difficult behavior comes from a need to prove something, not only to others but also to themselves.

Oftentimes, difficult interpersonal behavior comes from people who have this strong, almost compulsive need to show themselves and others that they are worth something. So it isn't that they are evil or intentionally unpleasant, but rather that they are often desperate.

From the Manager's Desk

True star performers who want to be the straw that stirs the drink are hard to deal with. You need to decide whether treating someone like a star is likely to make him or her less or more difficult. It's tough to know in advance.

A Reaction … I Need A Reaction

This motivation is actually linked to the other ones we have talked about so far. Believe it or not, some people seem driven by a desire to cause reactions in other people. It's almost as if they don't believe they are alive and breathing unless they can stir up the people around them. What's odd about such people is they don't seem to care whether they generate a positive reaction, like praise, or a negative reaction, like being yelled at. They seem to gain some psychological satisfaction from either.

Is it wanting to control others? Could be. A desire to be the center of attention? Sure. However, what is important with people who are driven to create reactions is to *not* give them what they want, which is some emotional reaction. That means keeping their behavior in perspective so you don't reward bad behavior.

Weird Biology, Weird Science

Some difficult people actually act out in difficult ways because of their biology. As scientists develop a better understanding of the brain, we will probably find out that at least some difficult behavior can be explained by biological factors.

We mention this here to help you understand that difficult behavior may not be under the complete conscious control of the person doing it. And so, you might add a dash of compassion to your negative reactions. The truth is that some people (and we don't know how many) can't help it.

Briefly, here are a few biological sources of difficult or erratic behavior. The first is *attention deficit disorder* (ADD or ADHD). Most people associate this with an older term, hyperactivity, which was used almost exclusively to describe children with poor

Employee Handbook

Attention Deficit Disorder, or ADD for short, is the term used to describe children (and now adults) who have low attention spans, are generally above average in intelligence, tend to be impulsive, are disorganized, and are generally difficult to manage.

Attention Deficit Hyperactive Disorder (ADHD) is another way of referring to the same things, where the "H" stands for hyperactive.

From the Manager's Desk

It's difficult, but if you can look at difficult people as people who are probably unhappy or out of balance rather than out to harm you, then you can be more of a helper than a punisher.

attention spans who are very difficult to control. While this is a controversial area, there seems to be some indication that ADD is not restricted to children, but also to adults. Their biology seems to result in poor attention span, impatience, boredom, and a tendency to create crises around them. The bottom line with ADD kids or adults is they can be very difficult, but are often of above-average intelligence.

Some other biological conditions that may cause difficult behavior include blood-sugar problems, brain tumors and other related brain maladies, and, of course, the influence of medications, recreational drugs, and alcohol. It's good to keep in mind that medications, in particular, can affect how people behave.

How Does Knowing All This Help?

There are several reasons why the information in this chapter is important. First, it allows you to obtain some perspective on difficult people and difficult behavior so you don't overreact and take such behavior in overly personal ways. You don't want to let your own emotions interfere with your management of difficult people.

Second, they have some direct implications for action, as you will see as you progress through this book. For example, it's useful to know that some people may have biological reasons underlying their behavior, particularly when medical attention is needed. Or knowing that some people's poor behavior is actually reinforced by the reactions of people around them may help you stop rewarding those behaviors. That can result in behavior change.

Third, understanding people who behave in difficult ways a bit more allows us to develop compassion for them. They aren't evil, but merely people who may be different from you and I. And rather than punishing them, you can step back and help them (and yourself in the process).

The Least You Need to Know

➤ Most difficult people aren't disturbed or crazy.

➤ Most people are difficult because of what they have learned or how they are rewarded for their bad behavior.

➤ Some difficult people simply don't know how to act in less difficult ways.

➤ Understanding some of the reasons why difficult people act the way they do can help make their behavior less personal.

➤ You need to consider the possibility that some difficult behavior is beyond the control of the person, particularly if it's a result of biology.

Chapter 4

Why Me, Lord, Why Me?—The Manager's Burden

> ### In This Chapter
>
> ➤ Don't take it personally
>
> ➤ Sometimes you may contribute to difficult situations
>
> ➤ How to tell whether you are part of the problem
>
> ➤ Managing brings extra responsibility
>
> ➤ It's in your own interest to be proactive

There are two common questions managers blessed by difficult people ask. Managers wonder "Why me, Lord, why me?" Faced with inexplicable difficult behavior, it's no wonder managers are puzzled. Maybe it's karma, sins in a past life, or perhaps a simple twist of fate. Or maybe someone upstairs is really annoyed … just kidding! The second question is a bit more serious, and it contains both a lament against unfairness and a legitimate question: What exactly is the manager's responsibility (burden) with respect to managing or addressing difficult situations? Both questions are important; the first, because feeling victimized by difficult people makes it harder to succeed, and the second, because the answers help you make decisions about what you should, and perhaps shouldn't, be doing. In this chapter, we are going to answer both questions.

It's Probably not Personal

Just to put your mind at ease, there are very few managers who are free of difficult people, so don't feel so darn special if you have a few of them around. The truth is, if you don't have difficult employees, a difficult boss, or difficult customers, you are

From the Manager's Desk

Don't overreact when faced with attacks and behaviors that seem aimed at destroying you. That may not be the motivation at all. Don't react too quickly and fight. Don't beat yourself up for causing the problem.

either dead or completely oblivious to what is going on around you. Neither of those scenarios is likely to enhance your career advancement.

Let's put this in perspective by saying that people who behave in difficult ways come with the territory of being human and being a manager. It's perfectly possible that your particular difficult person has nothing against you personally, or is reacting to a situation and targeting you as the cause, even if you've had nothing to do with it.

For example, both you and a co-worker apply for a promotion to the manager position. Congratulations! You won. Unfortunately, the used-to-be co-worker is now working for you, and despite the fact the two of you got along well in the past, everything's different now. He or she is disappointed and mad. Really mad. Now, who do you think is going to be the target of that anger? You. The weird part is that the same thing would probably have happened no matter who else was promoted.

It may appear personal, but often it's not.

Let's consider another situation. Your company is in a mild recession, and limits or eliminates pay increases for the current year. You do your best to explain to staff, but despite that Warren starts balking at assignments and you hear that he has been bad-mouthing you in private. Well, heck, you couldn't increase the raises; you just followed company directives. No matter. Warren is really angry, and has aimed that anger at an immediately available target—you.

Again, nothing personal here, although it may seem very personal.

Insider Secrets

Employees often become angry, frustrated, and difficult when something they had or expected to have is taken away or is not received. For example, a promised bonus not paid is more anger-provoking than if there was no bonus promised (never mind that the bonus isn't paid in either case). Moving from a private office to an open cubicle is another example. Even small changes of this sort can create problems, so it's good to be on the alert, no matter how trivial the change seems to you.

The point of discussing this is so you understand that many difficult situations occur because of circumstances, and that you, as a manager, are a handy whipping post for people who are angry and frustrated. It's particularly important to remind yourself that you have to deal with someone who makes personal remarks about you. Yes, they are offensive. Yes, they sound personal. But it doesn't mean that the person hates your guts, or the situation is beyond redemption. It doesn't necessarily mean that you have messed up.

... But It Might Be You

Ok, it's truth time. Who's that person who looks out at you from the mirror in the morning? Is it someone who never makes mistakes and never creates anger, frustration, and difficult behavior in others? Because you aren't perfect (are you?), that's probably not so accurate. The person who looks back at you isn't perfect, sometimes makes mistakes, and, yes, sometimes influences or creates difficult situations.

OK, so if that sounds right, then, once again, welcome to the human race. Some of the difficult situations that occur are in fact directly related to handling things in less-than-perfect ways. Sometimes you screw up, and you'd better face that head on. If you don't, you are going to accumulate difficult people until you are ready for the funny farm.

It's important that you take on the responsibilities of handling difficult situations. That doesn't mean beating yourself up or blaming yourself. It does mean recognizing when you have handled things badly, or recognizing that you have contributed to the building of difficulty. In an earlier chapter, we mentioned it takes two to tango and two to make a difficult situation into an all-out war. Remember this. If you contribute to difficult situations, you will be unable to fix them unless you recognize your involvement and seek to avoid making similar mistakes in future.

All right, let's get back to the bathroom mirror. Do you see someone who is surrounded by difficult situations? How many difficult people do you encounter? If you find that a number of your employees seem difficult, then maybe it *is* you. If you find a number of your peers are difficult, maybe you're a contributing factor.

This is always a touchy area. It's hard to take a good, honest look in the mirror and see yourself as others see you. But with respect to difficult people, it's a necessity.

From the Manager's Desk

While it may be that the difficult behavior you face isn't meant as personal, it's important to realize that you might have contributed to causing it. As a practical tip, the best way to find out is to ask the person whether you have done something that the person finds frustrating. Do it privately. Acknowledge you might have erred.

Here's why: Difficult people often create other difficult people. There are some people who are difficult enough that people react to them in contrary ways. You probably know a few. It's easy to recognize a difficult behavior when it's someone else's behavior. It's often very hard to identify or realize that you yourself might be difficult. What if you don't realize it?

If you are, in fact, a major cause of the difficult behavior around you and don't realize it, your future is dim. It may interfere with your career, but perhaps worse, you will be ignorantly miserable for the rest of your working life.

Identifying If It Is You

So, given our tendency to overlook our own shortcomings, how can you figure out whether or not you are a primary cause of your own grief? How can you find out what you need to change?

First, look for patterns of behavior or reactions from others. Do people say the same things about you at home and in the workplace? That's a dead giveaway that there is something going on. For example, if your spouse and one or two of your staff think you are hard to talk to or that you aren't a good listener, then there's a good chance you *are* hard to talk to and you could use some work on your listening skills.

Here are a few other reactions from others that you might want to pay attention to:

➤ People avoid talking to you or are vague.

➤ People seem to be intimidated in your presence.

➤ People clam up when you appear.

➤ People seem defensive with you.

➤ People often get frustrated in conversations with you.

Insider Secrets

Managers do strange things. One manager I know used to rant and rave about how staff members wouldn't let him know what was going on. He constantly proclaimed his much-vaunted open-door policy. Unfortunately, when staff members did come visit, he didn't look at them while they spoke to him, continued to hunt and peck at his keyboard, and generally showed disinterest. Talk about being the author of one's own aggravation!

Second, look for patterns in your own behavior and reactions. Here are a few questions to ask yourself:

➤ Am I often distracted or inattentive?

➤ Am I often more interested in talking than listening?

➤ Do I often use my position of power as a manager to get things done (issuing orders, coercion)?

➤ Am I easily upset?

If you answer yes to some of these questions, then it's likely that you're contributing to the development of difficult people around you. While there's no mortal sin involved in being distracted or talking or getting upset, it's likely that you are conveying an irritability, impatience, and lack of interest in those around you. That turns people off. When people get turned off this way, they tend to be less cooperative over time.

Third, ask people for feedback. It's impossible to understand how you affect people without getting them involved in helping you. Here's how to do it.

With your employees, and in private one-to-one conversations, ask each one how you could be of more help to them in getting their jobs done.

With your spouse (provided you get along well), just plain ask whether there are things about you that he or she finds difficult. (If you don't get along, don't ask this question.)

With your boss, ask him or her whether there is anything you should be doing that might make you a better manager or contributor to the company. Bosses really like this, so there's an added benefit there.

Clearly, all the feedback in the world isn't going to help if you don't really want to hear how other people see you. That's your choice, of course.

This Won't Work!

It's not a good idea to put people on the spot when asking for feedback. Asking "What's wrong with me?" isn't likely to give you very honest information from your staff. You can get around this by focusing on how you can be more helpful or useful. You'll get better information.

It's Your Choice to Change

Let's say you've figured out that, yes, you are contributing to the development of difficult people and difficult behavior in those around you. Then what? Are you doomed to misery? Are the people around you doomed, too?

No, people can change, and so can you. But should you? That's your call. If you are tired of people reacting badly to you, then that's good motivation to work on changing your own behavior. If you feel work is a struggle, or worse, one war after the other, perhaps you will be motivated to change.

The bottom line here is that if you see it as in your own interest to change what you do, you will do so. If you don't see a payoff for it, you probably won't, and I can't make you do so. I do think it's worth the effort, whether you are an occasional contributor to difficult situations or a chronic one.

To help you think this through, here are some benefits you may receive from becoming less difficult yourself:

➤ More productivity, fewer hassles

➤ Less stress

➤ More effectiveness on the job

➤ More respect and affection

➤ Increased job enjoyment

As a final point on changing yourself, we aren't talking about a personality makeover here. We are talking about focusing and targeting specific behaviors you decide to change. For example, if you want to become easier to get along with, don't commit yourself to being a nicer person. Commit yourself to being a better listener, or to involve staff more. Choose one or two limited areas to work on at one time, and try to change what you DO, not who you are.

The Manager's Extra Burden

Managers are like everyone else in that they have bosses and are employees of the company. They have whatever obligations nonmanagement employees have with respect to acting according to company policies. But the responsibility doesn't stop there. Managers carry additional burdens and responsibilities, and when you were hired to a management position, it was assumed that you would accept those extra responsibilities and carry them out.

Let's look at the extra responsibilities you have as a manager, and explain why it is important that you understand them and don't ignore them.

From the Manager's Desk

When the manager's extra burden gets you down, think about how good it feels to accomplish something special, such as solving a difficult-person problem.

Responsibility for Your Work Unit's Productivity

While your employees are the ones who do the work and create productivity for your work unit, you are the person who is responsible for the overall productivity and results your department creates. Your manager and the company hierarchy aren't interested in why your productivity is lower than it should be. They aren't interested in the collection of difficult people who work for you. They want results, and if you can't deliver them, who do you think they are going to come to? Is the Vice President going to talk to the receptionist if he or she causes customer service complaints? No, of course not. The VP will come to you, and expect you to fix the problem.

So it's more than a responsibility on your part. You will be held accountable if difficult people interfere with the productivity of your work unit. You're a bright person. I'm sure you can figure out the consequences of allowing one or more difficult people to reduce the effectiveness of your work unit.

This is the major extra burden carried by managers. The remainder of the extra responsibilities all derive from this one.

Responsibility for Staff Welfare

Whether you feel it's right or not, you have a legal, if not moral, obligation to attend to the welfare of your staff members. On the legal side, courts have indicated that management has certain legal responsibilities regarding things like work harassment, sexual harassment, and maintaining a safe work environment, both physically and psychologically. You and your company can be sued if you don't carry out those responsibilities. Let's be clear here. If you don't take action to deal with certain difficult situations that come to your attention, you can be sued even if you aren't the perpetrator of illegal acts.

The law attributes certain extra responsibilities to management.

Apart from the legal risk factor (which should be enough to encourage you to take on your responsibilities), when you allow difficult people to run roughshod in your organization, you indirectly cause harm to those who work for you. There is at least some moral obligation to use your additional power and influence as a manager to protect staff from difficult people.

This Won't Work!

People can sue anyone for just about anything these days. The most risk involves management inaction regarding sexual harassment and toxic work environments. If you are in doubt about your legal responsibilities, consult an expert.

Of course, there is the practical issue. If you allow difficult people free rein and don't execute your responsibilities, chances are that productivity will drop. Staff may leave and your turnover statistics will be high. Customer service may worsen. And guess who is accountable to the brass? You.

Responsibility for Mediation

Chapter 10, "Monkey in the Middle: Mediation and Arbitration," goes into more depth about the management function of mediation. Essentially, *mediation* refers to a process in which a third party works with two people who are in conflict or cannot settle an issue. The mediator (I call this person the monkey in the middle) is expected to assist in conflict resolution.

Employees look to you to solve certain kinds of interpersonal or productivity-related problems. When two people can't get along because one or both people are difficult, who do they come to? Often it's you.

You have that extra burden. If you feel that adults should be able to work out their own differences, you're right. However, if they can't and it affects staff productivity or morale or health, then the hot potato falls in your lap.

Employee Handboook

Mediation refers to a process in which a third party works with two people who are in conflict or cannot settle an issue themselves, and helps them come to an agreement. With mild difficult situations, managers often mediate in an informal unstructured way. In more complex situations, sometimes an outside mediator is best, because mediation is a fairly complex process.

If you refuse to involve yourself in the mediation process when approached, then you lose credibility and will be seen as shirking your responsibilities or as incompetent by your employees and your boss.

It's in Your Self-Interest

The reason we've talked so much about the extra burdens of management is to help you develop a particular mind-set about difficult people in your workplace. Dealing effectively with difficult people isn't an option, it is a responsibility of management. But it's more than a moral issue, or what's right or wrong. There are direct links to your willingness to address difficult people problems and your own self-interest.

Ultimately, though, you have to choose, and you have to make informed choices about how you deal with difficult people. So read this next sentence carefully. When you avoid dealing with difficult people or deny there is a problem when there really is one, you are the one who is going to pay the price.

You will be held accountable if difficult people affect the productivity of your work unit. You will be held accountable by the courts if you fail to take action in certain domains such as sexual harassment. Employees will blame you if you do nothing in the face of difficult behaviors among the people who report to you.

None of this is going to help your career or your sanity. It can even affect whether you keep your job.

You may ask the questions: "Is all of this fair?" or "Shouldn't adults behave properly without a manager pushing them?" The answer is, no it isn't really fair, and yes, adults should behave courteously and cooperatively. So what?

We can't work in a world of what should be. We have to work with the world we have. And you live in a world where you are held accountable. So if you are sitting there thinking about the unfairness of the extra responsibilities you carry, get over it. Or find a job with responsibilities you are comfortable with.

OK, that's pretty harsh. Still, if you aren't comfortable with these management responsibilities, you will be miserable, because you will allow difficult situations to grow and grow, until they become major problems. You'll get tired of explaining to your boss why your employees quit. You'll get tired of complaints. You'll get tired of the hassles.

This Won't Work!

The most common mistake managers make in dealing with difficult behavior is to ignore it until it's too late, or to deny there is a problem. Ignoring it allows difficult behavior to eat at the fiber of your organization.

The bottom line is that it is in your self-interest, as a manager, to accept the management burdens placed upon you. It is in your self-interest to take early action with difficult people and situations.

It's your choice. After you accept these responsibilities, you will be positioned well to deal proactively with difficult people and ensure that they don't cause damage as a result of the situations being ignored.

The Least You Need to Know

➤ Difficult behavior is often not about you.

➤ Realize that you might be a contributor to difficult-people problems.

➤ A common management mistake is to ignore difficult behavior until it's grown into a huge problem.

➤ Managers have extra responsibilities regarding difficult people and situations.

➤ It's in your own interest to address difficult situations early, and not ignore them.

Chapter 5

Keeping Your Feet on the Ground with Difficult People

In This Chapter

➤ The importance of the right mind-set

➤ The difference between blaming and problem solving

➤ How to think first rather than react first

➤ Tips for keeping your feet on the ground

One of the things that makes difficult people challenging is that they use techniques to put people around them off-balance. Their behavior causes people around them to become angry, frustrated, or even confused to the point that they don't know quite what to do. If you allow the difficult person to put you off-balance, you have much less of a chance of dealing with the troublesome behavior in a way that is going to create a win-win situation. When you get angry or frustrated, you make mistakes, say things you might regret, and take action without thinking things through. Or your tone and impatience can make the situation worse. By being off-balance, you end up as a contributor to the problem, rather than a solver of the problem.

Think of it like a dance. Imagine how difficult it would be to tango with a 120-pound weight on your left foot. Or how hard it would be hit a baseball while standing on a waterbed. It's like that. You need a firm base to deal with difficult situations effectively. It's very important that you approach difficult people and situations with the right mind-set, the right perspective, and the right attitude. You need to have a mental balance.

What kind of attitude or mind-set do you need to deal more effectively with difficult people? How do you adopt that mind-set so essential to success with difficult people? We'll provide the answers.

It Isn't Going to Work with Me

One interesting thing about difficult people is they aren't stupid. They will tend to be more difficult when they feel what they are doing is having an effect on the target.

From the Manager's Desk

When dealing with difficult behaviors or situations, particularly with people who try to control your reactions, it's critical to avoid overreacting. You need to send this message: "Your tactics aren't going to work with me." You don't reward bad behavior.

This Won't Work!

A common mistake people make is to believe that the other person makes them mad or angry. That gives the other person much more control over them than is necessary. Throw that idea out. The devil doesn't make you do bad things; neither does a difficult person. Don't give up control of your life.

You don't want to send the impression that the difficult behavior is getting to you. You want to send the exact opposite message—that the difficult behavior is not going to work with you.

What does the phrase "not going to work with me" really mean?

When and if you allow difficult people to see they are succeeding at getting what they want, they will continue to use difficult techniques on you. If a person succeeds in getting under your skin, you will probably send subtle or not-so-subtle messages that their tactics are working. That's exactly what they want psychologically. Your anger or frustration reinforces the nasty behavior, so they continue. You get more frustrated. They are rewarded and continue, and round and round it goes.

To combat this cycle, first you want to develop a mind-set or attitude that allows you to put the difficult person or behavior in perspective. It isn't going to be fatal (usually). It doesn't have to drive you nuts. And you don't have to allow it to control you, your reactions, your health, and your well-being. Remember this: A difficult person doesn't *make* you feel anything. Your feelings are your responsibility, and believe it or not, you actually choose to feel angry or frustrated. So you need to learn how to make better choices.

Some people think that's nonsense, but think about it for a moment. How come Mary reacts to difficult behavior with anger, while with Ted, it rolls off his back? Simple: because they think differently, and say different things to themselves. Mary, who gets angry, says things to herself that creates anger. Ted says different things to himself, things more likely to keep him calm and in control. You can learn how to do that. It's not magic. At the end of this chapter we'll get more specific about how to get there.

Second, you have to know how to convey the idea that the difficult behavior isn't going to work with you. That requires skill and knowing what to say in difficult situations. We'll focus on that part of the equation throughout the remainder of the book, when we get to handling specific difficult situations, and specific tactics and techniques.

The bottom line here is that you don't want to reward bad behavior. You want to show the person that you aren't getting suckered in, that you are cool and calm, and that, perhaps above all, you will not be manipulated or allow anyone to control your emotional state or your actions.

You are a responsible adult and you are going to act like one, in control of your own actions and reactions.

Blaming and Problem Solving—the Difference

Part of the mind-set needed to help you stay balanced, your feet firmly on the ground, involves understanding the difference between a *blaming mind-set* and a problem-solving mind-set. After you understand the difference, you must commit to a problem-solving approach. If you don't, you become a gasoline thrower.

I'm sure you have come across people who seem to be more interested in finding someone to blame when things go wrong than figuring out why it's gone wrong and ensuring that it doesn't happen again. In fact, we listed this as one of the difficult behaviors that people use that drive others crazy.

Employee Handbook

The **blaming mind-set** is a way of thinking that finds someone at fault, rather than focusing on preventing the problem from re-occurring.

You know the type. It's the person who says:

> "If you hadn't stalled so much, we'd be on time with this project."

Or,

> "Hey, you didn't tell me you wanted it that way. How am I supposed to know, read your mind?"

Another example:

> "Well, I finished the report last week, but Fred obviously didn't get it typed on time."

The person who is never at fault and constantly blames others for problems drives most of us nuts. It's easy to recognize when other people behave this way, but it's a lot harder for us to see it in ourselves. The truth is that most of us go through this blaming process now and again, particularly as we get more frustrated or feel under attack.

Employee Handbook

The **problem-solving mind-set** involves focusing on the present and the future, and focusing on solving problems, not finding fault.

As a manager of difficult people and situations, you don't have the luxury of getting into blaming mode. You can't use language, either intentionally or unintentionally, that conveys that you are focusing on trying to pin the "blame tail" on a handy donkey. If you do, you are almost guaranteed to make things worse. The irony of this is that things will get worse even when you're right about who is to blame—just talking in the blaming mode creates problems.

The other problem with a blaming mind-set, or use of blaming language, is that it doesn't get us closer to solving the problem. Take a look at the examples we provided. Let's try the first one: "Hey, if you hadn't stalled so much, we'd be on time with this project." How is this a helpful or useful statement? Does it help us figure out *why* there was a delay? Does it tell us how to prevent delays from happening? If you think about it, the comment is a jab, something that the person hearing it is going to react to in a negative, defensive, or aggressive way.

What's the alternative? Certainly, people mess up, and in the case of difficult people, they do things that cause problems for you and others. You can't ignore it. So, rather than using blame-oriented language and a blame-oriented mind-set, you use a *problem-solving mind-set* and problem-solving language.

Problem solving is different from blame finding in that it …

➤ focuses on the present and future, not the past.

➤ involves identifying causes and effects of problems.

➤ involves asking more questions to get information rather than stating opinions.

➤ focuses on thinking rather than emotion.

➤ is nonaccusatory.

Let's look at an example. Suppose Philip is difficult at a team meeting. He interrupts constantly and acts like he has a chip on his shoulder. You decide to talk to Philip after the meeting (these kinds of things are best done in private). A blaming tone and mind-set would sound something like this:

You: "Philip, you're always interrupting people at our meetings you're annoying, and you're making the meetings a total waste of time. I want you to stop before you cause more damage."

Weigh the odds. Do you think this is going to result in a constructive discussion about this difficult behavior? Probably not.

Now, a problem-solving mindset.

You: "Philip, I could be wrong but sometimes I think that you're a bit frustrated at some things around here, because you seem less patient at our meetings. Is that possible?"

Philip: "Yeah, I'm getting pretty tired of a few things, and I don't figure people are listening to me in the damn meetings. Frankly, I'd rather not attend."

You: "OK, why don't you and I see what's going on here and see whether we can find out about the listening part? Let's talk about the possibility of your going to only some of the meetings. Does that make sense?

In this example, you, as the manager, are staying on balance, not reacting emotionally, and trying to find out what is going on and opening the door to working with the person to find solutions. Notice: no blaming, no accusations.

Avoid the Lowest Common Denominator

People behave in difficult ways seem to succeed and feel rewarded when they can influence other people to act as badly as they do. Part of that is the "I-want-to-get-a-reaction" thing, and part is the need to control other people. When other people behave toward the difficult person in kind (poorly), it has very strong negative effects. It legitimizes poor behavior in the workplace, almost helping the difficult person justify his or her behavior.

As a manager, you have an even higher standard of conduct you must adhere to. Employees look to you to show them, through word and deed, what is appropriate behavior. If you drop down to the lower levels of behavior, the lowest common denominator, you tell everyone that's an OK approach.

For example, you have a chronically difficult person in your employ. One day over coffee, you're talking to a supervisor who reports to you, and you start making remarks about this difficult person—in other words, you are talking behind the person's back. Heck, all you are doing is hoping for a sympathetic ear, right? No harm, no foul.

This Won't Work!

Don't sink to the level of the difficult person. That only creates a war where everyone loses. Don't use difficult tactics to deal with difficult tactics.

57

Uh, uh. You have dropped to lowest common denominator. Now you are a problem causer rather than a problem solver. I hate to break it to you, but you've become as difficult as the person you were talking about. Another example:

> An employee yells at you in public. You yell back. Think of the positive effects of this versus the negative effects. In all probability, you will get none of the first and a whole lot of the second. You'll get an argument and a poisoned relationship, and you will ruin your ability to lead people in your work unit.

It's an unfortunate but almost universal truth that nasty, unpleasant people may use nasty, offensive behavior, but that managers or leaders cannot answer back *in the same way.* Later you will see that you don't have to tolerate or accept it or ignore it. What you should remember now is that, pure and simple, you can't respond in kind unless you're willing to live with a bunch of negative consequences.

If you're a sharp reader, you've probably figured out that avoiding sinking to lowest common denominator isn't easy. It takes self-control, discipline, and a willingness to learn new ways of handling your own anger.

Here are a few tips you can use for self-control.

Slow Down Your Talk and Responses

You can avoid getting caught up in the moment when communicating with a difficult or nasty person by slowing yourself down. This means deliberately slowing down the pace of your speech. By speaking more slowly, you give your rational brain a chance to think rather than allowing your emotions to take control.

Insider Secrets

Believe it or not, managers actually do really dumb things. I once worked for a manager who, on the surface, was a gentle, considerate, ex-hippie-type guy. Lovable. Except for the fact that in private conversations he would swear at employees, accuse them of various nefarious deeds, and do other strange things. I suppose he thought nobody would find out. Perhaps he felt that if employees were difficult, he would be more so. At one time the work unit had 17 people. Under his leadership it ended up with three.

Apart from slowing down your speech, allow more time between the moment when the other person stops talking and when you start. Use that time to think and figure out a constructive way to respond.

Slowing things down also can contribute to a less-urgent feel to the conversation, which can help the other person regain self-control.

You *can* learn how to do this. It's easy if you remind yourself.

Listen and Paraphrase

When people get into heated or potentially emotional discussions, they don't tend to listen. What they do is start preparing their responses while the other person is talking. That isn't going to help you. Rather than figuring out what you are going to say while someone is talking, try your best to listen and understand. The listening mind-set will help slow you down, and also slow down a difficult person trying to steamroll you.

After you have heard what the other person said, paraphrase it back to him or her. Again, this slows down the interaction and gives you more time to think, and also shows the person you are making an effort to understand. By using your thinking brain rather than your emotional brain, you're less likely to get knocked off-balance or to sink to the lowest common denominator.

Call Time-Out

If you feel you're getting too angry or annoyed to react constructively, call a time-out. Either schedule a better time when you (and hopefully the other person) will have had a chance to calm down. Even a short five-minute break for coffee can work well. Regroup. Think. Calm down. Then return.

What You Focus On You Get More Of

Understanding this principle is very important so you can stay in control, be constructive, and keep both feet firmly planted.

It's kind of a universal law: What you focus on is what you'll get more of. In conversations, what people focus on is what they are going to talk about. If you talk about the wrong things, you're going to steer the conversation in a negative direction.

From the Manager's Desk

Staying balanced requires not only a different mind-set, but also the use of certain behaviors; listening and paraphrasing, calling time-outs, and slowing down interactions are all techniques you can use to give yourself time to think rather than to react blindly. Start reminding yourself to use them, beginning now.

For example, if you talk about how angry you are, you're likely to spend even more time stuck being angry. If you talk about how poorly an employee has performed, in all probability you will get more bad behavior and worse performance.

From the Manager's Desk

You can save time and energy by making sure you focus on the things you really want to talk about when confronting difficult people. Better to aim at how to change things than to expend all your energy in argument and ac-cusations.

On the flip side, if you talk about more positive things, like how to improve something, then you're likely to get improvement. This law actually explains why problem solving is more effective than blame. In part it's the positive focus, and when we talk positively we get positive stuff in return.

But this law has a less apparent application. It isn't just about what you say to someone, but what you say to yourself and what is going on inside your head. If you focus on how unpleasant someone is or how stupid the conversation is, then that doesn't put you in the correct mind-set to stay calm and in control. Stewing, thinking about how bad things are, or worrying about things getting worse puts you off balance. That, unfortunately, leads to mistakes and causes bad things to happen.

So there are two parts. In conversations, don't focus on the stuff you want to get rid of; focus on what you want the person to do. Don't zoom in on the errors; instead, take a look at solutions. You'll get positive behavior and better results that way.

The second part involves what goes on in your head. It works the same way. Turn your thinking to positive, solution-oriented paths and you will keep your balance much more frequently. You will be less controlled by the other person and more in control of yourself.

Think Big Picture—Think Long Term

When dealing with difficult people, particularly when we get caught up in the frustration, we tend to focus much too narrowly, or in the "right now." We get carried away and forget that what we're doing now may have implications for other people in the future. It's important to keep this in mind. After all, there is a tomorrow and another tomorrow to think about. Managers have to take into account the effects of what they're doing, not just with the difficult person, but other employees. They have to consider the effects not just today but six months from now.

Using Self-Talk to Stay Balanced

Self-talk is at the core of staying calm and in control in the face of difficult situations. Simply put, *self-talk* refers to the words and thoughts we say to ourselves.

Even if you aren't aware of the exact words that you're saying to yourself, be sure that you have this quiet internal process going on within you. It's a very powerful force for helping you stay calm and changing your own behavior.

We can divide self-talk into two categories:

1. Negative self-talk makes it more difficult to find and use constructive solutions.

2. Positive self-talk is more likely to help you find and use constructive solutions.

Let's look at them in more detail.

Negative, Nonconstructive Self-Talk

Negative self-talk is inner dialogue that has a tendency to make you more angry, less in control, and less likely to step back and put difficult behavior and situations in context and perspective. Some general examples of this kind of negative inner dialogue include ...

Employee Handbook

Self-talk refers to the things we say to ourselves—our thoughts. Self-talk reminds us of how we should react and behave in various situations. Positive self-talk helps us respond constructively. Angry self-talk causes us to react destructively.

➤ vilifying or demonizing another person.

➤ labeling the person in a negative way.

➤ focusing on how angry you are getting.

➤ thinking about how unpleasant a conversation with that person is going to be.

➤ words and thoughts of helplessness.

This kind of self-talk is more likely to make you angrier, more emotional, and less in balance.

To be more specific, what do these statements sound like in your head?

➤ What an idiot Jane is!

➤ I wish this person would smarten up.

➤ Man, he drives me crazy!

➤ Oh, no, now I have to go talk to Fred.

➤ Maybe he'll quit; that's the only hope.

➤ This is stupid. I can't do anything with Herb.

Do these sound familiar? Most people use these at one time or another. Are there ones not listed here that you use? It's important to identify your own self-talk patterns and habits.

Positive, Constructive Self-Talk

Positive self-talk helps you deal with difficult situations because it relates to problem solving and the possibility of finding solutions and other positive results that you might create.

Some general examples include …

➤ reminding yourself the other person may have a valid opinion.

➤ focusing on the possibility of a solution.

➤ realizing there are two sides, yours and the other person's.

➤ looking at problem situations as a challenge rather than something to dread.

Specific examples sound like this:

➤ Won't it be neat if I can help turn Fred around?

➤ I'm sure there's a solution if only I search for one.

➤ I have to take special care to stay cool.

➤ I'm not going to let this person control my life.

Insider Secrets

Whether you're aware of it or not, you're talking to yourself (silently) almost all of the time. If you modify the things you say to yourself, you can learn to be more in control of your own behavior. Psychologists have recognized this. The technique psychologists use to refer to this process is called cognitive-behavior modification. It's been shown to be a very useful technique for helping people eliminate phobias, reduce stress symptoms, develop more effective anger control and change other behaviors that interfere with their lives. Many of the self-help books and tapes available involve changing that inner dialogue (for example, affirmations, relaxation tapes.

If you become more adept at modifying your own self-talk, you will find you can be much more in control. How do you go about changing what you say to yourself? Well, it's not easy and takes some diligence and work. First, you have to identify the negative self-talk you use (we all have some). Then you have to decide what self-talk phrases would be better, so you can use them to replace the less constructive ones.

Then, you have to try to catch yourself; when you use a negative self-talk phrase, replace it with a constructive one.

Some people benefit from planning out this process. Make a list of your negative self-talk phrases on the left-hand side of a piece of paper. On the right-hand side, write down the more constructive replacements.

If you do this consistently, over time you can succeed at making your internal dialogue more positive. It requires vigilance and a commitment of several months to work on it. That's because you are trying to learn new mental habits.

The Least You Need to Know

➤ You need to stay calm, balanced, and think things through rather than act too fast or reactively.

➤ Focus on positive outcomes.

➤ Work to change your negative self-talk.

➤ Avoid blaming and labeling.

➤ Slow yourself down when necessary.

Part 2
Managing Garden-Variety Employees

Most of the difficult behavior you encounter is likely to be of the "garden-variety" type. It's not malicious but, it's all around you. It's the silly little habits of others, procrastinating, arguing, negativity ...

It's important to manage these situations before they get worse. While this kind of difficult behavior is annoying, it can also impede employee morale and productivity. So, what do garden-variety difficult employees look like? And what can you do to manage the difficult situations they create in a proactive constructive way? Let's take a look at some answers to these questions.

Chapter 6

Identifying the Garden-Variety Difficult Employee

In This Chapter

➤ How garden-variety difficult people cause problems

➤ Using your interpersonal skills

➤ The limits to power (and how it gets you in trouble)

➤ Creating a good work climate

Now that we've outlined why it's important that you deal with difficult behavior promptly and the importance of a constructive mind-set, it's time to move on to practical issues. What do you do with difficult people? How do you handle different situations? What do you DO? We are going to start with what we call garden-variety difficult employees, and in Part Three of this book we'll address what you can do with more serious difficult people and behaviors.

In this chapter you'll find out how to identify garden-variety difficult behavior, how this kind of behavior impacts your workplace, and what tools you have at your disposal. We'll end with a discussion of how you might prevent difficult behavior in the first place.

Identifying the Difficult Employee

The *garden-variety difficult person* is not intentionally trying to harm others. So let's see how to identify garden-variety difficult behavior and what your options are in dealing with such individuals.

Employee Handbook

The **garden-variety difficult person** is someone whose behavior you consider difficult, but not in ways that are intentionally harmful, although the results may be quite destructive.

This Won't Work!

Garden-variety difficult behavior tends to spread like weeds as other people start reacting to and even picking up behavior cues. The danger is not so much in the present incident, but if it's allowed to continue over time, things can get worse and worse. Don't blow off minor incidents of bad behavior.

With difficult people who are consistently difficult, vindictive, and obnoxious, it's easy to identify that a problem exists. It's so "in your face" that you can't help but recognize a problem, and it's so nasty, it's easy to know you must take action.

With garden-variety difficult people, it isn't that easy. That's because they aren't all that consistent in their difficult behavior; they don't seem to harbor malice toward others, and usually they seem relatively normal. They just happen to be occasional pains in the rear end to people around them.

We can look at some of their behaviors. Here are some examples:

➤ Poor interpersonal behavior (interrupting, poor communication, occasional blaming)

➤ Negativity, cynicism

➤ Occasional poor work performance coupled with refusal to take responsibility (for example, it's never their fault)

➤ Occasional outbursts of anger

➤ Occasional whining and complaining

➤ Hesitancy to take on new work or volunteer

➤ Lateness, higher-than-expected absenteeism

If you look at these examples, (and perhaps you can add others of your own), you should see that none of these are, in and of themselves, enough to cause you great worry. It's not likely these things will create crises or that the person exhibiting one or two of them is dangerous in any real sense.

You can also see that most of these behaviors are not meant to cause harm to others. They are really just instances of people acting human and sometimes doing dumb things. Many times, a person simply lacks the skills to act appropriately, or someone loses his or her temper or emotional control for a short time. These are largely inadvertent mistakes.

However, garden-variety difficult people are not completely harmless. The fact that the people doing objectionable things have no destructive intent doesn't make their behavior less difficult. So let's keep this in perspective. No, they probably aren't dangerous, but neither are they harmless.

The Hidden Costs of the Garden-Variety Difficult Employee

When obnoxious kinds of behaviors occur, managers tend to ignore it or hope it goes away. The behaviors don't seem that serious—but they become serious when they're ignored.

Here's a way to think about it.

> Herb is generally a good employee but lately has become a little less reliable, a little less patient; in fact, once or twice in the last year he has been involved in rather loud shouting matches. Because Herb has been easy to work with in the past, you, the manager, excuse or ignore these behaviors, hoping to avoid what might end up in a confrontation—a mistake on your part.
>
> Herb finds his bad behavior unchallenged, and that's interpreted as a green light to continue acting in the same manner.

By ignoring the behavior, you reward Herb psychologically for the bad behavior. So what's going to happen? It's probably going to get worse; the behavior will be more frequent and more severe.

What are the results? Sooner or later Herb will do things that can no longer be ignored; for example, he might tell off an important customer or miss critical meetings. Then you have a major problem.

Consider also that the longer Herb continues his poor behavior, the more of a habit it becomes. When people do things for a period of time, they get ingrained or habitual, and that makes them far more difficult to deal with. Long-standing poor behavior is tougher to remedy than short-term varieties.

What are the effects of Herb's behavior on other employees? They see Herb getting away with bad behavior, and some employees will have a tendency to adopt what is tacitly accepted as OK. Herb gets to set a workplace tone, and you just might find others jumping on the bandwagon. Also, staff will expect the manager to intervene, to protect and help them. If you do not, then they blame you. They may see you as weak and incompetent. That's not a good position for any manager to be in.

So, if Herb's behavior is happening *now* and you ignore it, it is likely you are going to get …

➤ escalating poor behavior from Herb.

➤ more poor behavior from other staff.

➤ loss of face and credibility with other staff.

➤ more of a challenge when you do get around to facing the bad behavior.

So, when we apply the reality check principle to Herb (remember, that's looking at the current results of the bad behavior), we need to focus on the future possible outcomes. We need to look to what might happen if the behavior is allowed to continue without comment.

Take Action to Prevent Worsening Behavior

By now you've probably caught on that we believe in early action, even when the difficult behavior is relatively minor. By acting early, you prevent an escalation of the problem.

What actions can you take? You have several tools for dealing with difficult people. We will get more specific

From the Manager's Desk

Assess garden-variety behavior in terms of its future effects on you, your organization, and other employees before you decide to let it go without comment or action. Think *long term.*

in the next few chapters, but let's outline them now, and provide some specific tips for the use of the tools.

Your Interpersonal Tools

When we talk about interpersonal tools, we are talking mostly about the way you communicate with someone. If you use effective interpersonal communication skills, you are more likely to get through to a difficult person, to increase your influence,

This Won't Work!

Many managers believe the best way to manage a difficult situation is to take control and read the riot act. While that might have worked in the old days, now it's better to open good lines of communication before coming down hard.

and play a helping role rather than a "hit-'em-with-a-stick" role. Your interpersonal skills are the frontline tools you rely on when dealing with difficult and non-difficult people alike.

They include things like listening, questioning skills, empathy skills, taking on a helper role, and working in cooperative modes.

If we put aside the fancier language, what are we talking about here? Well, when Herb acts difficult, you'll go talk to Herb. Your success in doing this, however, is going to depend on *how* you talk to Herb. Here's how to do it right.

In conversation, before you do anything, your job is to try to understand where the difficult person is coming from. What makes the person tick? Is there some reason he or she is being difficult? That means you want to get the difficult person talking to you, while you talk less.

How do you do that? Here's an example that states a tentative observation along with a well-phrased question.

"Herb, I could be wrong here, but I see that you've been late for a few meetings, and I get the sense that you seem frustrated sometimes. That makes things tougher for others, and I'd like to know whether there is anything I can do to help. Got any ideas?"

See what you, the manager, have done? You start with a tentative observation (you can turn up the heat later if necessary). You explain that Herb's behavior is making things a bit difficult (note the calm language). Then you move into helping mode. Presumably, after Herb has responded, you can rephrase or use active listening to reinforce the idea of interest and assistance.

The information and reactions you receive will help you decide where to go next. The reactions will provide a good hint as to whether you need to become firmer and more insistent.

From the Manager's Desk

There is a basic rule in dealing with difficult people: Begin discussions with the most gentle and least forceful language and approach. You start off as a helper. Later, if it's clear that isn't going to work, you can increase the firmness of your response.

What other things are important in using your interpersonal skills to talk to difficult people? Here's a checklist of things to keep in mind.

❑   Avoid accusatory language.

❑   Talk about observable behaviors.

❑   Stay away from comments about the person's character or personality.

❑   Encourage the difficult person to acknowledge that it is in his or her interest to deal with the issue.

❑   Encourage the difficult person to offer possible solutions rather than imposing yours.

❑   At the end of your talk, summarize the gist of the discussion and ask whether the person agrees with your summary.

❑   If any potential solution is arrived at, make sure it's clear who will do what by when.

Formal Authority Tools

If your first line of defense involves the use of your interpersonal skills and building effective communication, perhaps your last line of defense involves the use of whatever formal power and authority given to you as a manager. We say last line because,

Employee Handbook

Formal authority tools refers to the things you can do because you're in management. Examples might include taking disciplinary action, laying down the law, and use of performance-management techniques.

as we've noted before, it's a lot better to resolve problems bilaterally (working together with a difficult person) than attempting to impose a solution because you believe you have the power to do so.

In the next chapters we'll provide some very specific guidelines about how to use tools like performance management or disciplinary action effectively. Right now we need to look at what *formal authority tools* you actually have. You may be surprised to find that being a manager doesn't give you much free rein.

So, You Think You Really Have Power?

I'm going to try to convince you that overusing what you think is your managerial power is really problematic. Why? Because I want to keep you out of trouble.

We're at a strange era in management history. In the olden days (well, maybe not so old), managers had a lot more power to take action against difficult employees. Now it's not the case. In past times, employees recognized the authority of management to make arbitrary decisions. Management decisions were more respected simply because they came from management. Nowadays, that's not so. Employees no longer tender that respect automatically. If anything, authority, power, and respect must be earned.

So the first problem here is that if you try to impose solutions too often, you may mobilize employees to fight back, to become uncooperative, to sabotage, and to eat away at whatever authority you believe you have.

Insider Secrets

Here's a thought. Whatever power and authority you have can be completely ignored by the people you think you have power over. Sure, you might be able to fire someone, but your staff can also become totally uncooperative and destroy you. Countless managers have been cut down to size by staff. Power and authority should be used sparingly. It's far better to have employees cooperate willingly because they respect you, than to have to stand over them carrying a big stick. And it's less likely to create employee backlash that occurs when too much power is used too often.

There's a second issue regarding the use of power and authority. These days, employees have a number of options to use if they feel you're treating them unfairly. And they aren't trivial options. There are grievance procedures, use of union resources, and the threat and reality of legal action. Whether we like it or not, employees have acquired more power, and these options require you as a manager to consider carefully whether you want to use power-based approaches to difficult people.

Here's the core issue. When you take formal disciplinary action—fire, dock pay, suspend, officially warn, or otherwise depend on what you believe is your management authority—you shift the playing field from working together to being on completely different sides. In other words, use a power-based approach to the problem and you encourage the employee to also use a power-based approach. If you try to use power, you get power back, and that's when you find that you don't have quite as much authority as you thought.

Sometimes the use of power makes things much worse.

So When Is the Use of Authority Warranted?

When is it appropriate to use the preceding outlined tools?

They're appropriate when you have exhausted other person-to-person attempts to resolve problems. They're appropriate when the difficult behavior is dangerous or exceedingly damaging. That's the "when" part. But there are some other things you need to consider.

Are you aware of the limits to your authority regarding the actions you might want to take? For example, do you really have the authority to fire someone? Will you be supported by your boss and the human resources department? If not, you would be foolish to try something that will fail.

Here's what you do in situations where you feel formal disciplinary methods are indicated. First, confer with your boss. Explain the situation, ask for suggestions, and find out what he or she wants to do. Second, contact the human resources department to find out your options and what they suggest. By doing this you will know, in advance, whether you really have the authority to do what you'd like.

Finally, it's always a good idea to be aware of any legal issues regarding formal management actions. Generally, human resources departments can advise you, but to be honest, sometimes they don't

This Won't Work!

One of the most damaging things that can affect your credibility as a manager is if you attempt to discipline an employee and have your decision reversed after the fact or do not get the support you need to carry it through. Before you take disciplinary action, consult with the right people to ensure you can do it.

know, either. If the formal actions you want to take are somewhat extreme (for example, firing someone), it may be good to consult the government office responsible for labor law in your area and/or a labor lawyer. We don't want to freak you out here, but you need to know both your authority levels and your obligations before you take drastic action.

Preventative Tools

We've talked about the importance of communication skills and tools, and the use of formal authority to deal with difficult behaviors when they have occurred. But let's face it. Isn't it better to prevent undesirable behavior in the first place? Sure it is.

How do you go about doing that?

Creating Norms

The term *norms* is a sociology term that refers to the guidelines and rules of conduct that people follow in a group. Sometimes these are formally mapped out. Often they are not so formally mapped out but are somehow understood by people. A simple way of putting it is that norms tell people "the way we do things around here."

In terms of prevention of difficult behavior, norms can be very important. When the norms of a workplace are well understood and supported by most employees, there tends to be less difficult behavior. When the norms are not well understood or not well supported, people behave the way they like, and that's not always a good thing.

It's important that everyone in your work unit understand what constitutes acceptable or unacceptable behavior.

It might seem that you could sit in your office and draft a set of guidelines, then pass them to each staff member as a set of orders. But it doesn't work that way. Norms or standards of behavior, to be most effective, need to come from the people involved. If they're imposed, they create backlash.

Employee Handbook

Norms are rules of conduct used by group members to guide their behavior. They can be explicit (formally written) or informal. People learn these rules by talking to each other and seeing what behaviors result in rewards or punishments.

So, how do you develop healthy group norms? If you're a savvy manager, you know that one of your roles is to facilitate employee discussions about desirable behavior in the workplace. Note the word "facilitate." That means that your role is to get good, constructive dialogue going among staff.

Here's what you can do. I recommend that at least once a year you hold a whole work unit get-together. The focus of the get-together is to discuss some or all of the following issues:

➤ How are we doing with respect to following the guidelines we created together?

➤ How should we treat each other?

➤ What can we do to make this a better place to work?

Don't know how to explain to staff why you're doing this? Here's a good catchphrase:

> "We can't treat our customers any better than we treat each other, so it's important that we share some ideas about how we should be dealing with our co-workers."

If you don't feel you have the skills or distance to conduct such a session, then consider hiring an external consultant or facilitator to do so.

There are two important things to remember here. First, the discussion or process is probably more important than any official document or record of the proceedings. The process should be one of focusing staff on how they treat each other (and you). We want them to think about it. Second, yes, it is a good idea to record and distribute the findings of the group.

The Power of Norm Creation

When people hold in common a set of guidelines about what is good behavior and bad, you're less likely to have people doing their own thing. Clear norms, based on employee involvement, help to keep these guidelines fresh in people's minds. But there is another important outcome associated with norm creation.

From the Manager's Desk

Where the work unit is troubled or under siege, it's much better to have an external person run a norm exploration get-together. Or, if you don't feel you have the objectivity or distance from work issues, see whether you can get someone from outside your work unit.

What we want is for your work unit to become more or less self-policing. Let's face it: You don't want to be the enforcer or arbiter of all the weenie, itty-bitty behaviors of people. You don't have time, and it's not practical.

When you have well-understood and accepted norms, work unit employees begin to self-police. They intervene when a person violates those norms. They apply a bit of pressure. And that's usually a good thing. When a difficult person hears from a peer that his or her actions weren't appreciated or consistent with specific guidelines, that can have a powerful effect.

When group norms are understood and their value recognized by most employees, it becomes less necessary for the manager to act as judge and jury. Other staff will help and step in when those norms are violated.

The Least You Need to Know

➤ Although garden-variety difficult people aren't short-term harmful, if allowed to continue they can cause long-term problems.

➤ Your first line of defense are your own interpersonal and communication skills.

➤ Your last line of defense is the use of power or authority.

➤ Always explore the limits of your power before you take power-based action.

➤ You can prevent some difficult behavior by helping employees create, buy into, and understand behavior guidelines or norms.

Chapter 7

Providing Feedback to Difficult Employees

<table>
<tr><td>

In This Chapter

➤ Why feedback is an important tool

➤ Different ways of using feedback

➤ How to share the feedback load

➤ How to give feedback that works

</td></tr>
</table>

It's an interesting thing about difficult people. While people who are intentionally destructive often know exactly how they affect others, garden-variety difficult people don't always realize or even consider how their actions affect the people around them. Perhaps they're self-centered, or don't consider the ramifications of their behavior at the time they do their stuff. Regardless, we need to consider this. If your difficult people are unaware of the effects they have, then one way of addressing this is to help them recognize and become more sensitive to the results of their actions.

How do you do that? The primary tool you have in your toolbox is *feedback*—information about the effects of one's actions on others or on achieving results. It comes from an outside source, from either other people or naturally in the process of doing a task.

In this chapter we're going to help you understand more about the use of feedback with difficult people and how to make sure that difficult people can learn about the negative (or positive) effects of their behaviors on others. You'll see that giving feedback isn't quite so simple as it might seem and that there are several feedback techniques that are unfamiliar to many people.

Feedback—a Major Tool for Change

None of us can improve our behavior or performance without understanding exactly what we need to change and what we need to change it to. This is such a basic process that we take it for granted. For example, when we drive, we constantly collect information from around us and alter our steering and braking according to the information we collect. Of course, it happens quickly so we don't notice the process of obtaining that feedback. When we drive, though, the feedback is part of the activity; that is, it is inherent in the task. Crash into a pole and you don't need anyone to tell you a mistake occurred.

Insider Secrets

Although we might not be aware of it, we are almost always taking in information from around us (feedback) and modifying what we do on the fly. The problem is that we (and difficult people) don't always pay attention to the right feedback or interpret it in the ways those who gave it to us expect. The feedback process works best when the recipient of the feedback is not defensive and is open to hearing it. But there's a responsibility on the feedback giver's side, also. The feedback giver needs to phrase the feedback in ways that make it easier for the recipient to hear. As a manager you have two responsibilities. To be open to feedback about you, and to give feedback so that it is constructive and easy to "hear".

There are many situations where the information (or feedback) from the environment is hard to figure out. Such is the case with many interpersonal behaviors or the ways a person communicates or interacts with others. Think of it this way. You go on a first date, and it's time to say goodnight. Do you kiss or not? What does the feedback or information from the other person indicate? Well, that's kind of hard to tell, isn't it? Often the information we get from people is ambiguous and difficult to interpret.

It's actually the same for some inanimate things. Consider health. A person with poor eating habits (high fat and calories, low nutrition) may let decades pass until the body provides its feedback in the form of a heart attack—and then it's too late. So you can see that sometimes the effects of behaviors are delayed.

While all of us need feedback to do things effectively, it's not always naturally occurring in the world around us.

So, let's get back to difficult people. Because some people are oblivious to how they affect others, one way of helping them change is to make them aware of the results of their behaviors. Given the opportunity and realizing that they affect others in negative ways can often motivate difficult people to change their behaviors.

The Different Faces of Feedback

Feedback involves sitting down with someone and giving some specific, nonconfrontational information about how the person may be affecting you and others. However, that's just one form of feedback, and while it's an important one, giving feedback that really changes people's behavior is a bit more complex than that. We need to look at the different dimensions of feedback, because that will allow us to better utilize the feedback-related tools we have available to us.

Two Feedback Dimensions: Factual and Emotional

There are two kinds of information you can convey to a person while providing feedback. The first, *factual feedback,* is information about the results or outcomes of the person's behavior and is based on factual observations.

Let's consider Rob, who is often late for meetings. You sit down with Rob and say, "Rob, it's possible nobody has pointed this out, but when you're late for a meeting, we all have to wait, and that means that some important things might not get done. None of us have the time to lose given the new XYZ project."

Notice that the feedback in the example is a statement of fact. That *is* what happens, and in this case you're providing that information to Rob.

Factual feedback is always appropriate with difficult people, provided it is, indeed, truthful and accurate; you also must deliver it in a way that doesn't cause the person to reject the information. We'll talk about that in a minute.

It's ideal for people who just haven't considered the effects of their actions on others.

Employee Handbook

Factual feedback is based on factual observations (what you see or touch, for example) and helps a person determine whether their behavior resulted in positive or negative results.

Emotional feedback is information about how other people react emotionally to a person's behavior.

The second dimension of feedback relates to the emotional side. *Emotional feedback* is information about the emotional reactions of others towards the person or his or her behavior.

It differs from factual feedback in that the information is about the internal states of mind and emotions of other people, and not the external facts.

For instance, let's go back to our example with Rob, the tardy meeting guy. If you were to say:

"Rob, darn it, are you late again? Man, that makes me angry!"

then that would be emotionally based. Why? Because you're talking about the effect of the lateness on your emotional state.

The thing about emotional feedback is that it is conveyed in two ways. The first is, of course, the words. When you say:

"When you're late, I get really angry,"

you're using the words to explain your inner state. The second is probably far more important. Emotional feedback is also sent through your nonverbal behaviors, tone, and general demeanor. Here's a list of the ways we send emotional feedback, often unintentionally:

➤ Raised voice, voice quality

➤ Physical behavior (red face, pounding on table)

➤ Facial expressions

➤ Tone of voice, sarcasm

➤ Other body language (rolling eyes, slumping, glaring)

Generally, the nonverbal ways of sending information about your emotional state are more likely to cause a reaction in another person. That's not necessarily a good thing. For example, if you try to deliver some factual feedback but your nonverbal signals indicate that you are very angry, then the person is more likely to react with defensiveness or aggression than if the factual feedback is sent without the angry nonverbals. In other words, the person may become more difficult.

Emotional feedback (talking about or showing your emotions) works best with garden-variety people who actually care about your emotional reactions. It's easy to see that "When you made that remark about me, you hurt my feelings" is a good thing to say to someone who is concerned about your feelings. However, saying the same thing to someone who hates your guts and likes to make you feel bad isn't going to have the same effect.

Insider Secrets

Psychological research strongly suggests that if your words and nonverbal behavior are in conflict (that is, inconsistent), the other person will rely or trust his interpretation of your nonverbal behavior rather than *what* you said. When what you say conflicts with how you say it, people believe the latter.

So, whether you use emotional feedback depends on the relationship you have with the person in question. It ends up as a judgment call.

Also, it is critically important that you don't allow your nonverbals to send a hostile message to someone when you're trying to deal with factual feedback. It will contaminate the feedback and provoke a blowup.

Sources of Feedback

There are three sources of feedback, and you can use all of them. The first source is you. The second is others in the workplace, and the third is in the tasks or results a person creates.

In other words, a person can receive feedback from you. A person can receive feedback from co-workers or customers. Or a person can receive feedback from the direct observable consequences of his or her actions. This last one is like the feedback we receive when we drive a car into a pole. Nobody has to *tell* us.

It may seem a bit academic to make these distinctions, but here's why we do it. You don't have to rely only on the feedback you provide directly to a person. What you want to do is to sensitize the difficult person to all three sources of feedback. This takes some pressure off of your back, and allows you to use indirect feedback methods.

Your job, quite simply, is to make the feedback information more obvious, so the person is better able to see it. Whether the information comes from you, others, or the task doesn't matter. In fact, it's best if all three are involved.

Feedback Strategies

Now we get to the fun part. What do you do? What specific feedback techniques do you have at your disposal?

Direct Feedback

Direct feedback is information you provide to a person directly (and usually in private). It may be factually based, emotionally based, or both. Here's an example of factually based feedback:

> "John, I've noticed that when it comes time to volunteer for job tasks, you seem to be hesitant to jump in. Perhaps it's because you feel a bit overwhelmed, and I would like to know what's up. Are you feeling overburdened?"

Notice the gentle tone and that the manager offers a tentative observation (not absolute words like "never" and "always"). Also notice the use of questions here to try to open up a dialogue, and the lack of blaming.

Here's another example, one which is more emotional:

> "John, I get a bit frustrated when I see that you aren't comfortable volunteering for new tasks. We need you (and everyone) to pitch in these days and take on new responsibilities, and I'd like to talk to you about your hesitancy."

From the Manager's Desk

I can think of no situation where direct feedback should be public. Always provide such feedback in private, one on one.

Notice again the gentle tone. There's no ranting, raging, or blaming. Also, despite the fact the manager is making a criticism, the manager is also indicating that John is valued and needed.

We'll come back to direct feedback in a moment and provide you with some guidelines to follow so you improve the chances the difficult employee hear the information in a less-defensive way.

Facilitating Feedback from Others

Most people are familiar with direct feedback. It's the feedback method most obvious and frequently taught to managers. People are less familiar with the other methods, and that's a shame. You don't have to be the only source of feedback. In fact, the more sources of feedback available to a difficult person, the more likely he or she will likely actually hear and act on the messages to make improvements.

There's a second source, and that's from other people in the organization (co-workers) or from people outside of the organization (customers). Because difficult people affect many people, it only makes sense to help the difficult person receive information from them, too.

How do you do it? Perhaps the most useful way is to use staff meetings to do so. Let's consider an example.

It's your weekly staff meeting. You have 10 employees present, including Martha, who has been curt with some peers and overbearing with some of the support staff (for example, the receptionist). Here's what you want to accomplish:

➤ Open the topic in a general way.

➤ Help Martha think more about her behavior.

➤ Do all this without singling out Martha publicly.

➤ Provide a safe forum for discussion.

Here's what you might say:

"I've noticed that people seem a bit on edge and curt or even sometimes rude to each other. That bothers me, and I think it affects all of us directly or indirectly. I'd like to talk about this, and perhaps we can develop a small list of guidelines about how we should treat each other. To start off, I have a few questions for you. The first is, 'Do you feel that we could treat each other better?' The second is, 'How should we go about making this a more comfortable place to work?'"

Notice here we're not singling out anyone and we're trying to encourage discussion and dialogue. Within that dialogue we'll find that information about difficult behavior gets passed to Martha in an indirect way, without necessarily singling her out or humiliating her.

Of course, there's no guarantee Martha will see her own behavior as part of what's being discussed. There's a way around this. After the meeting, and in private, you can talk to Martha about the discussion and be more specific. You can combine facilitation of feedback with your own direct feedback. That drives the points home for Martha.

Customers can also be used as a feedback source, if the individual interacts with them frequently. You can use customer service questionnaires to obtain this information, or, better yet, have the difficult person (and perhaps co-workers) periodically ask for feedback from their customer contacts.

This Won't Work!

Many people aren't skilled at giving good feedback. If you have employees who are very frustrated, they may blurt out inappropriate comments about the difficult person. To avoid this, provide some guidelines or rules for the discussion. You can use the guidelines listed later in this chapter.

Cueing Attention on Task Feedback

Because one of the problems underlying difficult behavior is that the difficult person is oblivious to its effects, it's important that they be made aware of the consequences of their actions. While direct feedback and facilitated feedback from others involve the perceptions of people, task feedback is more objective in that it concerns the results of the actual job or tasks the person carries out.

Your role with this form of feedback is to encourage or *cue* the difficult person to examine the consequences of his or her behavior on actual job tasks. For example, if you're dealing with someone who constantly procrastinates, you need that person to consider how the stalling affects getting the job done, customer satisfaction, and his or her own mental state. Encourage people to focus on the outcomes of their behavior, and they're more likely to realize it's in their own best interest to change.

Here's an example of how you might do it.

Employee Handbook

Cueing means focusing a person's attention on some relevant results of their own behavior.

Let's use Martha's procrastination. During a private conversation with her, you say, "Martha, it seems to me that you might be making things more difficult for yourself and I'd like to help. Have you noticed that when you delay starting projects, you end up with a lot of stress? And that sometimes your delaying results in missed deadlines? I'm wondering if we can talk about how to avoid those situations, if we work together. First, can you think of other problems that might happen if you are rushed or start things late?"

Notice again, the gentle tone. What we want here is for Martha to identify the outcomes of her own behavior, or to think about it, at least. When she acknowledges that procrastinating isn't a good thing, then you can get to solutions.

To get to that point, she has to look at the results. And your job is to help her look at those consequences.

We've looked at three different methods of using feedback with difficult people. Now we need to look at how feedback should be delivered so it's likely to be heard. So let's turn to guidelines for effective feedback.

Giving Feedback That Gets Positive Results

No matter what the source or method, feedback delivered badly just isn't going to result in positive change. There are right ways and wrong ways to do it. We'll look at some guidelines to keep you out of trouble and to ensure that giving feedback doesn't make things worse. These apply to you directly when you give feedback or when you're cueing to focus a person's attention on consequences. They also apply to others who may give feedback when prompted by you. In that situation, they can be used as guidelines to be followed in public or group feedback environments.

Feedback That's Somewhat Controlled by Recipient

Ideally, the recipient of feedback should be in control of it, at least to some degree. That means that the receiver should have a choice whether or not to accept the feedback and to determine a good time for it. The reason is obvious. Feedback given when the receiver isn't ready for it or doesn't want to hear it is likely wasted, seen as an intrusion, and will likely be rejected.

How do you do this? Here's one way:

> "Martha, I'd like to talk to you about making sure things get done on time. I need your help. Would this be a good time to talk about it? Or perhaps we might set a time?"

Here's a firmer one:

> "Martha, I have some real concerns about what looks like delays in starting some projects, and I need to talk to you about it. Let's set a time when we can sit down and talk about it."

Or, in a relaxed setting with someone you have a good relationship with:

> "Martha, I'd like to give you some feedback on your job performance. We can do that now or set a time to meet."

From the Manager's Desk

The best way to ensure the feedback receiver has some control is to ask them whether it's a good time to talk about the topic or to ask them to set a good time.

This Won't Work!

While feedback should be under the control of the recipient, you as the manager have a responsibility to get it done. Don't allow feedback sessions to be put off indefinitely. There needs to be a balance of control.

No Overload

People have a tendency to save up complaints until they get so annoyed, they blurt them all out at once, overwhelming the recipient and causing him or her to go on the defensive. *Don't do that.* Feedback should be short and to the point.

This is one reason why you're better off dealing with difficult behaviors as they occur. If you deal with them promptly, you're less likely to be so frustrated or angry that you do that "blurting-out" thing.

Feedback Should Be Specific and Refer to Behavior

We reiterate the importance of focusing on behaviors and not personalities. All the research on feedback tells us that general feedback, or feedback about personality characteristics, just doesn't work very well.

For example, telling someone you think they are acting in a rotten way isn't going to cut it. It's going to create a mess. However, discussing the person's tone of voice when he or she talks to other staff members is better. Telling someone you don't think he or she is a team player is worse than useless. Talking to someone about his or her seeming unwillingness to volunteer for job assignments is much better.

See the difference?

Balance Positive and Negative

We've focused on feedback as a tool to correct difficult behavior. But feedback isn't used only when there is a problem. It is also used to tell people when they're doing the *right* things, not just the wrong things.

This is very important. People need to know what they're doing wrong, but they also know what they're doing right so they can continue to do it. Try to balance feedback to include both things that could be improved and things that are well done.

Insider Secrets

There's no such thing as constructive criticism. There is a misconception that if we say things like "I'd like to give you some constructive criticism," people will want to hear it. They don't. When you use that phrase, people wait for the other shoe to drop. Don't use it. It makes people feel manipulated and lied to.

And, lest we forget, when we provide feedback about things that need improvement and people do indeed improve, we'd better darn well congratulate them on their success. Provide that positive feedback.

Frame the Feedback

You can phrase feedback so it is nasty, manipulative, and likely to make the other person angry or defensive. Or you can phrase it so that it is likely to be heard and elicit the changes you're looking for. What determines the reaction is the phrasing and how you present, or *frame*, the feedback. Here are some tips:

➤ Use phrasing that suggests you want to work with the person, not do something to him or her.

➤ Ask questions. Get the other person talking.

➤ Don't talk as if you have all the answers. Don't make absolute statements. Make tentative ones (for example, "sometimes" rather than "every time" or "you never …").

➤ Don't accuse; rather, share observations.

➤ Stick with behavior, not personality.

➤ No blaming—focus on problem solving.

➤ Make offers to help

➤ Ask for their help

Recap Together

In direct feedback situations, end the discussion with some sort of recap or summary of the key points you have discussed, any decisions you have made together, and any obligations either of you have accepted. Get the employee involved in the recapping or ask her whether she agrees with your summary.

This helps focus on the key points, and ensures that you are both on the same wavelength when the meeting is done.

The Least You Need to Know

➤ Some difficult people are difficult because they're unaware of the effects of their actions on others.

➤ Feedback is information that helps a difficult person become more aware of how his or her actions affect others and job success.

➤ You can deliver feedback yourself, facilitate it so it comes from others, or help focus the attention of the difficult person on the consequences of his or her actions.

➤ Regardless of its source, feedback should not overload the recipient. He or she should have some control over it, and it must be framed as positively and helpfully as possible. You and the employee should be on the same side.

➤ Don't forget that feedback isn't just for when things go wrong. Be sure to give positive feedback, too.

Chapter 8

Parrying the Difficult Thrusts

In This Chapter

➤ Dealing with whiners and complainers

➤ Handling personal attacks

➤ Setting limits for difficult behavior

➤ Turning the naysayer around

➤ Dealing with meeting disrupters

It's time to get more specific. We are going to look at some difficult situations that you've probably come across and introduce more specific techniques for dealing with difficult people and their difficult behavior.

As you go through this process, keep in mind that we haven't yet touched on more severe difficult behavior, and in this chapter we're still talking about the garden-variety difficult behavior that pops up in every workplace.

Have Some Cheese with the Whine

One thing that drives managers nuts (and probably everyone else on the planet) is when an employee chooses to complain, whine, or otherwise act like he or she is constantly being wronged in some way. It's not surprising. It's kind of a hot button when an adult behaves like a child.

Let's introduce Paul. Come on out, Paul. Oh, heck, he doesn't want to come out, he's too busy, and he doesn't hesitate to tell me how he's overworked, underpaid, and gets no respect. And he has a habit of sounding like a whining child. Oh, here he comes. Here are a few things that folks like Paul do and say:

➤ I never get the good assignments.

➤ People don't listen to me.

➤ Everyone's out to get me.

➤ People don't like me.

So what do I do? Where do I start? The first thing I need to do is determine whether this is a really important problem that I need to deal with. Remember the reality check principle? OK, I need to look at the results of his behavior. First, it bugs me. I can't stand the whining that occurs almost every day. Well, that's not really enough to make this a serious problem, so are there other results? Yes.

I know if I ignore this, things will get worse. Paul's coworkers are showing impatience with him, and Sarah told me that she can't stand working with him. Also, I hear that he's been whining to outsiders about how badly he's treated on the job. It's not a good image to project to customers. I know that if this continues, people are going to start ignoring him and might just get so fed up they do try to get back at him. That's going to make Paul's behavior worse.

OK, that's good enough for me. I can't sit in my office and allow this.

From the Manager's Desk

Before meeting with an employee, get the right mind-set. Remind yourself to maintain your cool and to focus on problem solving and not blaming. Don't get into a "I-hate-this-situation" mind-set. This isn't life or death.

We're going to introduce several communication techniques here that are going to help me (and you) not only deal with this situation, but also similar ones. Feedback is only one of the methods we'll be using.

Beginning the Process

First, I'll set up a meeting with Paul, negotiating with him to arrive at a time and place and setting aside a specific amount of time. This is important so the meeting is neither cut short nor extends too long. I'd use the phrasing used in our discussion on beginning feedback in Chapter 7, "Providing Feedback to Difficult Employees."

When Paul arrives, I try to make him more comfortable with the usual amenities (coffee, for example). Then I start.

Empathy Responses

Empathy responses refer to things you can say that show that you understand the emotions of the person you are talking to. You have to prove you understand, so you need to be specific. Here are some examples:

➤ It seems to me that you feel you aren't being treated as well as you would like.

➤ I'd guess you are pretty upset at the moment.

➤ I get the impression that you feel I may not respect your work.

Employee Handbook

Empathy responses refer to things you say and do to prove to another person that you understand his or her emotions.

Why are empathy responses important? Because we want the employee to be open to what we have to say; in this case, if we show we understand where Paul is coming from, it's more likely Paul will be more open to our comments. It also defuses hostility and makes it less likely Paul is going to spend the entire meeting whining some more.

OK, so here's how I start this meeting I'm having with Paul:

> "Paul, thank you for coming. Here's what I want to discuss with you. Over the last few weeks, I get the impression that you feel you aren't being treated the way you would like, or that you feel your work isn't valued here. I want to talk about your feelings, and about the way you seem to be expressing them. I guess the first place to start is to ask you, how are you feeling about things?"

Let's imagine Paul denies he is feeling uncomfortable. That's not an uncommon response. Now we're going to shift into feedback mode.

> "OK, Paul, I may be mistaken, but what I see is that you often talk about how overworked you are [or whatever you have observed, being as specific as possible]. I've also heard from customers that you have complained about our work unit to them. How do you think those kinds of things affect people's perceptions of you, your coworkers, and the work unit?"

What we've done here is the beginning of our next technique, called "returning responsibility."

Returning Responsibility

Returning responsibility involves communicating to the employee that he or she is expected to take on at least some responsibility for solving the problem.

Employee Handbook

Returning responsibility means that you communicate to the employee that he or she is expected to be an active participant in problem solving.

From the Manager's Desk

When a difficult person doesn't respond to a gentle, less-forceful approach, you have the option of gradually becoming firmer and using your management power to set out guidelines and expectations. But save any ultimatums until you've tried other, usually more productive, approaches.

What I'm doing with Paul is simply asking him to figure out the consequences or outcomes of his complaining behavior. I want it from him.

Returning responsibility involves some other tactics. For example, in any setting, when I hear Paul complain, I'm going to ask him to suggest how to resolve the complaint. If Paul says he's overworked, I'm going to ask him how we can address that. If Paul says nobody pays attention to him, I'm going to ask him what he might do to change that, or why he thinks people might be ignoring him.

What I need to do, both in the meeting and at every other instance of complaining or whining behavior, is to send the message that I'm not going to be suckered into arguing or solving the problem alone, but that I expect him to come up with possible solutions. Then we negotiate.

Now, pay special attention. I've started really gently. I began by trying to show Paul I understand he may feel wronged but haven't agreed that his perception is accurate. When Paul denies the problem, we shift to talking about his behavior (which is really the issue). If he denies that part, then I will become firmer in the feedback cycle, explaining what I expect, and how I would like him to alter his behavior. We'll talk more about what happens if that doesn't work in a later chapter.

What's important here is I start out with the least possible force. I also send the message, both in the meeting and later on, that I expect Paul to take some responsibility for fixing the problem. If that doesn't work, I still have the option of becoming firmer in stating my expectations and consequences if they're not met.

Personal Attacks

In-your-face attacks are obvious, open attacks on you, your competency, and your personal characteristics, or they are simply abusive. They include behavior like offensive language.

In terms of a reality check, this is a no-brainer: It's not acceptable behavior. Let's look at two separate situations—when the verbal attack occurs in private and when it occurs in public.

Before we do, let's also assume that the nasty person doesn't do this too often. If so, that's considered venomous or more severe difficult behavior, and we will address this in a later section.

Private Attacks

Let's go back to Paul. Despite my best efforts to handle his situation, he loses his temper at the meeting. He makes some remarks that are personal. One thing he says is that the only reason I got my management job was because I knew someone upstairs. Then he throws in a few swear words. Not good.

I'm going to start with the empathy technique, but we're going to introduce a second technique called assertive limit setting.

My first response is to respond calmly by saying:

> "Paul, I know this is a difficult subject, and you're angry."

Then I'll wait and see whether his behavior changes to a more reasonable tone.

If it doesn't, I move to the limit-setting component.

Assertive Limit Setting

Assertive limit setting involves setting limits for a person's behavior and setting out the consequences if that behavior continues.

It goes like this. You say:

> "If you to continue to [insert the behavior you want to stop], I will have to [insert the action you will take]."

Here's an example we could use with Paul:

> "Paul, if you continue to swear, I'm going to end this meeting, and we will have to meet again tomorrow and the next day until we resolve this."

Or:

> "If you continue to make comments about my management skills in a rude way, I am going to have to move to a more formal process for dealing with this issue."

Employee Handbook

Assertive limit setting involves setting and communicating boundaries or limits, and communicating what will happen if a person goes beyond what is acceptable.

This Won't Work!

Angry people want you to react with anger, because that tells them their inappropriate behavior is getting a reaction. Don't— don't argue, don't get excited. If you need to calm down, call a brief time-out to get coffee.

What's important here is that these limits are put forth calmly in a nonthreatening way. Again, remember: We don't want to be sucked into an argument.

If Paul does not behave more appropriately, then you enact the consequences. In a private meeting, if a person shows no indication he is going to behave as you have requested, don't continue. It will only get worse.

Before we move on, consider that when setting limits, you need to be specific about the behavior you are unwilling to accept. Don't say, "If you don't smarten up …," or even, "If you don't calm down …." Name the specific behavior (for example, swearing, raised voice, personal comments).

Public Attacks

If you or other people are attacked publicly, your first priority is to stop the behavior as quickly as possible. Do not allow it to continue, because it will escalate. You can empathize, and quickly set a limit. If that limit isn't adhered to, you can speak to the attacking person privately, making it clear that this behavior will *not* continue.

If you are in a meeting and the attack continues, then it may be necessary to adjourn, if that's possible, or leave, if it's a meeting you have less control of. Do not lose your cool. Do not argue.

Regardless of how you handle it at the time, you need to follow up privately with the person. At that point, no doubt you will want to set limits for future behavior.

Dealing With Minor Back-Channel Problems

Gossip! Covert conversations held when the focus of that conversation is not present can create big problems, because this stuff creates a sense of mistrust for everyone. After all, while people enjoy talking about a person behind his or her back, they also wonder what people say about them when they aren't around.

Applying our reality check principle about the effects of back-channel gossip, is there sufficient reason to take action? Probably, although most workplaces have some of it. So what do we do?

Apart from the techniques already mentioned here, which can be applied to a particular person (feedback, empathy, limit setting), there are a few others we can introduce.

Modeling Behavior

How you behave with respect to back-channel discussions and gossip affects what other people do. In other words, you should be modeling the behavior you want, acting in the same manner you would like other staff to use to deal with back-channel discussions and gossip.

Insider Secrets

Gossip and back–channel communication can range from fairly harmless to hugely harmful. They erode the sense of trust needed in a highly functioning workplace. They can also encourage taking sides, and over the long term can eat at the foundation of your team or organization.

Here are a few techniques to create an anti-gossip climate.

When an employee talks to you privately about a problem with another employee, your first response should be to ask,

> "Have you discussed this with Tom yet?"

If the person hasn't tried to work out the problem directly, then you indicate you won't be involved until that conversation takes place. That models the correct behavior and sends the message that "at our company, we don't talk about people behind their backs. We try to work it out one-to-one *first*."

Second, if someone tries to communicate gossip to you (either publicly or privately), here's what you say:

> "Freddy, I don't think it's constructive to talk about things or speculate about people this way. I really don't want to hear gossip about people."

Mobilizing Group Pressure

While many people enjoy occasional gossip and back-channel talk (provided they aren't the subject), most will also recognize that it isn't constructive. But you probably have to mobilize that way of thinking, so people actually contemplate how destructive these kinds of remarks can be. How do you do it? Here's an example.

Use a staff meeting and allocate about 30 minutes, maximum, to discuss gossip and back-channel communication. Introduce the topic by mentioning that gossip and indirect communication can be harmful. Point out that while many of us like to gossip about others, we often wonder about what people say about us when we aren't there.

Work with the group to establish some general guidelines about gossip and how difficulties should be handled in a more direct fashion. Ask them to come up with the guidelines. This process sensitizes staff to the issues, and allows others to ignore or refuse to take part in gossip when it occurs.

Skill Building

Believe it or not, when people are approached with gossip, it's likely they don't know what to do to interrupt the conversation or what to say so they aren't pulled into it. Even if they don't want to hear it, they don't want to be rude to the person spreading the gossip, and will usually sit through it even though they don't necessarily agree with it.

So teach them. Give them a few phrases they can use in these situations.

This is best done as part of the aforementioned group meeting. You can suggest how people might handle a situation where they're exposed to gossip and want to contribute to stopping it. (See the section "Modeling Behavior" earlier in this chapter for an example.) Or, you can ask employees at the meeting how they think these approaches should be handled.

> ### From the Manager's Desk
>
> By making use of group pressure and getting other staff to help out, you can eliminate the rewards or reinforcements the gossip (or difficult person) receives for his or her behavior. Not only do you send the message that it isn't going to work with you, you get other staff to send the same message.

The Work and Responsibility Avoider

You know the type: the person who doesn't want to go the extra mile—or even the regular mile. This is the person who looks at his shoes when you ask for volunteers. This may also be the person who always has some excuse for poor performance, exhibiting the "hey-it-isn't-my-fault" syndrome.

OK, so first apply the old reality check principle. Is this a real problem worth addressing? Look at the consequences. Is it causing resentment on the part of other more responsible employees? Is it interfering with getting jobs done? Or is it just an occasional annoyance from a person who really is overworked? You decide whether this requires action (it usually does if it occurs over an extended period of time).

The most important technique here is one we mentioned earlier, and that is the returning of responsibility, coupled with a no-blaming approach. What we want to do is send the messages:

➤ Looking down at your shoes isn't going to work with me.

➤ Blaming others isn't going to work, either.

Here are a few specific things you can do.

When Paula makes excuses or claims overwork as a reason for not taking on necessary responsibilities, respond like this:

> "OK, Paula, I understand you feel overworked [or a similar listening response]. So, let's sit down and figure out what we can do about that. Why don't you think about it, come up with some suggestions as to how we can get the work done, and let's meet tomorrow at 9 A.M."

This Won't Work!

Don't assume the work or responsibility avoider is lazy or a poor employee. There may be other reasons why the person is avoiding work. One of the most common ones is a lack of confidence. In some cases it's worthwhile to ask, privately, why he or she doesn't want to do a specific job.

See what you are doing? You're shifting the responsibility to solve the problem to the person who claims it is a problem, and you are doing so in a gentle constructive way. And you are sending the message that you expect people to take responsibility for solving problems, rather than complaining or avoiding work.

Or, as in the previous situation, you can conduct a discussion among employees about how work should be assigned, again establishing some guidelines for the group that are generated by the group.

The Meeting Disrupter

The meeting disrupter can make meetings a horrible experience for all attendees. These folks use a number of techniques to focus attention on themselves, or are hypercritical, or take conversations into irrelevant areas. How do you handle these?

First, apply normal meeting management procedures. Always have an agenda that specifies the expected outcomes of the meeting, not just what will be discussed. There should be someone who has the responsibility to see the agenda is adhered to. You need not follow a rigid rules-of-order process, but you do need someone to follow up.

From the Manager's Desk

It's OK for the chair or you (the manager) to interrupt someone who is speaking inappropriately. While it may seem rude, the other meeting attendees will appreciate it. If you have an agreed-upon agenda, then you use that to justify the interruption.

Employee Handbook

An **A-1 executive decision** is one you make as a manager with formal power and authority.

It's not a bad idea to rotate the chair of the meeting among staff. This helps meeting disrupters see how difficult it is when others at the meeting are less cooperative.

The reason the agenda is so important is that it is used to justify decisions to move on as well as to stop potential meeting disrupters from getting the meeting off subject.

For example, if Dianne goes off on a tangent, the chair (or you) should jump in and say, "We really need to make some of the decisions outlined in our agenda, and while Dianne's points seem important, they aren't directly relevant to the decision we need to make. So, let's get back to ..."

In more extreme cases, where a person may be nasty or do things like rolling the eyes or giving other nonverbal signals, then private feedback is indicated.

In the preventative vein, we suggest that at least once a year you have a meeting to establish guidelines for behavior at meetings. Get your staff to brainstorm how they want to be treated at meetings. Make sure these guidelines are present at each meeting so the chair can use them to point out that the guidelines are being contravened. This makes it easier for people to speak up.

Finally there may be times when you need to make what we call an *A-1 executive decision*. That means that you, as a manager, have a responsibility to intervene and use your clout to make a decision when it is clear the conversation is destructive or pointless. Generally, this power is best used sparingly. Remember that if you're annoyed by the progress of the meeting, it's likely that others are as well, and they will sigh inwardly with relief if you end the pain.

The Naysayer

The *naysayer* is the person who always finds what's wrong with an idea, or always has reasons why something won't work. Rarely does he or she provide better ideas, but is more comfortable reacting and shooting down the ideas and enthusiasm of others.

Before we talk about how to handle such people, let's not assume that such folks are totally useless. They can serve as the canary in the coal mine, helping others to step back and think about possible flaws or problems rather than jump into the group agreement mentality. So, we don't necessarily want to shut these people up completely, but we do want them to become more constructive.

OK, first the reality check principle. Is your naysayer a problem? What are the consequences of doing nothing? Still feel you need to do something? OK.

The best way to handle naysayers is, once again, to return responsibility to them. What you want to do is get this message across:

> "It's OK to point out flaws in ideas, but if you do, it is expected that you will have an alternative, and yes, I'm going to ask."

So, if Jean says: "That's never going to work," or "Heck, we tried that years ago, and it failed miserably." Here's a response:

> "Well, Jean, if you feel it isn't going to work, can you suggest a better option?"

Or if you want to open up a general dialogue, you can say:

> "Can anyone recall what happened when we tried this last time?"

The latter is tricky because it invites others in a group (if it is a group) to jump in, and removes the spotlight (and the rewards) given to the naysayer.

This is an extremely powerful approach. If the naysayer is simply enjoying the spotlight or has nothing positive to contribute, this approach is likely to encourage them to stop being so darned critical. If they do have good ideas, then you're turning them from the negative to the positive.

If that doesn't work over time, you have the option of giving the person private feedback.

This Won't Work!

Managers often expect instant results when dealing with difficult people. That's bad. Think of stopping difficult behavior as a long-term thing that's going to have an effect over time (often months). No technique is going to create instant results.

The Least You Need to Know

➤ Always apply the reality check principle before acting.

➤ Empathy helps put you and the difficult person on the same side.

➤ Returning responsibility is a powerful technique for gently indicating the person is expected to take on responsibility to solve problems.

➤ Mobilizing group pressure is a way to set guidelines, and have other employees involved in ensuring they are followed.

Chapter 9

Using Performance Management to Help

> **In This Chapter**
>
> ➤ What performance management *is* about
>
> ➤ Common misunderstandings about performance management
>
> ➤ The important parts of performance management
>
> ➤ How to use performance management with difficult people

One of the most important tools you can use to address difficult behavior in the workplace is the performance-management process. Unfortunately, performance-management techniques are among the most misused management tools around. Somehow, our understanding of performance management and performance appraisal has deteriorated to make the process less than useful, or even damaging.

In this chapter we are going to look at how performance management can be used properly and effectively. We'll address some common misconceptions about it. And, of course, we will explain how you can use performance management to address difficult behavior in the workplace.

Performance Management Isn't What You Think

Many managers lack a good grasp of the *performance management* process, so let's spend some time explaining what it is and isn't.

Employee Handbook

Performance management is an ongoing communication process, undertaken in partnership, between an employee and his or her immediate supervisor that involves establishing clear expectations and understandings about work results and work behavior.

First, let's expand our definition a bit. We indicated that performance management is about communication and establishing common understanding and expectations between you and each employee. What are these common understandings about? Here are the things that are important.

Performance management is used to create common understanding about ...

➤ the essential job functions the employee is expected to complete.

➤ how the employee is expected to contribute to the welfare of the company, the work unit, and the team.

➤ what doing the job well means.

➤ how the employee and manager will work together to improve, sustain, or build on existing employee performance.

➤ how job performance will be measured.

➤ identifying barriers to performance and removing them.

This Won't Work!

Never, ever mistake performance management for performance appraisal. Appraisal is only a small part of performance management, and doing appraisal alone is going to cause you problems down the road.

Of course, performance management is more than that. It provides a forum for giving feedback to employees, both during the year and at the end of the year as part of the performance-review process. It's a forum for identifying and solving problems. It helps the manager get information he or she might need in a timely way.

You should be seeing a common thread here. It is a working-together process, a communication process, and a problem-solving process. In these ways it is very consistent with what we already mentioned about techniques you can use with difficult employees. Both performance management and dealing with difficult people follow the same principles.

What Performance Management Isn't

Before we map out the steps in performance management, let's talk about some of the common misconceptions both managers and employees have about it.

First, performance management isn't something a manager does *to* an employee. In fact, if that's how you approach it, it loses most of its value as a management tool. It is done in partnership, because if it's done well it benefits everyone: you, the employee, and the company.

Second, performance management, and by extension performance review or appraisal, is not a club to force people to work better or harder. This ties in with the notion that you can't make someone work harder or behave differently. You need the person's cooperation.

From the Manager's Desk

Performance management is a powerful tool when it is used correctly. Most managers need to upgrade their understanding of the process. We recommend you locate a good book on the subject to guide you and upgrade your own understanding, because it really is a book-length topic.

Third, performance management isn't used only when there is a problem with performance. Performance management allows the employee to receive feedback about his or her job performance. As we said earlier, people need several things from feedback. They need to know what they are doing well so they can continue to do it, what they need to change, and what is expected of them. That means performance management must provide a forum for both congratulating employees, and helping them change their less-effective behavior.

Fourth, performance management isn't about the paperwork or the forms or the human resources department. It's about what is said between manager and employee: the communication process. No forms or paper or computer software can replace that.

The Links Between Performance Management and Managing Difficult People

How does performance management tie in with managing difficult behavior? First, there's the preventative function. By establishing mutually agreed-upon standards, your difficult employee knows what is expected of him or her. By reducing misunderstandings, you reduce the probability of ineffective behavior.

Second, there is the ongoing feedback function. This serves two purposes. Obviously, because good performance management involves communication all year, the employee gets ongoing feedback that can help in keeping things on track. Equally important, the manager receives information from the employee, and that allows the manager to intervene early and solve problems early.

The performance-review process (often done formally at least once a year) allows you to attach consequences to good behavior and bad. You can reward the good, and problem-solve or apply sanctions for the bad.

Finally, because the performance-management process is a formal one, it allows you to fulfill some legal requirements when and if you need to take disciplinary action. We'll talk more about this issue in the next section.

The Important Parts of Performance Management

A lot of managers and employees think performance management is the same as performance appraisal. That's dead wrong and a recipe for disaster. Performance appraisal is but a small part of the larger, more prevention-oriented, performance-management system. So, what are the other parts? Let's go through them and point out how each step in the process relates to managing difficult people.

Employee Handbook

Performance planning refers to an annual (or more frequent) discussion between the manager and each individual employee to make sure both people understand and agree upon the employee's job responsibilities, goals, and any other expectations the manager has for his or her employees.

Performance Planning

Performance planning is the first step in the performance-management system, and a very important one. Let's define it. Performance planning refers to an annual (or more frequent) discussion between the manager and individual employee to discuss job responsibilities, goals, and any other expectations the manager has for his or her employees.

At the end of the meeting, the employee should be clear about …

➤ his or her major job responsibilities.

➤ how performance will be measured.

➤ when job tasks should be completed.

➤ how the employee's job contributes to the goals and objectives of the work unit and the company.

➤ how the employee and manager will work together to deal with any problems that come up during the year.

➤ how manager and employee will communicate about performance during the year.

➤ expectations about how the employee will behave interpersonally and with respect to the team.

Generally, someone will record the results of the meeting, so there is a physical record of the things that have been agreed upon. This is very important.

So, how does this help in the difficult people arena? First, as we've said before, one of the benefits is preventative. The employee knows what is expected of him or her. That allows garden-variety difficult people (who aren't really intentionally nasty) to try to alter their own behavior. That's good. It's kind of like aiming the person at the bull's-eye.

From the Manager's Desk

When setting expectations or standards, try to make them as specific, clear, and measurable as possible. If you can't do that for everything, just keep in mind that there may be some "fuzzies" in there that will require judgment and opinions.

The second benefit has to do with taking action during the year when and if a person doesn't fulfill the agreed-upon expectations. If you need to provide feedback on some bit of difficult behavior, it's a lot easier to do so if you have the agreement beforehand. You can use that agreement to validate your comment. By making reference to the agreement, your comments will seem less arbitrary and more fair than if you just pull a complaint out of the hat.

For example, it's easier and more effective to say:

> "Paul, in January we agreed that all of us should refrain from interrupting each other at meetings. I noticed that last Monday, you were passionate about the subject at hand and broke into the discussion several times while Mary and Fred were speaking. I'd appreciate it if you would allow other people to finish before you have your say, and in turn we'll make sure you don't get interrupted."

If you just pulled out this "rule" out of the blue, then it's going to be less effective.

There's another very important issue related to performance planning and difficult people. When you have a record of agreed expectations, it protects you if you need to take disciplinary action later on. There are two important requirements regarding disciplinary action. They are:

➤ that there be communication to employee about expectations (and also about performance problems throughout the year).

➤ that there be a record (or documentation) of both expectations and any communication between manager and employee about performance problems.

Insider Secrets

Many companies give specific forms managers are expected to use to do performance reviews. Many of those forms are useless, but you may still be forced to use them. Here's the solution. Regardless of the forms, make sure you always focus on the communication, face to face, with each employee. That's how you can succeed in spite of poor tools someone makes you use.

If you lack one or both of these and an employee files a grievance or takes other legal action, you might find you don't have a leg to stand on. So, the performance-planning stage and the recording of the results can be used to support other actions, if they ever become necessary. While there is no such thing as absolute legal protection (who can figure how courts will rule?), they are very important.

Ongoing Performance Communication

All too frequently, managers focus on performance reviews and forget what is probably a more important part of the entire performance-management process—ongoing performance communication throughout the year. It's a simple thing. *Ongoing performance communication* is a two-way process to track progress, identify any barriers to performance, and provide feedback to employees. It's also a way for managers to stay informed about what's going on.

What does ongoing performance communication look like? You might have short monthly meetings with employees to discuss their work progress. You could have regular project team meetings, or perhaps you'd prefer something less formal or structured. You can use informal communication (for example, spur-of-the-moment conversations over coffee or making an effort to talk to each employee regularly). Of course, you can also communicate when there is a specific issue to discuss. For example, a job well done or a particular issue that pops up can be the stimulus to initiate a discussion.

Employee Handbook

Ongoing performance communication is about talking throughout the year about employee progress, any barriers to successful performance and a chance to share information and feedback.

Regardless of how you do it, let's not underestimate the importance of this communication process. It's very important and it *is* part of the manager's job. Here's how it fits in with the difficult-people problem.

First, when you have this regular two-way conversation, you learn about problems more quickly. If someone is habitually late on deadlines, you need to know that as soon as possible, not at the end of the year, when it's too late to do anything about it. Second, we know that the best feedback is feedback that occurs as quickly as possible. If a person excels or causes a problem, the feedback should occur as quickly as possible. That helps them, and it helps you. Finally, if you do have to take disciplinary action, the ongoing communication you and the employee have had will provide some legal protection.

This Won't Work!

If you think performance management and all this communication is too much for a busy person like you, consider this. What are the costs of not doing it in terms of poor performance, crisis and fire fighting, aggravation, and lost productivity? It's a pay-me-now-or-pay-me-later scenario.

Documentation, Data Gathering, and Diagnosis

Because performance management is useless unless it results in better performance or better behavior, we need to have a way of recording any conversations with employees and gathering information that can be used to improve performance. Documentation refers to the record keeping. Data gathering refers to getting information you need to figure out where a problem lies. Diagnosis involves figuring out why the problem occurs.

Documenting simply refers to establishing a paper trail that indicates when you had performance-related conversations with an employee, the content of that conversation, and any agreements that come from the discussion. That's about as simple as it gets. It doesn't matter how you record the information, whether it's on a specific form or in a note, provided both you and the employee have signed off on the summary.

Data gathering is simply the process you use to figure out what is going on. For example, you may want to collect information from customers, direct observation, other staff, and the employee. But

From the Manager's Desk

Make it a standard practice to have an employee acknowledge any documentation you have shared with them, or any other records of communication you may need for disciplinary purposes. Usually, managers get the employee to sign that they have been shown the information or that they have had a specific conversation. Employees need not agree to sign.

what information do you need? That depends. Generally the information you should collect will help you ...

➤ identify that a problem exists.

➤ identify the importance of the problem.

➤ understand the consequences of the problem.

➤ pinpoint the real cause of the problem.

➤ solve the problem.

Let's consider an example. Let's say you manage a call center and you notice that Joan seems to be generating some customer complaints. First, you need information about the number of complaints related to Joan and those related to other staff. What? There's no difference? OK, so your data shows you there isn't a problem with Joan. But what if there have been more complaints about Joan than anyone else? Do you conclude that Joan is difficult or unskilled or unmotivated? No, you don't. If you do, you are likely to *make* Joan difficult or unmotivated. You need to determine the cause if you can, so you look at some other data. You learn that Joan is actually handling more calls per hour, and many of them come from the most challenging customers. So it may be that Joan's complaint rate is a result of going too quickly or that she is dealing with more challenging calls. You might continue to look at other data to discover the cause.

We shouldn't underestimate the importance of trying to find real data here. If you assume it's some sort of problem with Joan and the true cause lies elsewhere, then Joan is going to be exceedingly upset. And if it is a problem with something Joan is doing, then you need to know how to help. And for that you need information.

The Performance Review

Most managers are familiar with the terms "performance review" or "performance appraisal." If performance planning is the first step of performance management, performance review is the last. A *performance review* is a meeting between employee and manager to discuss how the employee has done over the past year (and sometimes more often). Some form of documentation of the discussion is produced which both manager and employee sign.

Here are a few things to remember about this process. First, the cardinal rule: no surprises. The employee should already know where he or she stands before walking into the meeting. How is this possible? Well, as a great manager you've been communicating all year, right? So the meeting is just a way of formalizing and recording things.

The second rule is also important. Many managers use the performance review to lecture the employee on his or her behavior. That is absolutely not the point. You should be talking less than the employee because you want the employee to self-evaluate and provide feedback on his or her own performance. After all, who is the person who is always present when Mary does her job? Well, Mary is!

Remember that the review is supposed to be a discussion or dialogue, not a lecture. If, during the performance-planning stage, you have established clear, common expectations for Mary's behavior, then Mary should be able to compare her performance against those standards. You should be the helper in the process.

Employee Handbook

A **performance review** involves regular meetings (at least once a year, but can be more often) to discuss how the employee has done during the year, or since the last review.

Using Performance Management to Solve Performance Difficulties and Soft Problems

Let's pull this all together. Joseph is an employee who has been somewhat difficult to work with in the past for two reasons. First, he affects his work team performance because he is sometimes rude and impatient. Second, his actual work production is slightly below that of his peers. So we'll separate the issues.

Addressing the Productivity Issue

As part of the regular performance-planning process for each of your employees, you meet with Joseph. You tell him you'd like to set some benchmarks for measuring his job performance so that he will be able to see how he's doing throughout the year. You negotiate some criteria, one of which has to do with the number of widgets he produces (or sells). You document that discussion, and both you and Joseph indicate agreement about that particular measure.

Each month you meet for a few minutes to discuss how Joseph has been doing. By and large Joseph tells you, but you also might be collecting production information so you will have some objective data. Let's say Joseph is below target in the first month. OK. In the ongoing communication process, you and Joseph work together to find the source of the problem and resolve it. Again, all this is documented with some short notes.

Insider Secrets

There's an old axiom. It's easy to measure the unimportant but it's hard to measure what's really relevant. That's the case with performance management. It's easy to measure how many phone calls a person makes. It's hard to evaluate how well a person communicates during the phone calls. Nothing is perfect. Sometimes you have to use fuzzy criteria.

The problem continues. Despite trying to work with Joseph, by the time you get to the end of the year (and the performance review), things haven't improved. At the performance-review meeting, you discuss what has happened during the year and specify any consequences for Joseph if he doesn't meet the agreed-upon targets. There's nothing new there. Then you document that discussion.

Of course, you could use disciplinary action and consequences any time during the year, also. Obviously, you can't wait a whole year all the time.

If you do have to use some form of disciplinary action, then you have got the information and documentation you need to do it effectively and with less legal risk.

Addressing the Softer Team Issues

As we've pointed out, people are difficult in a wide variety of ways. Sometimes their difficult behavior relates directly to their productivity (or lack of it). But probably more often and more aggravating is the difficult behavior that isn't directly related to productivity, but in the ways some people interact with others.

So what about Paul, the guy who does his job pretty well but makes everyone around him miserable? What if Paul actually reduces the productivity of others but performs well personally? Can performance management be used in those circumstances?

Yes, it can. However, it's harder than dealing with productivity or direct job-related results. Here's why. If Paul is supposed to produce 100 widgets and produces 50, it's possible to observe it, count the production, and document that productivity problem in a relatively objective way.

But what if Paul reduces the productivity of others because he's constantly arguing? Or if by his behavior, he makes meetings miserable or contributes to low team morale? We can't measure that very well and our observations are bound to be more subjective. That means more room for disagreement and more room for argument between you and Paul.

Still, you can build in performance expectations about contribution to teams and interpersonal behavior, and you can use them in performance management. You need to establish expectations about personal and interpersonal behavior as part of the performance-planning process. That's the difficult part, but just because it's tough and we can't do it perfectly doesn't mean we shouldn't do it at all. I think it's perfectly reasonable to set some standards regarding behavior at meetings or how employees interact with each other. The trick is to make sure you and your employee(s) are on the same wavelength.

It's important that you understand that such standards or expectations are going to be quite subjective.

Just as with a direct performance-related problem, all the other steps are important. In fact, one that increases in importance is the observation and documentation component. If you need to address interpersonal behavior with an employee, it's best to have notes on when and what specifically happened.

From the Manager's Desk

Always remember that with respect to interpersonal and team-related behavior, whether something is good, bad, or neutral is in the eye of the beholder. Don't delude yourself into thinking *your* opinion is objective. It's not. It's your opinion. Treat it as a perception that could be incorrect, not an absolute.

Let's see how this might work using Joseph as our example and Joan as his manager.

> Joan thought it would be a good idea to establish some norms (remember that?) regarding how staff should treat each other, and how staff should contribute to the welfare of their team. She met with staff as a group and they drafted a few items meant to be applicable to everyone. Here are a few her staff developed:

➤ Communicates in a timely manner with team members

➤ Does not hoard or withhold resources

➤ Is respectful of others (in use of language, etc.)

It's good to note these are pretty subjective and general, but it's not practical to have several hundred standards or expectations.

Joan, being no fool, decided to incorporate these into everyone's performance planning. So in her planning with each employee, she indicated that one of the criteria to be used in reviewing performance would be the items the group formulated. The reference went like this:

> "Employee is expected to follow the team and interpersonal guidelines that apply to the entire work group."

She did that in her meeting with Joseph, and they signed off on the performance-planning documentation.

Over the months, information came to Joan about some of Joseph's behavior. Some of it she heard from others. Some of it she saw directly. Once or twice she heard Joseph speaking to a coworker in an unpleasant way. There was one instance of Joseph berating a coworker in an insulting way.

Joan looked into the instances that she'd heard about from others, and decided there could be a potential problem. She documented the incidents she'd heard directly, and anything she could verify about the third-party complaints. She applied a reality check to the process, and determined the inappropriate behavior was potentially damaging.

From the Manager's Desk

Hard productivity-related issues and softer interpersonal-communication problems often go together, but not always. Sometimes it is your most productive employees who are disruptive. That doesn't excuse it or justify your ignoring the situation. At some point even productive employees who are difficult can cost more than they produce.

Then the ongoing communication process kicked in. She set up a meeting with Joseph (or it could have been a regularly scheduled status meeting) to bring up the subject. She told him that it appeared he wasn't following the guidelines and explained specifically what Joseph needed to change and how she would help him.

Again, that conversation was documented.

Now in Joseph's case, he was able to modify his behavior enough to eliminate the problem. However, if he had not, then the process would have continued, but the manager would become firmer and firmer. At some point (often at the performance review) Joan would lay out any consequences or disciplinary action that would apply if the behaviors didn't change. Everything would be documented so that any legal requirements for communication and documentation were satisfied.

In the end game, if the problem became severe, at least Joan would have some ammunition to support her choice of action.

So, to sum this up, the use of performance management and the end game (which is applying consequences) works like this. We use the performance-management process first to get the employee to change *with* our help and support. When it is clear the employee is unwilling or even unable to do that, then the process may change from helping the person to reducing or eliminating any damage they might cause. And, yes, sometimes that mean letting someone go.

> ### The Least You Need to Know
>
> ➤ Performance management is an important formal and informal tool for managers to apply to difficult people.
>
> ➤ The most important part of performance management is NOT performance appraisal. Performance appraisal is just a time to summarize what's happened during the year.
>
> ➤ In the event you have to take disciplinary action, you may be required to furnish proof that you have communicated with the employee about the problem, including written documentation of specific times and incidents. Performance management helps here.
>
> ➤ Performance management only works if there is year-round communication.
>
> ➤ If you think you don't have time for this process, what would you rather do? Invest a little time to avoid major problems, or ignore things until you have a major long-term problem?

Chapter 10

Monkey in the Middle: Mediation and Arbitration

In This Chapter

➤ The difference between mediation and arbitration

➤ When you should NOT be directly involved

➤ How to use the mediation process

➤ When to step in

Here's the situation. Bob and Terry report to you. Bob and Terry seem to be like oil and water. If Bob says white, Terry says black. If Terry says the earth is round, Bob says the earth is flat. They argue publicly and interfere with each other's work. Except for these clashes with each other, both are decent workers. It's like two monkeys heaving bananas at each other—and the bystanders are getting showered by the pieces.

What's your responsibility here? How do you go about addressing the situation?

What sets this scenario apart from others we have talked about so far is that you are not the target for either Bob or Terry. In this chapter we're going to look at two tools, mediation and arbitration, that you can use (and sometimes *must* use) to address on-going conflict between two employees.

Deciding When to Step In—Whose Banana Is It?

As with most difficult situations, your first step is to apply the reality check principle we've talked about. Ask yourself whether the conflict between Bob and Terry is one that deserves or requires action on your part.

Start with the consequences of the conflict and the difficult behavior connected to it:

➤ Is the conflict affecting the work output of Bob and Terry?

➤ If you do nothing, what's likely to happen?

➤ Is the difficult behavior a small annoyance or is it having an effect on others in the workplace?

The bottom line: Whose problem is it? Just the two people directly involved, or do you, as a manager, have to take some ownership?

When thinking about these questions, don't limit your consideration to the two people directly involved. Consider the effects of the difficult behavior on your entire work unit. That's very important, and it's easy to forget that the actions of even two people can negatively effect the productivity, attitudes, and morale of your entire staff.

This Won't Work!

Be aware that involving yourself in a conflict between two employees may end up with both employees targeting you. That comes with the territory. In situations of serious conflict, you probably have to intervene regardless.

There are two more factors to consider.

1. How will you be perceived by your employees if you do nothing? Because most employees expect (fairly or unfairly) that management will step in and do something about disruptive situations, will doing nothing end up with your losing credibility with your employees? Will they turn on you if you do nothing?

2. While doing nothing in the face of such situations may cause problems, doing something may also cause problems. When a third party intervenes in a conflict, there is a tendency for the warring parties to target the third party. It's very upsetting to try to help remedy a situation between two people only to find that both people start attacking you!

Let's assume that you've come to the conclusion that you need to address the situation between Bob and Terry because it's causing fallout for others, and it's affecting the ability of your work unit to achieve its goals. So, what options do you have?

Mediation—What Is It? When Does It Fit?

The most powerful technique managers use to intervene in conflict situations between two employees is called mediation. What is it?

Mediation is a process where the parties involved in a conflict are brought together to negotiate their own solution in a nonadversarial, noncoercive way, assisted by a third party. (That may be you or someone outside your work group or organization.)

It's important to understand the key points in the definition:

Employee Handbook

Mediation is a process where a third party, the mediator, tries to facilitate a process where the disputing parties can solve their problems in a nonadversarial, noncoercive way.

1. **Both parties must consent to the process.** The idea behind mediation is that the two parties, because they are so emotionally involved, need to be brought together so they can work to find a solution. There must be no coercion.

2. **A mediator must be neutral.** If you are the mediator, your sole objective is to help the two parties solve the problem. That means refraining from judgment about who is right or wrong.

3. **Mediation is future oriented.** At the end of a successful mediation, both parties should know what they have agreed to in terms of specific behavior changes they must make in the future. As Dan Dana, sometimes referred to as "Dr. Conflict," and a conflict consultant and mediator says, the purpose of mediation is "not to identify guilty parties and assign blame, or to punish either party for past behavior, or to determine who is right or wrong."

Insider Secrets

The skills involved in successful mediation can be quite complex. We recommend that you upgrade your existing skills (no matter what the level) before you start mediating. Here's a great resource. The Mediation Training Institute International provides a number of training and hard-copy resources. You can get more information on the Internet at www.mediationworks.com or by calling 1–800-DRCONFLICT. Much of the material in this chapter is based on the institute's work.

When Is Mediation Likely to Work?

You don't want to waste your time mediating problems that aren't likely to be solved through a mediation process. In fact, trying to mediate problems that are not suitable for mediation is likely to create more frustration and anger.

Dr. Conflict suggests asking the following questions before entering into the mediator role.

From the Manager's Desk

There is no point starting the mediation process if it's bound to fail. Ask yourself: Do the parties have the authority to solve the issue? Do I have the skills to mediate? Is there some root cause that we need to address first?

First, is illegal, unethical, or behavior related to company policy involved as part of the conflict? If so, then disciplinary or corrective action needs to occur, either before or along with mediation. For example, if Bob uses racial slurs towards Terry and your company has a policy regarding this offensive behavior, the first step is to deal with it as a policy issue.

Second, has the problem arisen from either party's failure to perform his job responsibilities (whether it be from lack of job skills or knowledge)? If this is a root cause of a conflict, all the talk in the world isn't going to remedy the lack of skills. In this case, attack the root cause first. Training and coaching are better choices to start with.

Third, has the problem arisen from some personal problems that are not being addressed (for example, family crisis, drug or alcohol problems, or other emotional problems)? If that's the case, these issues should be dealt with first. The person with those problems should be referred to the appropriate professional help—often an employee assistance program (EAP).

The fourth question has to do with authority and ability to solve the problem. Is the problem one that the parties, individually or together, have the authority to solve? In other words, it may be that the problem has to do with issues that only someone with more authority needs to address. If that's the case, the person with the needed authority needs to be involved.

For example, two employees disagree on their respective job responsibilities. Because neither employee has the power to change the job descriptions, neither really has the power to negotiate a solution. In this case, the manager of the employees needs to make a decision, rather than play the role of mediator.

Deciding to Mediate

After you have identified there is a problem between two employees that may require action, your first step is to determine whether mediation is appropriate. We've already mentioned the importance of the reality check as something that will help you decide whether any action is needed. Here are a few things you can do as part of this decision process (again from Dr. Conflict):

➤ Know what mediation can accomplish and what it can't.

➤ Identify the organizational problem to be solved.

➤ Determine whether the problem is subject to mediation.

➤ Consider costs and consequences of continued unresolved conflict.

➤ Weigh costs and benefits of using managerial mediation.

➤ Consider alternatives to mediation.

➤ Determine who is in the best position to act as the mediator.

Let's consider the last two items on the list, because they are important. First, what are your alternatives to mediation? You can ignore the problem. You may use your management prerogative to threaten one or both parties, separate the parties, or terminate one or both parties. You may choose to counsel each party individually and encourage them to work it out themselves. Or you can use a full-fledged mediation process, or arbitrate (we'll discuss that at the end of the chapter).

Each of these has pluses and minuses, although to be honest most of the power-based ones are likely to backfire or cause unexpected and undesirable consequences. For example, firing and replacing employees can be costly. Or, threatening employees tends to turn both parties into an attack mode, with you being the victim.

We also need to look at who is best positioned to mediate an employee-employee conflict. Sometimes it's best to involve an independent third party, rather than attempt to mediate yourself. Here are some situations where you are better off going outside:

➤ If you don't have a good relationship with both parties, or where one or both parties cannot trust your neutrality, fairness, or ethics, you are unlikely to succeed because mediation requires neutrality.

This Won't Work!

Probably the most common mistake managers make when involving themselves in a conflict is attempting to force people to act differently. Sometimes it works. Often it masks the problem even if it appears to work. It's always best to exhaust other "gentler" options first.

This Won't Work!

If you have some form of vested interest in the outcome (someone winning or losing), definitely don't mediate. You need to be neutral. Anything less and you must disqualify yourself from the process.

➤ If you actually *do* have a bias or an opinion about who is right or wrong, and can't step back from that, then it's best to retain someone who is more objective and distanced from the conflict.

➤ If you lack the mediation skills, then look for outside help if the problem is a serious one. There's no shame in that. Let's face it. Few of us are trained in this area. Knowing your own limitations is important here.

OK, so now that you have made the assessments regarding whether mediation is appropriate, let's look at the steps involved.

Hold Preliminary Meetings

In mediation you don't grab each person by an ear and sit them down and lecture them. There's a preliminary get-started stage that is absolutely critical.

Preliminary meetings involve meeting separately with each party to the conflict before meeting as a threesome. Dr. Conflict defines the purpose of this meeting as follows:

From the Manager's Desk

At some point before the three-way meeting, each person should receive, in writing, a short list of expectations regarding what you will do and how they should conduct themselves during the three-way. For example, it might include things like "refrain from personal attacks," and "talk to each other, not me."

➤ To allow each party a chance to give his or her side of the story without interruption by the other party, and without argument. This has two purposes. It gets information into the hands of the mediator. It also allows each party to let off some steam.

➤ To give each person an accurate perception of the mediation process, your role and theirs, and what the process will look like. One of the important things is to provide some assurances to each party that his or her interests will be addressed in a nonjudgmental way.

➤ To clarify the actual problem and define it so it can be addressed.

➤ To get a commitment to attend and participate in a three-way meeting (or get consent for the process).

What is your role in the preliminary meeting? First, it's to explain the process, how it will work, and how each person will be heard. Second, you need to get each person talking to you. Use a lot of listening techniques and empathy-type statements (for example, "I can see this situation upsets you").

So then what? Both parties agree to participate in a three-way meeting and seem clear about how the process will work.

Logistics and Establishing Context for Three-Way Meetings

It's worth paying attention to some of the logistics of conducting a good three-way meeting. Here are some things to consider.

Where should the meeting be held? The setting should be as neutral as possible, so it shouldn't occur on either party's home turf. The environment should be fairly comfortable and large enough to avoid a sense of claustrophobia. It should allow both individuals enough interpersonal space so they feel comfortable.

The location should also allow privacy. Mediation involves a strong bond of confidentiality and privacy. Pick a location where the discussion cannot be overheard (don't forget that people sometimes may raise their voices).

From the Manager's Desk

You should choose a location and time that ensure your meeting will not be overheard, even if the parties raise their voices. Privacy and confidentiality are critical here.

When is a good time for the meeting? Have it when people are as free from distractions as possible and when they are alert and not overfatigued. Meeting at the end of the day or first thing in the morning may be problematic. It depends on the people involved and when they function best.

Who should be there? Some managers feel more comfortable having a fourth or fifth party attending—another manager or a human resource person, for example. This is probably not a good idea. It's best to stick to the two feuding parties and the mediator, unless there is an extremely compelling reason to involve others. As the number of attendees increases, so does the difficulty in orchestrating the mediation process.

Ensure that no interruptions will occur. No phone calls, knocks on the door, or requests to pull one of the involved parties for a job task. Period. Interruptions destroy continuity.

OK, the ground has now been prepared.

The Process

Now we come to the most difficult part of the mediation process, which is facilitating a constructive discussion between the two combatants. Again, I need to advise you

---

that not everyone can be an effective mediator and that it takes a good deal of discipline, emotional control, and interpersonal skills to be good at it. Also, a caution: It's not possible to teach you all the skills of mediation in a single chapter. If you need additional help, contact Dan Dana at www.mediationworks.com on the Internet.

While I can't guide you step by step through the process, I can give you enough information to give you a fighting chance and aim you in the right direction. Again, this is based on the suggestions of Dr. Conflict.

This Won't Work!

If things get heated—and they often do—it's wise to avoid overreacting. You can try to guide the conversation onto a constructive path, but there may be heated exchanges. Your job isn't to quash those but to ask questions that lead the parties into something more constructive.

Working to the Breakthrough

Dr. Conflict talks about the need to create a *breakthrough*, or vitally important attitude shift required to move to problem solving as part of mediation. He describes this breakthrough as a "mutual shift in attitude from 'me-against-you' to 'us-against-the-problem.'" In other words, when and if the combatants can reach a point where they give up bashing each other or trying to win, they realize that the only solution is to work together against the problem.

He goes on to suggest that this breakthrough usually comes about as a result of sustained, direct dialogue between the two parties. Note that means they need to talk to each other, while your role as mediator is to encourage them to do so.

Dr. Conflict also goes on to make a rather daunting observation. He suggests that the dialogue that, in part, brings about such a breakthrough does not have to be passive. It may be "confrontative, hostile, and argumentative." That's a bit scary, because most of us shy away from those kinds of interactions. Perhaps it's necessary because the emotional content of the conflict needs to get vented somehow, before the parties are ready to move ahead to solving a problem together.

Tasks and Roles of the Manager-as-Mediator

Dr. Conflict suggests there are a number of primary tasks that fall to the manager-as-mediator. First, he says that the moderator needs to prevent withdrawal. That means the facilitator must exercise influence to keep the parties present and keep them from copping out or becoming less attentive or committed to the dialogue.

Second, the mediator-manager is responsible for ensuring that conciliatory gestures or statements of voluntary vulnerability are not ignored or punished by the other party. What the heck does that mean?

Dr. Conflict defines *conciliatory gestures* as the "magic of mediation." They refer to statements made by one party that indicate the person is opening up or allowing himself to be more vulnerable.

Conciliatory gestures indicate movement of position to a more cooperative stance. They include apologizing, taking responsibility, expressing positive feelings, and other similar expressions.

Because this is so important, let's look at the examples Dr. Conflict uses:

➤ **Apologizing:** "I'm sorry that my comments in the staff meeting embarrassed you."

➤ **Owning responsibility:** "I see now that I have contributed to the problem. I didn't see that before."

➤ **Conceding:** "I'm willing to meet with you, if we can do it at a time that's convenient for both of us."

Employee Handbook

Conciliatory gestures indicate movement of position to a more cooperative stance such as apologizing, taking responsibility, expressing positive feelings, and other similar expressions.

➤ **Self-disclosing:** "I've been worried about what you might do to get back at me, and so I've been avoiding you."

➤ **Expressing positive feelings for the other:** "You are a competent and skilled professional."

➤ **Initiating both-gain problem solving:** "How do you suggest we solve this?"

So, your task is to extract these kinds of statements out of the participants and to make sure that other person does not use these concessions to attack. In other words, you need to keep the conversation focused on solving problems in the future, not the past. There's that no-blame theme again.

Finally, one of the major roles of the mediator is to wait. Weird thought, isn't it? Because the mediator is *not* directly responsible for creating solutions and agreement, the solutions and underpinings of any agreement must come from the parties involved. So, effective mediation may depend more on knowing when to shut up and wait, rather than on what you actually say.

Don't take the responsibility away from the parties involved. Don't rescue them with solutions. And always remember that in these situations, there will be times of silence and that you must allow these to unfold. It's up to the parties to figure out what to do with them.

There's no question it's hard to avoid filling in the silences, but it's the only way the parties will formulate their own solutions.

Insider Secrets

It's true silence is golden; so is patience. Particularly in mediation. Get comfortable with the silence and understand that it doesn't mean that nothing is going on, but perhaps people are reflecting on their own behavior. That's a good thing. Sometimes silence comes just before some important insight. We live in such a noisy society that many of us are uncomfortable with silence that goes on too long. We tend to want to fill it up with words. Keep in mind that people need a chance to think and reflect and that often creates gaps in conversations. Wait them out.

This Won't Work!

An agreement that is vague and unclear may be worse than no agreement at all. The reason is that if there isn't clear understanding of the meanings of the agreement, it's likely the conflict will erupt again, this time even worse than before. Even worse, the parties will have less faith in the mediation process.

Framing Agreements and Following Up

If/when the parties come to an agreement during the mediated session, that agreement should be clarified and recorded somehow, and each party should receive a copy. The agreement should be as specific as possible and refer to the changes in behavior each party has committed to.

So, what happens after an agreement is struck? It's a good idea to have follow-up meetings to discuss how the agreement is working, and whether any other issues need to be addressed. This allows further problem identification, and also shows that you are serious about making it work.

So, that's the bare bones of manager-as-mediator. It's a nonjudgmental process that requires great skill and discipline on the part of the manager.

Arbitration, or When Someone Just Has to Decide

Compared to mediation, arbitration is at the opposite end of the spectrum. It doesn't rely on the ability of the two parties to solve their own difficulties. It uses authority to decide the issue.

Arbitration refers to a process whereby a third party gets the facts of the issue, then makes a binding decision on behalf of both parties and the organization.

So, in a sense, the arbitrator is the judge. While the mediator avoids judgments, the arbitrator makes judgments and a decision. Often that decision will include who does what with respect to solving the problem.

Arbitration Tips

Here are some basic things to consider about the arbitration process.

First, it's best if both parties consent to arbitration. It's also best if they agree *who* should arbitrate. Sometimes that might be you. Or, one or both parties might prefer that it be someone who is uninvolved.

Second, the parameters should be clear ahead of time. Both parties should understand that you will make a decision and that the decision will be binding (except, of course, if one person prefers to resign, or something like that).

Third, to arbitrate, it's best if you talk to each person individually, for the same reasons that apply in preparing for mediation. If you feel it's appropriate, you can bring the parties together and talk to them together.

Fourth, any decisions you make should be specific and help the parties change their behaviors. Avoid vagueness.

Employee Handbook

Arbitration refers to a process whereby a third party makes the final binding decision about the issue, usually after considering each side's position and obtaining the facts.

From the Manager's Desk

Even if you have enough authority to impose a solution, it's best to have the parties agree in advance that they will abide by your decision. That makes it more of a cooperative venture and will lend more credence and power to your solution.

Finally, be aware that because you end up as judge and decision maker, one or the other of the parties may shift hostility toward you. In fact, it's possible both parties will do so.

Mediation Versus Arbitration

Throughout this book, we have applied the principle that the least use of power and authority is desirable, not for moral reasons but for practical reasons. Managers don't want to play daddy or mommy. There is an expectation that employees will behave like adults, but sometimes they need help. Mediation supports that expectation because it treats the combatants like adults who can solve the problem between themselves (albeit with some help). Mediation is meant to empower the people involved.

There are situations, however, that cannot be solved through a mediation process. In mediation, the solution isn't in your hands and if the combatants are unable to come up with a solution and the problem is serious enough, then the solution has to come from somewhere.

That's where the arbitration process fits. If you have the ability to use mediation effectively, that's a good long-term strategy. If you lack the time or ability, and the problem *must* be solved, an arbitration process is probably a usable alternative. However, arbitration or making a decision for people can create hard feelings and other problems down the road.

The Least You Need to Know

➤ It's in your interest to intervene as a third party when there is a conflict between staff.

➤ Before intervening, assess the cost of doing nothing.

➤ Mediation involves helping the combatants find their own solution, not you providing one.

➤ Mediation is difficult and requires discipline, skill, and patience. If you lack any of these, get someone from outside to do it instead.

➤ When you need a resolution fast, or when mediation fails, you can impose a solution via an agreed-to arbitration process. However, that can have negative long-term effects.

➤ The outcomes of both mediation and arbitration need to be stated clearly and specifically so both parties can abide by the decision.

Part 3
Managing the Venomous Difficult Employee

These difficult employees are the backstabbers, the politickers, the verbal abusers, and the outright liars. I hope you don't have any of these around you. If you do, you'd better know the in's and out's of dealing with them. These folks are nasty and intend to cause damage. What can you do to protect yourself from the damage the venomous employees can cause?

You can still try working cooperatively with them or you can use more formal ways of discipline. We'll also talk about the issue of workplace violence, because that's always a concern.

Chapter 11

Indentifying the Venomous Difficult Employee

In This Chapter

➤ What sets venomous employees apart

➤ Personal attacks and some suggestions

➤ Dealing with sabotage and insubordination

➤ A tricky way to deal with backroom politicking

In previous chapters we focused on the garden-variety difficult person and his or her difficult behavior. Now we turn our attention to venomous employees and the behaviors they use to make life miserable for those around them. As a capsule comment, dealing with garden-variety difficult behavior is like water torture. There's no one large incident, but many small ones. It's death by a million wee mosquito bites.

The venomous difficult person is different. It's not death by mosquito bites—it's more like dealing with a howitzer. The venomous person isn't being difficult accidentally, but is acting with some degree of aggression and malice. While the garden-variety difficult person may be destructive (usually by accident), the venomous person is destructive intentionally.

In this chapter we'll look at the difference between venomous and garden-variety difficult people, characteristics of venomous behavior, and ways to address specific situations.

What Separates Venomous from Garden-Variety

The *venomous* difficult person behaves in destructive ways with the intent of causing damage to others around him or her.

Employee Handbook

The **venomous difficult person** behaves in inappropriate or destructive ways in an intentional way. There is intent to damage others, which is absent with the garden-variety difficult employees.

It's not a case of the occasional poor behavior. It involves a sustained (over time) attempt to get back at people, control people, or damage the work unit or individuals. The behavior may be aimed at you, the manager, or other employees. It could be aimed at the company as a whole, also.

One thing that separates venomous difficult behavior from the garden variety is intent. The garden-variety person may be inept, lack skills, or occasionally cause problems in an accidental way, but the venomous person *wants* to cause problems for others.

A second distinguishing point is that venomous people act difficult over time. Their difficult behavior is sustained. It's almost possible to rely on their lousy behavior. After a while you can predict their reactions, because you will have seen them before.

A third difference is the degree of difficult behavior. While garden-variety and venomous people share certain difficult behaviors, the venomous person stands out because his or her behavior is more extreme.

For example, John, a garden-variety difficult person, loses his temper and responds with a brief outburst. Mary, a venomous type, has much longer, more extreme outbursts. John might gossip a bit and inadvertently make unpleasant comments about someone else, but Mary does so consistently and in a much nastier way. John may resent the fact you are promoted to the manager position and grouse about it quietly. Mary picks up her weapons and goes over your head to try to prove you incompetent (ouch!).

There's one more difference that's important. Because garden-variety difficult people don't intend to hurt people, they are a bit easier to work with. Talking reasonably and helpfully to a garden-variety person can often result in behavior change. That's because, at least in most cases, the garden-variety person is not out to get anyone. A little guidance, a little feedback, perhaps some skill building, and garden-variety difficult people can change what they do. The venomous person is less likely to respond to gentler approaches and help, particularly if his or her axe to grind is with you. If Mary is out to get you personally, she is less likely to respond positively to the techniques that work with the less difficult.

That brings us to a difference in how we deal with venomous behavior and people. As you will see later, we still try to deal rationally and reasonably with the difficult person, using good interpersonal skills, feedback, listening, and other techniques. However, with the venomous we must be aware that heavier tactics may be in order; we probably will need the support of others in the organization. That might be your own boss, or the personnel or human resources department.

There's your first tip. Because venomous people are, in essence, fighting a small war, you need to garner and secure your allies.

This Won't Work!

Gentle techniques and dialogue are less likely to work with the venomous person. Often this type of person is playing a power game or a controlling game. You may have to respond with consequences or sanctions much earlier with someone like this.

Why the Venomous Employee Is So Dangerous

It's pretty obvious that any person who tries to harm you or other people is going to have the potential for serious work disruption. Because venomous people tend to be a bit more obvious, it's easier to identify them and less likely you will miss their behavior. It's still worthwhile to talk about both the "in-your-face" problems these folks create, and also the more hidden outcomes.

You don't have to be a physics professor to understand that someone who is abusive, manipulative, and aggressive has a profound impact on other people.

Here are some of the more obvious effects:

➤ Wastes the time of others
➤ Reduces work unit productivity
➤ Increases stress levels for everyone
➤ Creates an untrusting environment

While these are significant in and of themselves, you need to be aware of the less-obvious effects.

1. **Aggressive, manipulative people bring out aggression and manipulation in other people.** Think about it. If Mary is nasty and abusive to others, you can bet that sooner or later, even nondifficult people are going to fight back. Then you have a situation where there is not one difficult person to deal with, but several.

2. **Because venomous behavior tends to be more obvious, employees know when it is occurring.** They expect management to take action, to offer some semblance of protection. If you do not act, your credibility as a manager is damaged. In the eyes of the victims or even bystanders, inaction is an abdication of your responsibility to your employees. That makes it harder for you to manage your staff, both the difficult and not-so-difficult employees.

3. **Venomous people can increase your legal liability.** In many places there is a legal obligation to provide a safe workplace free of certain kinds of abuse (for example, free of sexual harassment). Venomous people can create a sufficiently toxic environment that a union or other employee may decide to bring legal action against the company and, yes, against you as a manager. That provides a compelling reason to take action promptly.

As an aside, the key to avoiding such lawsuits, or at least protecting yourself, is to show that you and your company have taken actions to address the problem.

Insider Secrets

Employers (and management) are obligated by law to provide a safe work environment. The key legal issue here is that, once aware of a problem, you must make reasonable attempts to remedy the situation. For example, if sexual harassment occurs in your work unit, you are aware of it, and you do nothing, then you and your company can be sued (probably successfully). The same legal obligations may exist with respect to racist remarks and behavior, sexist comments and behaviors. If a court finds you and your company took no preventative action, or through inaction allowed such things to continue, it could hold the company, and individuals, liable. Best to focus on prevention and try to stay out of the courts.

Why are these effects so important to you? As we noted in an early chapter, most of us tend to shy away from direct confrontation with difficult people. Heck, who wants to get involved in battles? So, we deny the problem until it's totally out of control. While you might be able to ignore occasional difficult behavior from a garden-variety difficult person, you aren't going to get away with it from a venomous person. It's not going to go away. And if you do ignore it, you become a victim.

Let's move on and look at some of the tactics of the venomous person, and some important things you need to do to deal with them.

Techniques of the Viper

In this section we'll look at some of the most common tactics and techniques of the venomous person. We'll explain the behaviors to you, and make some suggestions about your priorities and some actions you can or need to take.

Abuse and Personal Attacks

Abuse and personal attacks are behaviors designed to demean, belittle, harass, or insult another person. They can be "in your face" and include actions like swearing, yelling, threatening, or intimidating, or they can be a bit more subtle, possibly implied rather than explicitly stated.

You will know when the first type is aimed at you. If you observe such attacks made on others, you aren't likely to miss it or misidentify them, either.

The second type, the more subtle attack, is trickier. So let's look at some examples.

> Consider a meeting where Mary stands up, and says, "If you really knew what you were doing, you would…." Is this an attack? Is it abuse? Absolutely. Why? It's an insult, although it's framed in such a way that it is somewhat indirect. It really says, "You don't know what you are doing because you aren't doing what I want." It's an accusation couched in a tricky language format.

Employee Handbook

Abuse and personal attacks are behaviors designed to demean, belittle, harass, or insult another person. Sometimes an abusive person will hide the behavior under the guise of "humor." Sometimes not. These behaviors can be "in your face" and include actions like swearing, yelling, threatening, or intimidating, or they can be a bit more subtle, implied rather than explicitly stated.

Here's another one, Mary again.

> Mary stands up, directs her gaze at you, and says, "Most of us really want to succeed here and work hard to make it work. It's too bad we aren't appreciated."

Wow. What about this one? Is it abuse? Yep! It's really dirty pool. The attack (on you and your nonrecognition) is implied by the words and the eye contact. What's really dirty is it is an attack dressed up in what might appear to be a compliment concerning the rest of the staff. It's not. People who use this kind of sneaky tactic aren't doing it for fun. There's intent here.

Want another one? What about nonverbal attacks?

> In this example (again a meeting), Mary doesn't say anything. She sighs loudly and rolls her eyes when you speak. Finally she gets up and walks out of the meeting you are chairing and doesn't come back for 30 minutes. You make the mistake of asking her why she left. She says, "I had something important to do."

From the Manager's Desk

Be particularly alert to the more subtle attacks. Often our first response to them is one of uncertainty or disbelief. These more subtle attacks are no less abusive than a person telling you to "bleep off."

Again, pretty nasty. First, there's the nonverbal behavior done in such a way that other people can't miss it. Second, her statement of having something important to do implies that the meeting, and by extension, you, are NOT important. But she didn't actually say that with her words. However, everyone knows exactly what she has done and implied.

Do these sound familiar? How do you handle abuse, whether it be directed at you or at another employee? What's your *first* priority?

Your first priority is to stop the abusive behavior immediately. You can't allow someone to take shots at you or at another person, because doing nothing implies that such actions are acceptable. You can't do nothing because that makes you appear weak to the abuser and to anyone observing the process.

Your first step is to communicate what's acceptable and not acceptable and make a clear request. For example:

> "We've all agreed that personal attacks aren't permitted at our meetings. As the manager I have a responsibility to everyone, and I'm not going to allow insults, bad language, or similar behavior. Now, let's get back to the issue."

A second option involves setting a limit and specifying consequences if the limit isn't observed. If the abusive behavior occurs in a staff meeting, here's how you might handle it.

> "We're not here to blame each other or to attack each other. If this behavior continues, I will adjourn the meeting or request that those breaking our guidelines leave."

Here's a third option.

> "I think this conversation is getting heated. Let's take a ten-minute break and then return and deal with the agenda we've agreed upon and stay away from personal remarks."

At the break you might take Mary aside and indicate privately that her remarks are inappropriate and unacceptable.

What if the abusive comments occur in a private meeting between you and John?

Same priority. Stop the nasty behavior. Request the person stop the behaviors (be specific). If the person continues to berate you or insult you, lay out the consequences of not acting more appropriately. In severe cases, end the meeting.

From the Manager's Desk

When you see abusive behavior occur, your first priority is to stop the behavior as quickly as possible, and indicate it's not acceptable.

It is rarely appropriate to argue or to continue a conversation that's abusive. Don't argue about the person's behavior. If they don't see they're being nasty, don't argue. State the consequences, apply them if needed, and end the conversation if it doesn't take a turn for the better.

Not all abusive conversations can be turned around at the moment. Often it's best to enforce a cooling-off period.

What's your next priority? It's getting backup and support. After you have identified someone is frequently abusive (or even if it's a single but extreme instance), you have to take care of some business behind the scenes.

You need to determine what level of support you will receive from your boss or from other players (for example, the human resources department), and then mobilize support by informing those parties what is going on and what you would like to do about it.

This Won't Work!

Don't assume you have the support of your boss without checking first. Support has a tendency to be situation specific, and on occasion, somewhat political. Keep supporting players informed and find out exactly what they will support and what they won't.

Employee Handbook

Outright sabotage refers to attempts to damage or impede the work of others, or to damage the reputation of others. **Insubordination** is a deliberate refusal to carry out a legitimate job task or reasonably alter job-related behavior when those changes have been requested by the manager.

In other words, you are preparing to use whatever tools your organization has to support you (including your own authority, backed by the authority of your boss).

You need to know what kinds of support and backup are available to you. You also need to ensure the abusive party doesn't try to use those same tools and play office politics on his or her own terms. Quite simply, you must go to others as needed—and get there first.

After you know how much support you'll get and what actions will be supported, you will know where you stand and what your options are.

You'll find that obtaining backup and support is a theme that pops up regardless of the specific activities of the venomous person.

Outright Sabotage

Outright sabotage refers to attempts to interfere with the work of another person or the reputation and perceptions associated with the targeted person. It could involve hoarding of resources, for example, or bad-mouthing the target to a customer, or spreading rumors. Or, if you, the manager, are the target, it might include refusal to do assigned tasks (either directly or indirectly, something we would refer to as *insubordination*).

We need to clarify something about sabotage. We aren't talking about someone who on occasion makes errors or doesn't do what's required. Heck, that happens all the time, and while it may be garden-variety difficult, it isn't venomous. Here, we are talking about intention. When someone spreads rumors about another person, that's not by accident. Saying that the senior partner lives with a bevy of farm animals isn't something that accidentally comes out of someone's mouth.

This distinction of intent is critical with respect to insubordination. Before you conclude you are dealing with a sabotaging, insubordinate employee, you need to ask some questions:

First, is this person doing this to deliberately harm?

The second question is a kind of additional reality check: Does it just appear deliberate because the person is unskilled or has poor work habits, or because the expectations I have about his or her work are unrealistic or unreasonable?

You must explore this before you decide there is insubordination occurring, because you may be required to provide documented evidence that the behaviors have been repeated and deliberate.

If you conclude that the actions of the person are deliberate, you must consider the person a potentially hostile employee (kind of like a hostile witness). As with the abuser/attacker we talked about earlier, one of the first key steps is to obtain and mobilize backup within the organization. Your boss needs to know what's going on. You need to know whether your boss will support disciplinary action if the situation continues. And all this should go on prior to approaching deliberately destructive people.

Why? You need to begin from an informed position of strength. You don't want to threaten punishments or even mention consequences you can't deliver if the behavior doesn't change. You simply need to know your options, so you can present them to the employee in a clear way. You can't do that if you don't know where you stand.

Your most important tool is one we've already talked about. It's performance management. Performance management allows you to communicate formally with an employee about his or her behavior, and gives a structure to document that behavior and set out consequences.

Essentially, sabotage (particularly of work tasks) is a performance issue, and that's how we'll address it. We are going to apply all the steps of the performance-management process, begin-

This Won't Work!

Starting a disciplinary discussion without knowing where you stand and the degree of support you'll get from your boss is akin to putting a noose around your neck. Many a manager has discovered they are left dangling when their own bosses have "chickened out."

ning with making it clear to the individual that certain behaviors are unacceptable. We are going to work with the person to resolve the issue, and we are going to document those actions. Finally, if no success comes from this process, we will communicate the consequences that will occur as a result of continued poor behavior, then ensure that those consequences occur.

Backroom Politicking and String Pulling

Backroom politicking is a technique some venomous people use to erode your support internally through the use of back-channel communication, often with others in the company at the same level or the levels above you. However, it might also include lobbying employees or trying to turn others against you.

Here's an example.

> Tommy is well acquainted with the divisional manager who happens to be your boss. You find out that Tommy has been passing negative comments about you to the boss.

Here's a slightly less-obvious one.

> Fred is trying to get his pet project funded, but you've indicated it isn't a high-priority item. So Fred goes over your head and tries to lobby other managers to support the pet project.

There's not much worse than having someone who avoids or questions your authority by using these kinds of backroom techniques. It creates a situation where you may lose credibility in the eyes of your boss and your employees, particularly if the backroom politicking succeeds.

Employee Handbook

Backroom politicking is a technique some venomous people use to make themselves look good, or gather more power at the expense of others. This in–cludes the use of back-channel communication with others in the company at the same level or the levels above you.

So, how do you handle this? You do something completely different than with the other situations we've discussed in this chapter. You are going to try to cut off any re-wards or reinforcement the backroom person gets from doing these kinds of things.

How? You don't start with the person using the backroom techniques. You start with the people that person is talking to.

Let's talk about Fred. He's the guy with the pet project, and you find out he's been talking to Martha, the division head who is also your boss. You go to Martha and say:

> "Martha, I know Fred has approached you about the XYZ project he wants to do. I could use your help on this. If Fred keeps coming to you with these kinds of issues, it's going to make it impossible for me to do my job, and that means lower productivity. Is it possible for you to refer any of Fred's concerns back to me, so Fred deals with me rather than you? I really need to be directly involved in any of these discussions. Or, maybe the three of us could meet if you think we need to revisit the initial decision."

It's very important that you do this calmly and without any emotional outburst. Now, if Martha agrees, you have cut off the "ear" listening to Fred's complaints. When Fred talks to Martha about this, Martha simply says:

> "Fred, I'm not going to override the decision, so you need to talk to your direct manager."

Bingo! No audience there. No reward. No reinforcement.

I suggest you try this route first, even before you talk directly to Fred. After you have Martha's support, then you go to Fred and talk about the problems his behavior may cause, and the possible outcomes if he continues.

You're probably wondering what to do if Martha doesn't support you and continues to provide an ear and even overturns your decision. You are in big trouble. Your problem isn't Fred. Your problem is that you work for an incompetent or difficult boss. We'll address that when we talk about difficult bosses in Chapter 15, "The Nutso Boss."

The Pinocchio Problem

Wouldn't it be great if noses really grew when people lied or were dishonest? The reality is that people lie in a variety of ways and expect to get away with it. People lie about their jobs and why they didn't get their work done. They lie about the facts of situations (or at least they often recount them with considerable error). They may even lie about you and what you said or did.

Little white lies are one thing. However, when a person lies about you (or coworkers or why jobs aren't done), that's a problem that becomes serious. Venomous people often lie about things, or distort reality to suit their own causes.

Let's provide a tip or two right now. First, never confront or challenge a liar in public.

> If, for example, at a meeting, Diane lies about something you said, don't call her a liar. Challenging a person directly (even in private) is not likely to generate enough rapport to avoid an ugly confrontation. What, you say? You won't stand for dishonesty? Here's a way of dealing with it so that it allows Diane a face-saving out.

> When Diane says something that's not accurate or not truthful about you, then you say: "Diane, I think we have different recollections about what was said at that meeting. I recall it [then you put forth what you feel is the truth]. Is it possible that's more accurate?"

Insider Secrets

When we witness lying or are lied to, we tend to have strong emotional reactions. We want to even the score, or exact revenge when we feel we are being played for a fool. It's natural, but that idea of vengeance or retribution almost always makes things worse. It's better to allow some face-saving for the other person. By humiliating someone you will make an even more bitter enemy. Don't try to pressure or bully a person into "fessing" up. It almost never works. Be the better person. In other words, deal with the problem and its effects and put aside the desire for vengeance. You'll build a better reputation as an honorable person.

You shift the discussion to accuracy and not lying. That's far less confrontational and much more likely to avoid a terrible scene.

What if Diane lies (or you believe she lies) about why a job hasn't been completed? Again, shift the emphasis from whether Diane is right or not to a discussion of how you might prevent the problem from recurring. Boot the ball back to her. Here's an example phrase.

> "Diane, obviously there's some disagreement as to what happened, but my concern is the job didn't get done, and that's not OK. We need to agree on how to prevent this from happening, because it is your responsibility to make sure your job gets done."

With liars, often the best course of action is to finesse the problem indirectly. We want to send a message to the person that lying just isn't going to work with you, and we can do that more effectively without direct confrontation.

Doesn't that drive you nuts? We all want to see liars have their comeuppance and to answer for their misdeeds. The reality is that an attitude of punishment or retribution is only going to make the situation worse. Stay focused on the issues more than the lying.

If you find that doesn't work, then a more direct, confrontational approach may be needed. But be aware that intentional liars aren't prone to admitting they lie to you. They fight back. That's why it's best to start with indirect approaches.

Tying Up the Venomous Person in a Nice Pink Bow

Here are some basic principles for dealing with venomous people:

1. In some situations, it's best to deal with venomous people indirectly, or to avoid direct confrontation. Leave face-saving outs for people. If you need to come down harder, later, then you can still do so.

2. Consider also that you will have difficulty dealing with the truly venomous without support within your organization; from your boss, from the hierarchy and perhaps from human resources. You need backup to succeed. That backup and support should be in place before you take action directly.

3. Keep your personal feelings in check. We all feel affronted by destructive people and want them put in their places. That's not your goal. It's not about getting even. It's not about punishment. It's about dealing with a work problem that interferes with getting the job done. You must, absolutely must, not make it a personal issue. If you do, you become difficult or even venomous yourself.

4. Performance management gives you a formal basis to deal with venomous behavior that affects job performance (for example, situations of insubordination). The entire process must be used, from the initial discussions of expectations through the observation and documentation process to the actual performance review or appraisal.

Above all, you need to demonstrate you have attempted to deal with venomous behavior and the employee has been made aware of your concerns.

The Least You Need to Know

➤ Managers and companies have a legal obligation to maintain a safe and healthy work environment.

➤ Venomous people intentionally try to harm.

➤ Backroom politicking is best handled by eliminating the sympathetic ears.

➤ Outright sabotage is best dealt with within a performance-management process. Often it can be treated as a performance problem.

➤ Put aside ideas of vengeance or comeuppance for liars. It's not about getting even or punishment.

Chapter 12

Can You Create Win–Win with These Folks? And How!

In This Chapter

➤ Is a cooperative approach worthwhile?

➤ How you can win with win–win

➤ How to start a win–win

➤ How to find some common ground with a difficult employee

Here's a question for you. Given what we said in the last chapter about venomous difficult people and some of the techniques you can use with specific situations, is it possible to turn situations around with these types of employees without using power-based approaches?

This is an important question. If it's not possible to work together with a venomous employee, then it's hardly worth the time and bother. You might as well go straight to a disciplinary, more formal approach.

In this chapter we'll answer that question, and we'll talk about what you can do to build a bridge with a venomous person.

Is Win-Win Possible with the Venomous?

Before we talk about whether it's possible to create a situation where both you and the difficult person work out a solution that is win-win, we should take a closer look at what the term means.

Win-win means that both parties in a dispute or problem situation end up constructing a solution that works for them. Some people suggest that the only way this can happen is if both people get what they want and need. Another way of looking at it, and one that's better for us, is that both parties come to a decision they can live with, even if it doesn't give them everything they want.

Employee Handbook

Win-win means that both parties in a dispute or problem situation construct a new and innovative solution that gives them what they both want or need.

Win-win has some advantages over using an imposed solution or using managerial authority to force a solution.

1. The idea behind win-win is that the problem situation is resolved. That means it doesn't reappear in some other form, because you have addressed what's underlying the problem. An added bonus: When you fix a problem with win-win, you also improve the relationship between you and the employee. That's gotta be good!

2. If you succeed at creating a win-win situation, you avoid the risks associated with a unilateral management decision, or the use of disciplinary action. When you use power and authority to solve a difficult person problem, chances are that the difficult person will become more difficult, will use whatever power he or she has to fight you, or will initiate a union grievance process or legal process to strike back.

Let's look at an example to see these advantages in action.

Mel works in a department as a receptionist. He reports to Roberta, who manages five other staff members. It's a union shop. Roberta faces a problem. Mel has been less and less productive over the last months, but even worse, he has been doing some things that indicate a venomous situation may be developing. He's made it known that he feels his talents aren't being used properly and that Roberta has made promises she hasn't kept, and once or twice he has gone over Roberta's head to the division head to complain about possible discrimination.

This situation has all the makings of one that will result in possible grievances or even legal action.

Roberta's a sharpie. She's catches this stuff early. So what are the choices? She can read the riot act (Lord knows it's justified), but that's likely to result in the involvement of the union. Or she can try to work with Mel to find out what's going on and see whether there's a way to solve the problem.

Roberta sets up a meeting with Mel and broaches the subject in a nonconfrontational way. She says to Mel:

> "Mel, I'm getting the sense that you're frustrated or unhappy about your work and what you're doing. I'd like to talk about that and see whether I can help in some way."

From the Manager's Desk

While we are presenting win-win techniques in our section on the venomous, they can work in most other difficult-person situations. Use the approach once you've determined it can succeed.

Unfortunately, because Mel is so darned upset, he doesn't react well to this. That's common. He goes off on Roberta, commenting on her management incompetence and implying that she is out to get him.

Now we come to a critical point. If Roberta overreacts, it's over; but she doesn't. She indicates she understands Mel is upset and she'd like to work *with* Mel to come up with some solution that will work for everyone. She sticks to this until Mel calms down somewhat.

Insider Secrets

It's pretty normal for win-win discussions to be a bit rocky. After all, it involves at least one (and probably two people) who are frustrated. While it may not be fair, it's smart to give the frustrated person some room to be nasty. Sometimes a good squawk tires the person out! Then he or she is ready to solve problems.

In the subsequent conversation, which is at times heated, Mel is encouraged to state his frustrations—and, boy, he's got a bunch. He says he was promised an opportunity for promotion and the promise has been broken. He says Roberta's lied to him.

But one key point comes up. Mel needs more challenges in his work, and it's clear if they don't occur he is going to become more cynical, more of a problem, and more venomous.

So, using a good deal of listening and then negotiating, Roberta suggests that she can help Mel develop his skills in areas like desktop publishing so he can take on more responsibility and eventually be promoted. Roberta also suggests it might be a good idea for Mel and Roberta to see whether there are other positions in the company that might be more suitable to Mel's ambitions and career desires.

And guess what? It works. Mel leaves feeling more hopeful, and also promises to come to Roberta if he has a problem he needs to discuss rather than keeping it to himself or using back-channel politicking. In the end, Mel and Roberta agree to a transfer to a position that has more of a career upside. So both win. Mel gets an opportunity to develop and follow a more desirable career path. Roberta prevents a nagging and expensive problem from escalating. And the company may benefit from a more skilled and happier employee. Above all, the complications of legal action are avoided.

So that's a specific situation where there are clear advantages to creating a win-win situation.

Disadvantages of Win-Win Attempts

Win-win requires the cooperation of both parties. You can't legislate a win-win solution. So the major dis-advantage occurs when an employee is not willing to work in this way. You end up digging a dry hole—and it gets deeper and deeper with no results.

This Won't Work!

Don't throw out a win-win attempt until you at least give it a shot. You might be pleasantly surprised at the result. After you get through the initial anger, it's possible to see about-faces from difficult people.

But it's hard to tell in advance whether a venomous employee will work with you. The only way to find out is to try. Sometimes the nastiest people can show remarkable turnarounds when approached in this way.

The other disadvantage is that it tends to be time consuming up front. You and the employee may need to put in considerable time, at least at the beginning, to roll back the hostility, work through it, and get to solutions.

Finally, working towards a win-win solution requires that you apply some advanced interpersonal skills and have a considerable degree of self-discipline. The self-discipline is critical so you don't get pulled into destructive conversations when an employee dumps on you at the beginning of the discussions.

So Is It Possible? Is It Worth It?

Only you can answer these questions for your specific situation. It's going to be a judgment call. Let's list a few questions you should ask yourself to determine whether the process is indeed possible:

➤ Do you have the skills and self-control you need to work with someone who may anger you?

➤ Have you caught the situation early enough so that it's not a hopeless case?

➤ Do you have a sense the person is difficult or venomous because of personal or health reasons? If so, you might not be able to address those problems yourself.

➤ Is the person capable of rational, calm discussion? (This is a tough one—sometimes you can't tell until you try.)

➤ Has the person involved the union or other third party (for example, a lawyer)? If so, it's probably too late.

Even if you think it's possible to work win-win with your venomous employee, given the time and difficulty in going with this technique, you must decide whether it is worth the investment. You do that by answering these questions:

➤ What is the likelihood of success?

➤ Are other methods better (for example, laying down the law, disciplinary action, ignoring the situation)?

➤ If it does succeed, can you live with working with this person afterward?

Let's say you decide that it's possible and it's worth it. I'm going to walk you through the how's of doing it well.

Win-Win—Breaking Through with the Approach

The *initial approach* is probably the most critical phase of creating win-win. If you do it well and the employee buys into the process, you lay the groundwork for a successful win-win resolution. We'll use our example of Mel, the disgruntled employee, and Roberta, the manager, to help you.

When Roberta approaches Mel for the first time to begin some conversation, she wants to convey a lack of pressure, a willingness to listen, the intention to help, and a lack of judgmental comments. That means no blaming, focusing on creating solutions, and, at least at the beginning, trying to get the door open.

Employee Handbook

The **initial approach** is the bedrock or foundation of creating a win–win situation. It is the first contact made by the manager towards the employee to present the option of working together and to get a commitment to do so.

From the Manager's Desk

The first contact in a win–win process may not work out. If the initial meeting goes badly, you have two choices. Give up and move to a power approach, or be tenacious and schedule another try.

In our example earlier, Roberta approached Mel with the following:

> "Mel, I'm getting the sense that you're frustrated or unhappy about your work and what you're doing. I'd like to talk about that and see whether I can help in some way."

See the helping tone. Roberta didn't mention the difficult behavior Mel was using. That can come up much later after she's established a communication bridge. At this point either Mel will respond positively or not. If the first meeting isn't working, Roberta stops it by saying:

> "OK, perhaps we both need to think about what to do about this so we both can live with a solution. Let's stop now, and we can both think a bit, and meet again tomorrow. How's two o'clock?"

This allows a cool-down phase. It allows Mel to take some time to think about the situation. Notice the emphasis on "we." Also notice that Roberta hasn't offered a choice of whether or not they will meet but *when* they will meet. She sent the message the process will continue without being overbearing.

Let's assume they meet at two o'clock and Mel is still not ready to enter into some sort of cooperative win-win situation. Shucks, it happens. Then what? Roberta can give up, but she has one more technique to apply. She's going to map out why it's better that they solve it together. Here's what it sounds like.

> "Mel, it's probably better for both of us if we work together on this because, look, we're both unhappy with the situation. But I can't work with you unless you want to solve this together. If we can't do that, then the only other option is to get into a disciplinary process, because it's obvious your unhappiness is affecting your work. I don't want to do that unless it's necessary, and I'm sure you don't. Let's try, at least. Let's stop this discussion for now. When we meet on Thursday, I'm going to ask you whether we can work on this together, or whether you want me to start documenting some of your performance difficulties. That way you get to choose which way you want to go."

Insider Secrets

Believe it or not, it isn't always obvious to angry people where their own best interests lie. That's why it's a good idea to map out the options to someone, to explain the benefits of working something out together, rather than going to war. Then let the person think about it for a while.

By providing an either/or situation, Roberta helps Mel think this through. Does Mel really want a war? If not, Mel is likely to come back prepared to talk.

Here's some tips for the approach:

➤ Don't wait too long to start. The longer the situation goes on without intervention, the harder it is.

➤ Keep the approach meetings fairly short, particularly if it isn't going well. If it does go well, the meeting can be longer because you don't want to lose momentum.

➤ Consider documenting the meetings or keeping notes with times, dates, and discussion details. If the process fails, you'll need these in any disciplinary process.

➤ Stay cool and focused on solving problems. Don't let the person pull you into arguing.

➤ If the person acts unpleasant or makes personal remarks, refocus him or her on the problem. Here's a statement you can use: "If we both get angry, we can't solve this, and we both lose. Let's get back to the issue."

➤ At the end of the approach meeting, summarize any commitments each of you has made and any ground rules you have agreed to follow. It's a good idea to do this in writing, also.

If you follow the tips above, you may be very pleasantly surprised. Some of the apparently nasty people will work with you if you approach them in just the right way.

Looking Under the Rock—Figuring Out What's Going On

After we've built the groundwork during the approach and have gained a commitment to the process, the next step is to get the employee's perceptions, feelings, and reactions out in the open. If the approach phase is completed easily and in a short time, you can begin this in the same meeting. If the approach has been a struggle, schedule another meeting to do this. Here's what it sounds like.

Roberta and Mel meet again. Roberta starts.

> "Mel, thanks for agreeing to try to work out this problem. I'm confident that we can come up with something that fits for both of us. The first thing I need from you is to find out what's going on. Why are you unhappy? Is it something I can address?"

This is probably the only time Roberta is going to invite Mel to vent. It has two purposes. One is to get the emotions out (and hopefully out of the way). The second is that Roberta really needs to know. So, how does Roberta react when Mel unloads all his complaints, some of which are pretty personal?

Roberta responded calmly and with empathy. Here are some responses.

From the Manager's Desk

OK, OK, I know it's not pleasant to allow someone to vent at you. But it's important. The feelings must be dissipated first before you can have calm, rational discourse. Put your mental asbestos suit on.

"Well, Mel, no wonder you aren't happy with the way things are."

"I can see how you might come to the conclusion that I'm interfering with your career."

Here are some critical hints for this phase:

➤ **Don't interrupt.** Let the person go without substantial comment. Listen.

➤ **Don't correct errors of fact.** That may occur later, but may result in arguing.

➤ **Don't argue.** Your turn comes soon.

➤ **Let the other person have his or her say.** This is giving him or her a chance to vent.

➤ **At the end of the employee's turn, paraphrase what he or she said.** Ask whether you're correctly understanding what they've said.

There is an exception to these suggestions. If the person loses control, seems threatening, or becomes unstable, then you can try refocusing on the commitment and ground rules. If that doesn't work, set some assertive limits. And if that doesn't work, it's probably time to fold, and give up on the win-win process.

Your Turn—Presenting Where You Are

Let's assume the employee (in this case, Mel) has had his say, calmed down, and is acting reasonable, and you've both agreed you understood him correctly. Now it's your turn. Wait! Your turn to what? No, It's not your turn to present your emotionally based attack. It's not your turn to argue. It's not your turn to pull the conversation away from finding solutions.

It is, however, your turn to state your position. Here's the way Roberta did it with Mel.

> "OK, now I understand better, Mel. Here's where I'm coming from. I want to come up with a solution that works for you, but it has to work for me also, and I don't have total flexibility here. Believe it or not, the company doesn't always let me do what I think best. First, Mel, I think we can use your talents better, and if we can't maybe you and I can figure out where you might be able to learn new things and follow a different career path. So we agree on that one. But I need something from you. We need to work this out between the two of us. That means that I need you to stop talking to Patrick (Roberta's boss), and I need you to stop bringing up your unhappiness with other employees. I don't think we can succeed without that. Are you willing to do that for now?"

This Won't Work!

A win–win negotiation requires *all* of the pieces we've described. Don't skip any of them.

From the Manager's Desk

When presenting your needs, make sure you indicate where and how your needs and the needs of the employee fit together or coincide. You do this to build hope and focus on the areas where agreement exists.

Here Roberta is stating her needs. If Mel doesn't agree to these, than in all likelihood, the win-win process stops here. In a way this is a simple test. The best way to determine whether someone is willing to go win-win is to see whether they will agree to meeting at least some of your needs.

If Mel agrees, then there is a further exchange of needs and positions related to the reasons for Mel's unhappiness. Mel says what he needs (for example, a chance to learn new things, more recognition, a chance for promotion). That's different from solutions. We aren't there yet. We're establishing what the solution must bring about. In turn, you get to present any of your needs or the company's needs.

Collaborative Problem Solving

Now you've mapped out the "problem space" and each person's needs. The next part is working out what solutions might be possible. That's actually a hard part to explain because the process varies from person to person.

What you are trying to do here is generate ideas together that will provide for the needs of the employee, you, and perhaps the company. It's a give-and-take process that can involve brainstorming. Here are some tips:

➤ Try brainstorming—getting a bunch of ideas without making judgment—then go back and look at your ideas in detail.

➤ Encourage the employee to take into account your needs.

➤ Make sure you take into account the needs stated by the employee (as best you can).

➤ Be slow to judge, and quick to listen.

➤ If something doesn't work for your needs or those of the company, clarify why.

➤ It doesn't matter whose solution eventually wins out, because you want to solve the problem. Usually the outcome is a result of both party's ideas.

Solving problems together requires good communication. The preceding ideas above will help you get that communication going, and help you generate creative ideas.

The End Game—Commitment and Follow-Up

Let's assume you and your employee come up with a solution both of you can live with or, better yet, one you're both excited about. Well, there's many a slip between the cup and the lip (whatever that means). Agreement is good, but you have to make sure it happens. There's two parts to this: summarizing the commitments and follow-up.

Make sure any agreements or solutions are summarized clearly verbally and preferably also in writing. It need not be a long document (short is better), but it's probably something you both want to sign as a note of understanding (rather than a binding contract). Include (both verbally and on paper) any commitments you have made and any specific actions you have agreed to take. Likewise, any commitments on the part of the employee need to be understood and recorded.

We aren't done yet. You need to have some way of making sure things improve, and that whatever solutions you've agreed to are being implemented to the satisfaction of both parties. Set up periodic (usually short) meetings to discuss how things are going. Here's how Roberta set these up with Mel.

> "Mel, I'm really glad that we've come to an agreement on this, but let's not stop talking until you and I are both happy with the results. What I'd like to do is meet in a month to see whether there is anything we need to change, to find out whether things have improved. Hopefully we'll only need a few minutes."

At the follow-up meeting, the following can be discussed:

➤ Are both parties happy with how the other person has carried out the agreement? (If not, fix it.)

➤ Is there anything else that needs to be done?

➤ Any barriers cropping up to the solution? If so, deal with them.

➤ Boy, we should be congratulated for turning this around!!!

And that's about it. Continue follow-up until it is deemed no longer necessary.

This Won't Work!

A common error is to assume that once an agreement is struck it will happen without problems. It's absolutely critical that you have a follow-up plan in place so you can identify glitches and fix them.

From the Manager's Desk

Make sure you can actually keep your commitments. Sometimes that means talking to others needed to make the commitment happen. There's nothing worse than agreeing to something and having to tell an employee "Sorry, I couldn't get that approved."

The Least You Need to Know

➤ Win–win can work with even venomous employees.

➤ You need to assess the likelihood of success.

➤ Win–win requires great skill levels and self-discipline on your part.

➤ The initial approach phase is probably most important but all steps are needed.

➤ When the going gets rough, refocus on the benefits of working together and on the problem itself, not on personalities.

Chapter 13

I Fought The Law and ...?

In This Chapter

➤ Find out what laws you need to be aware of

➤ The laws aren't black and white

➤ How to use the steps of progressive discipline

➤ Learn about your responsibilities regarding workplace climate

When a manager faces a difficult situation with an employee, whether it's venomous behavior or just plain poor performance, your options for dealing with it are somewhat constrained by legalities. It could be that what you want to do with a problem employee could get you in trouble. You need to know what you can do and how to go about it so you are protected.

In this chapter we'll help you learn about the law as it applies to difficult employees and situations in the workplace. You don't want to fight the law and lose. In fact, you don't want to fight the law at all. You need to know your rights and obligations so you don't get into the courts. Period.

The Legal Swamp

Before we get into more specifics about laws as they pertain to difficult situations in the workplace, there are a lot of things you need to know about the law and how it works. In a moment you will see why this section is so important.

Before we do that, here's the standard disclaimer. I'm not a lawyer, nor do I play one on TV. Nothing in this chapter should be taken as legal advice. When in doubt, consult a lawyer.

While it may seem that laws permit you to do the things you want to address difficult situations, it's not that cut and dry. That's because a number of laws may need to be considered, not just one.

For example, the laws in your area may specify that you can terminate someone for no cause at all; other laws may affect whether you actually can do that. While the labor law may say you can fire someone, if you have a contract or implied contract with an employee, contract law enters into the equation. Or, while you may be able to fire someone with no cause, if you don't do it properly, you may run afoul of employment equity or antidiscrimination laws.

Insider Secrets

Even if your labor laws state you can fire a person without cause, that doesn't mean you can do so without getting yourself in hot water. Contract law and antidiscrimination statutes can still provide reasonable grounds for a dismissed employee to sue you.

That's why it's so important to have informed expert advice from someone who is a lawyer (and doesn't play one on TV).

Layer upon Layer of Law

I have no idea where you live, and what country's laws apply to you and your situation. That makes a big difference.

For example, the laws differ by country. Dismissal laws in Canada, the U.S., Britain, and Australia are going to be different enough that you can't rely on applying the principles from one to another. Not only that, but local laws (states, provinces) can also differ. In the U.S. alone, some states allow firing an employee without cause, while others (albeit the minority) require more from an employer.

As another example, in the U.S. and Canada, labor law generally is part of state or provincial jurisdiction. However, there are still federal laws that apply, such as antidiscrimination laws.

So, when considering disciplinary action with a difficult or nonperforming employee, you need to consider or be advised about ...

> ➤ the federal laws that apply.
> ➤ the local laws that apply (state or province).

But that's not all. Contract law also comes into play. Let's say your difficult employee has signed a five-year contract that specifies terms of dismissal. After a year, you realize the employee is a total bust—nasty, incompetent, and venomous. Your local laws say the person can be fired at any time, but that's not what the contract says. You may have your hands tied if the contract specifies terms different from the minimum requirements outlined in the laws of your jurisdiction.

It gets still more complicated. It makes sense that a signed contract is binding on the parties involved, right? But contract law can take effect even when there is no formal contract between the parties. How can that be?

If your company has employment policies about the process of dismissing an employee, they may be considered by the court as a binding contract. So let's say your company has an employee handbook that says that no employee will be dismissed without just cause, but you live in an area whose labor laws say you can dismiss without cause. Well, guess what? The courts may consider your employee handbook as a binding contract.

From the Manager's Desk

The policies in an employee handbook can be interpreted as a binding contractual agreement. Make sure these policies don't tie the hands of management. If you hit a snag, it's good to notify the human resources department or originator of your policies to discuss it.

So, now we have four layers: federal laws, local laws, explicit contracts, and implicit contracts.

There's yet another layer that applies for companies that have unions. Collective bargaining agreements may come into play, so that's another thing you need to know about as it applies to your situation. There are also grievance procedures and policies.

So there we go. Five layers of law you need to take into account when dealing with the difficult employee. Is it any wonder we suggest expert advice?

How the Law Really Works

There is a dangerous misconception about how law works. Naively, some people think that what the law *says* is actually what is important. Despite what we would like to think, the law is not black and white. The application of the law and the interpretation of the law are the important parts. And that's done by real people, whether they be judges, juries, tribunals, or grievance panels. What does this mean for you?

This Won't Work!

Do not assume that because one law seems to support your action, you will prevail in the courts or legal proceedings. It's people who decide, people who make the judgments, and that's unpredictable.

It means you can never predict with absolute certainty how the law is going to be interpreted for a particular situation. The courts look at each case individually, drawing from the statutes and how other courts have decided similar cases in the past. They make judgments by weighing the different laws that may apply and come up with a decision. In civil suits it can get even worse because you may not be dealing with a judge schooled in law and precedent. It may be a jury that decides. And we never know what 12 citizens will do in court.

Even the advice of lawyers can be misleading. That's scary. Lawyers don't know with certainty how a judge or a jury will apply the existing laws. As a good lawyer will tell you, there are no guarantees when something goes to court.

It is a swamp, and a somewhat dangerous one. Certainly it's an unpredictable one. So what's the solution? If we never know for sure whether the courts will support a specific decision, what do we do? No managers want to get their butts sued when there is always a chance those butts will lose.

The solution, such as it is, is not to get into the legal system if you can possibly avoid it. That means doing things according to the best available practices so an employee isn't given an opportunity to begin legal action. By doing things properly, you discourage lawsuits.

Disciplinary Issues—Do You Have Protection?

Before we jump into the generally accepted protective steps you need to take when initiating disciplinary action, let's talk about where the landmines lie. Let's assume you live in the U.S. (although this may apply to other countries), and you live in a state that is at-will, which means you don't have to prove cause for dismissal.

On what basis can employees fight back?

According to Title VII of the Civil Rights Act of 1964, employers are prohibited from discrimination on the basis of race, sex, color, religion, or national origin. The Federal Age Discrimination Act protects employees from age discrimination, while the Americans with Disabilities Act protects disabled people. In addition, the National Labor Relations Act protects workers' rights to form unions or band together to protest working conditions. Other prohibitions are getting added to the mix, or will be. The most notable, and one that is being contested in various jurisdictions, is sexual orientation.

What does this have to do with your venomous or nonperforming employee? If your employee falls into any category related to Title VII, they may contend that the disciplinary action you took was not related to their job performance or work behavior, but to their gender, color, ethnic origin, religion, and so on. And guess what? They don't have to prove that's so. It is *your* responsibility to prove the disciplinary action you took was based on performance. That's right. An employee can accuse you and unless you can prove otherwise, you're likely to have a problem. Whether you agree with this or not, you need to understand it.

> **From the Manager's Desk**
>
> If an employee accuses you of discrimination as a result of disciplinary action, it will be your responsibility to prove that isn't so. The only way you can do that is prove that the action is a result of work-related or performance behavior. Hence, you need to keep records of specifics.

The laws protect employees in other ways. For example, some jurisdictions have what are called *whistle-blower* protections. A whistle-blower is a person who attempts to inform others about illegal or dangerous practices occurring in the workplace.

If you attempt to fire a whistle-blower, even if it's a result of poor performance, it may appear that you are doing so because of his or her whistle-blowing activities.

> **Employee Handbook**
>
> A **whistle-blower** is someone who exposes illegal or dangerous practices in the workplace. Some governments offer protection against dismissal if a person speaks out.

Similarly, some jurisdictions prohibit disciplinary action that is retaliatory in nature. For example, if an employee consistently speaks out about what he or she sees as sexual harassment, the employer cannot retaliate for that speaking out. Neither can an employer terminate an employee for participating in any investigation or proceeding under the relevant statutes.

Again you may be saying, "How does this apply to my situation?" It comes down to this. Whether the difficult employee wants to use employment equity laws or whistle-blower statutes or any of the preceding, it is going to be up to you to demonstrate that the employee wasn't disciplined for any of those reasons, but was disciplined for bona fide performance problems.

In effect, it doesn't always matter what's true. What matters is what you can prove it to the body or person judging the action.

The Disciplinary Prophylactic

Keeping in mind that you need to prove any disciplinary action is not a result of discrimination but rather related to performance, how do you protect yourself? You use what is called *progressive discipline*. Progressive discipline refers to a series of steps that involve progressively firmer warnings and sanctions coupled with providing opportunities for the employee to address unacceptable behavior.

Employee Handbook

Progressive discipline is a process wherein an employee is notified of inappropriate behaviors and where the sanctions and warnings become firmer and more severe. For example, a first warning may have no immediate consequences. If the person doesn't change, then the next warning may involve the possibility of a short suspension.

There are several key principles here.

1. **Documentation.** You must have documentation indicating the nature of inappropriate behavior, when it has occurred, and how you addressed it. You need this to be as specific as possible, down to dates and times and records of conversation.

2. **Communication.** You need to communicate properly with the employee. You must be able to demonstrate you have communicated what is unacceptable. So you need to document any communication you have with an employee who may be subject to disciplinary action.

3. **Evidence.** You must provide evidence the employee has had an opportunity to change his or her behavior, and that you have made the effort to assist.

So what are the recommended steps?

Oral Warning

The initial step is to provide an oral (and usually informal warning) to the employee describing what is wrong, and requesting that a change be made. The warning should be specific and make clear what specific behaviors or actions must be changed, and the consequences for not doing so. Generally, this informal step does not include entering a note in the employee's personnel file. However, you might want to record that the meeting took place, when it occurred, and what was said.

Formal Oral Warning with Documentation

This differs from the preceding oral warning because it includes an entry into the employee's file. As a manager you go to this step when the oral warning has not resulted in the needed changes.

Insider Secrets

When managers delay action or ignore poor behavior, they tend to skip too many of the progressive discipline steps and get themselves handcuffed or at risk legally. Don't be hesitant to have informal discussions about behavior early on. Delaying makes the eventual encounter more emotional, and the manager who has let things go too long may be driven more by emotion than by a desire to solve the problem. As a result, the manager may communicate a very harsh initial penalty rather than start with a small one.

For all warnings that have been formally documented and entered into an official file, you should always have the employee acknowledge that he or she has received the warning. Many managers will have the employee initial the paperwork to signify receipt. It should be clear to the employee that acknowledgement of notification or receipt does not indicate agreement. Some companies may permit the employee to add his or her own comments to the file.

Written Warning

The written warning is a formal document that goes in the file. With the oral warning steps, you generally record the basics of the communication. With a written warning, the entire problem should be described in a written format. You should include a description of the problem behavior, again as specifically as possible. It should reference and document any oral warnings and/or conversations you have had previously. It should spell out exactly what will happen if no improvement occurs. In addition, it should explain why the behaviors are unacceptable, and suggest some courses of action to remedy the situation.

Final Warning

If none of the preceding steps have worked, then a final warning can be issued. It must be written, and the employee must acknowledge receipt. At this point, whatever consequences you had indicated to the employee earlier will be imposed.

For example, if you indicated the employee would be suspended unless the behavior changed (in your first written warning), then this is the time to impose the suspension. Make sure you provide a date by which you expect the employee to implement the desired changes.

Other consequences, ranging from mild to more extreme, include entering a permanent note in a personnel file, removing a person from a high profile project, sending the person home for a day to "think," through to longer suspensions and dismissal.

Termination

In the event none of this has worked, it's crunch time. If there has been no improvement after the final warning has been issued and you have already used other less-severe sanctions, you have the option of termination.

Provided you have followed the preceding guidelines, you should have enough documentation to protect yourself from accusations that the dismissal is a result of non-work-related issues, such as discrimination.

Insider Secrets

Do you know what it costs to hire someone or replace a dismissed employee? It depends on the job. The more complex the job, the more expensive. Some estimates put the replacement cost at the equivalent of one to two years' salary for the position.

Before we move on, let's discuss the cost of termination. Termination should be a last resort because it's downright expensive, and some of those costs are hidden—that is, we don't always think about them. It's expensive to replace an employee. We have to advertise, review applications, interview, and complete the hiring process when we do find someone new. Not only that, but it can take as long as six months to a year for a new employee to get up to speed and perform at a high level.

Termination should be a last resort.

Hey, You Have *Another* Legal Responsibility

All this legal stuff is pretty daunting, and, I'm sorry to say, there's more. Apart from the legalities of disciplinary action, you have another legal responsibility.

Management (that's you) has a responsibility to ensure a safe and secure environment for employees. In the past that has been restricted to physical safety. You probably know that you can't have dangerous or ill-maintained machines, poor air quality, et cetera, and expect to be free of lawsuits or sanctions.

What's changed is that the principles of the safe and secure workplace have been extended to non-physical safety issues. The most obvious area is sexual harassment. We know you wouldn't sexually harass an employee, right? But you have an additional responsibility. Not only must you, personally, not harass people sexually, but you must ensure that employees don't harass each other.

From the Manager's Desk

Prevention is important. It may be helpful to demonstrate you have done your best to prevent things like sexual harassment and verbal abuse through preventative training and communication of corporate policy to staff.

Here's an example:

> Bob constantly hits on Marie for dates and uses sexual innuendo with her. She informs him that she doesn't like that.

If it continues and you do nothing, you may be sued successfully. Not only are you responsible for ensuring a psychologically safe environment, ignorance and being oblivious are not excuses for inaction. Let's say you didn't know about Bob's harassment. That may not matter. You may still be liable.

You are expected to know what's going on and to take positive steps to ensure this kind of behavior doesn't occur. Certainly, you aren't a miracle worker and can't be responsible for everything, but you may need to demonstrate that you have a sexual harassment policy in place, that Bob (and all employees) are aware of it, and that when any problems are brought to your attention you take appropriate action to remedy it. For example, you might be expected to have introduced relevant training into the workplace as a preventative measure.

This Won't Work!

Ignorance is no protection under harassment laws. The law looks at whether you as a manager should have known about a potential problem. If it's reasonable to have known and you still weren't aware, too bad.

This may extend into other areas, and there's a clear link to dealing with difficult behavior. What are the implications?

First, difficult behavior that affects the psychological welfare of others may require you to take positive and proactive action to deal with the specific situation, and to prevent it from occurring in the first place.

Second, if you do not take action and the courts deem that you should have, you can be liable. You may ask, "How do I know in advance what the courts will think about any specific difficult behavior?"

Sorry, but you can't know that. In the area of sexual harassment, there are enough cases to have a good idea about it. In other areas, such as verbal abuse, the law evolves and changes.

Because of this level of uncertainty, many employers are instituting training on topics such as sexual harassment and what constitutes appropriate behavior in the "respectful workplace." They are doing so for three reasons.

From the Manager's Desk

Just because some inappropriate behavior doesn't affect your bottom line doesn't mean you can ignore it. The law may require action. Factor this into your reality check when looking at difficult behavior.

1. Some employers truly want to create a positive environment for staff, because that probably results in better productivity.

2. Some companies feel a moral and ethical obligation to create a positive work environment.

3. Using preventative strategies like training before any problems occur demonstrates that your company has fulfilled its legal obligation (to some extent) to provide a safe work environment. That can protect you if you or your company is sued.

For the same reasons, companies are developing policies about proper workplace conduct and making sure each employee receives a copy and acknowledges receipt of the copy.

Both strategies are important. Developing a policy shows that the company has discharged part of its legal responsibilities. Making sure each employee gets a copy and acknowledges receipt provides legal proof that the company has taken positive action to communicate the policies.

Is There Any Good News Here?

I know some people will read this chapter and feel upset or distressed or even angry about what the see as meddling of government. Everyone is entitled to an opinion, but regardless of yours, you have a reality to consider. Things are what they are, and you need to know this stuff.

The question is, in all of this is there any good news? Sure, even though we probably have to search for it:

➤ While there is some protection for employees, keep in mind that it probably applies to you as an employee. After all, managers are employed just like line staff.

➤ While nothing is certain in labor law, nothing is certain in life, either. It's like anything else. If you make an effort to understand what you can and can't do and do things that conform to all legal requirements, you're much less likely to experience legal attacks.

➤ By understanding the legal issues involved and acting accordingly, you can deal with employees with more confidence. You will be less likely to freak out when an angry employee threatens to sue, because you know the chances of a successful lawsuit are small.

Let's end this chapter by reiterating what we said at the beginning. There is no substitute for professional legal advice. You may read a book or two and think you have it down. The human resources department may advise you, but are they lawyers? Be aware that law is complicated and a little knowledge may be a dangerous thing.

The Least You Need to Know

➤ Labor laws differ from place to place, and there are several layers of law.

➤ Progressive discipline is a way of covering some of the legal bases.

➤ In a legal dispute *you* (management) must prove that disciplinary action was not discriminatory; the onus is not on the employee.

➤ Management has a legal responsibility to ensure a safe and healthy workplace.

➤ Ignorance of things like sexual harassment or similar difficult behaviors may not protect you.

➤ Take proactive steps regarding work environment. Train people, have clear policies, and communicate those policies to all employees.

Worry About the Other Shoe Dropping— Violence

> ### In This Chapter
>
> ➤ Chances for violent behavior on the job
>
> ➤ Dismissing potentially violent employees
>
> ➤ Predicting workplace violence
>
> ➤ Corporate strategies for a safe workplace
>
> ➤ Management strategies for a safe workplace

It's scary. More and more we're hearing about employees who commit acts of violence in the workplace, either without apparent provocation or in dismissal situations. The first thing we should say is that although workplace violence is a serious concern, the majority of violence in the workplace is perpetrated by strangers, primarily as part of other criminal activity, such as robbery. The odds are slim that you will face violence in your role of manager, although even that depends on a number of factors.

In this chapter we will look at the issue of workplace violence. Is it predictable, and how can you do your best to prevent it, particularly in disciplinary situations? We'll provide as many tips as possible.

An important note: Violence is no laughing matter, and whenever possible, dealing with it should be left to professionals. The information in this chapter is for information tion purposes only. It should not be construed as advice about your situation because no book can tell you what to do. We'll try to offer possible courses of action, often

recommended by experts in workplace violence, but ultimately you are the one who has information about your specific situation. When in doubt (and you should often be in doubt about workplace violence), contact law enforcement, security experts, or other professionals.

View from the Bridge—Some Background on Violence

We need to put workplace violence in perspective. We need to look at any hint of violence as serious, and not ignore the possibility. On the flip side, we don't want to run around in terror, thinking the next employee who walks into the office is going to do something crazy. Both extremes put you at higher risk.

Ignoring a threat is just plain dumb. In fact, some of the literature on workplace violence suggests that it is more likely to occur when smaller work problems have been ignored or handled badly.

Being overly paranoid or reactive can also be problematic. Apart from the misery of living in fear, it may encourage you to use a heavy hand in some situations, creating a siege mentality for you and those around you.

One more point on this. It's an unfortunate truth that the methods we take to defuse hostile situations through interpersonal communication and dialogue are the opposite of what we do when we shift to a concern about safety. Heavy security, for example, or even immediate removal from the premises of a dismissed employee may enrage a stressed-out person or push him over the edge. So, there's always a trade-off. The more power you use to protect people, the more likely the potentially violent person will feel a loss of dignity. When someone is stripped of self-worth, he or she is more likely to act violently.

This Won't Work!

The very techniques people use to protect themselves from violence may increase the chances of violence occurring. That's because the use of power is often violence provoking. Use minimal force at all times, but when there is a clear threat, focus on safety.

To address the issue of risk, it might seem that violent crime is increasing. We hear about it all the time in the media, but that's partly a function of how the media works. We don't hear of the thousands of instances where employees have been dismissed in an amicable manner with no problems. We do hear about the one person who flips out and attacks a manager. While it's no consolation, over the last few years statistics show that violent crime in general has been dropping in both the U.S. and Canada.

Now, the bad news. According to U.S. Justice Department, workplace violence is the leading cause of death on the job for women, and No. 2 for men. Sounds terrifying, right? We need to look more carefully at the numbers to gain a perspective here. First, the majority of those deaths result from other crimes that go wrong, such as robbery. That's why most workplace homicides occur in service and other high-risk areas that are frequent targets for robbery. Second, our North American workplaces are extremely safe, and there are few occupational deaths from accidents. So because there are so few deaths from other causes, it makes homicide look far more frequent than it would otherwise.

Insider Secrets

The numbers on workplace violence can appear alarming, because most people aren't statisticians. They need to be put in context to understand them, and then the picture isn't quite so alarming. Still, workplace violence is *always* an important issue.

The point about all of this: Don't freak out about the statistics, but at the same time don't ignore the possibility of violence. We'll look at things you can do to reduce risk in the rest of this chapter.

Violence, Disciplinary Action, and Dismissal

In the last chapter we talked about legal issues related to disciplinary action and outlined the steps of progressive discipline. We're going to extend that discussion a bit, and talk about workplace violence that occurs as a result of a dismissal or termination process.

The chances of becoming a victim of workplace violence related to termination are probably pretty low. But there's a catch. If you do it badly, or in a way that humiliates the employee or results in feelings of desperation and being trapped, the risk factor increases significantly. So let's talk about how to do it right and the things to avoid.

First we'll consider an example from hell, one that might drive even a relatively normal employee to extremes.

John is manager of a work unit of about 30 people. Garry works for him. John is a bit of a gruff guy. He moved up from the ranks below, and could be called the "salt of the earth." Not a great communicator, not even much a manager, he's more one of the guys with a fancy title.

As a manager, John is a bit explosive. He yells when he gets excited, swears on occasion, ridicules employees in public, and does similar things that set a tone of hostility and disrespect. Not surprisingly, some of his employees have taken his cue and act in similar ways.

This Won't Work!

When a manager sets a climate of verbal abuse and disrespect, there may be an increased chance of violence.

It's not a great place to work, but nothing's perfect, right?

Back to Garry. Garry is a somewhat moody employee who has just purchased a new home. His attendance is fine, but sometimes he gets involved in the horseplay, and the truth is his work production is terrible. Because John is a rule-by-power guy, he figures he'll wait just so long and drop the hammer. John hasn't worked with Garry to address the problem. He hardly talks to him about the problem except to make occasional snide remarks to him.

So, it's Tuesday and John's had enough of the poor productivity. He calls Garry into his office, leaves the door open, and says:

"Well, Garry, I'm fed up with your lack of productivity, so this is your last day. You're fired and if you think you are going to get a good reference from me, no way, brother. Security will walk you to your workspace so you can get your personal effects, and your check will be mailed to you."

OK, try to pick out the problems in this scenario. What are the chances that Garry is liable to haul off and hit John right away or become sufficiently upset to return with a gun to even the score? Has John created a high risk scenario? Yes. Let's look at what John should have done.

Preventive Measures and Dismissal

John's first error is establishing a work environment where hostility and abuse are acceptable. This increases the risk of violence in general. One thing a manager should do is work to create an atmosphere of respect and nonabusive behavior. Abusive verbal behavior can lead to violent behavior, so dealing with it at the source is the

best path.

John's own behavior should have been different. He should serve as a role model. Second, any abusive or disrespectful behavior occurring in the workplace should be dealt with using the progressive discipline scenario described in the previous chapter.

Now, let's consider what *didn't* occur before the fateful Tuesday meeting. By not communicating earlier with Garry about the performance problem, John has set several wheels in motion that increase the possibility of immediate or delayed violence. By avoiding communication about the issue over the last year, John has increased his own anger levels, so that when the conversation does take place, John makes it personal. It's like the teakettle. It gets hotter and hotter until it blows the top off to release the energy.

Perhaps what's worse is that the dismissal meeting comes as a complete surprise to Garry. He gets no time to improve his performance. He's had no chance to adapt to the idea or prepare himself emotionally or financially. That's a situation ripe for violence.

Now, let's turn to the actual meeting behavior. Take a look at what happens. The words and tone used by John are very personal. His words aren't supportive, regretful, or helpful—quite the opposite. Garry is going to see himself as a victim, with John as the attacker. And rightly so. John isn't just conveying information here. He's sticking in a figurative knife and twisting.

In dismissal situations, it should be clear that the decision to terminate is not an emotional one born of anger or vindictiveness but a carefully weighed decision made on the basic facts. No personal attacks, no arguments, no threats.

From the Manager's Desk

Use an armed or security escort only when absolutely necessary. It conveys mistrust and can heighten the tension. It can also add to the humiliation of the employee.

This Won't Work!

Some managers think that dismissals should be short, ugly, and abrupt, the rationale being that it's better to get it over with. An overly short or abrupt dismissal can make things much worse. It makes the manager and the company seem inhuman and cold. Use the employee's reactions to determine whether there is any point in continuing and when to end the meeting.

The general tone is important. When an employee is dismissed, it helps to offer support services such as outplacement counseling, job-hunting training, psychological counseling, and so on. By doing so, the manager is less likely to come across as the enemy or a victimizer.

Finally, the statement John makes about the letter of reference is completely out of line. It's a threat, and threatening someone is the best way to produce violence in people prone to violence. Here's a completely different alternative. During the termination meeting, John offers to negotiate what will go into a letter of reference (if any is to be offered). This helps introduce some hope in a desperate person, and again tries to establish a cooperative bridge, a sense of working together.

This Won't Work!

It's easy to get so frustrated and angry with a person that you allow your personal feelings to affect how you treat the person during a dismissal meeting. Don't. Stay calm and objective. If you can't, then let someone else conduct the meeting.

If Garry feels his firing means the end of his world as he knows it now, he's dangerous. If he feels there is a future for him and he isn't boxed in, he's going to be a lower risk.

Let's consider dignity and humiliation. John seems to go out of his way to humiliate Garry. He does so in his words and tone. The dismissal is semi-public, because privacy hasn't been secured. Then Garry is going to be escorted out of the building by security guards in plain view of his co-workers. How much is this guy going to take?

Dismissal is a business decision. It's not personal, and it's not about humiliating someone, getting even, or making someone look stupid. That's the fast track to becoming a victim of violence.

Other Tips

Are there other things to do to reduce the probability of workplace violence connected with dismissal? Yes.

1. *Exhaust all other possibilities before moving to dismissal.*

   Remember that you hired the person, and you have some responsibility in the matter. Train, talk, coach, and help. At least the employee will recognize that you aren't being vindictive if you try helping first.

2. *Catch abusive behavior early.*

   Yelling, personal abuse, and similar behavior may indicate a proclivity for violence. Have a policy in place that specifies what is inappropriate behavior, and try to nip it in the bud using the tools we've already mentioned. The policy must apply to everyone, top to bottom, and be enforced consistently.

3. *Be honest during performance appraisals and the performance-management/feedback process.*

   Don't tell a poor performer he is doing well when he isn't. That creates surprise if you come down with a heavy hand. And that can contribute to violence.

4. *Be prepared to offer any support services available.*

   Plan to do so in a dismissal meeting. If you can provide job-search training, offer it. If you can provide counseling, do so. Garner your support resources before the meeting so you know what you can offer.

5. *Don't conduct a dismissal meeting without planning it all out.*

   Decide who needs to be there. Will there be someone to witness it? Will the employee be asked to leave immediately? How will severance be handled? Who will say what?

6. *Keep the dismissal meeting short, perhaps 15 minutes or so.*

   You want to convey information, how you and the company can help, and to project as supportive an image as possible. This is not the time to negotiate or argue or harangue, because you've already made a final decision. With an upset or angry employee, the longer a meeting goes, the more volatile the situation can become. Take your cue from the employee. Ask yourself: If we continue, is this meeting likely to get easier or worse?.

7. *While you need to explain the reasons for dismissal, nothing stops you from also mentioning any areas of strength the employee has shown.*

   The dismissal process is hard on the employee's ego. Mentioning any positives cushions the ego blow. It also shows you aren't trying to destroy the employee. Talking about positives can make the discussion seem less "personal."

8. *Provide the basic information in written form.*

   The employee needs to leave knowing where things stand and to be able to reference details on paper. For example, severance arrangements should be specified in writing, as should any other significant details such as continuation (or termination) of benefit programs. Have this prepared in advance of the dismissal meeting.

9. *Consider dismissing at the end of a day and/or on a Friday.*

   There is some advantage to not exposing the employee to the humiliation of having to leave in front of his or her co-workers. However, the downside to this is that the dismissed employee may have less access to supportive friends.

From the Manager's Desk

Poor dismissal techniques put you and your staff at risk. Learn how to do it properly. Consider getting some training. At minimum, consider practicing the dismissal process with a colleague in a role-playing process. Be prepared.

10. *There are pros and cons to having the person escorted from the building by security guards.*

   While it may be helpful in high-risk situations, it's also incredibly humiliating. Unless there are warning signs of potential violence, consider letting the ex-employee leave the building alone, and come back after hours to get his or her belongings. Or, give him or her a choice.

11. *If the ex-employee contacts you for clarification, respond as quickly and promptly as possible.*

   Losing one's job is disorienting and anxiety provoking. By delaying responses to questions, you increase the person's level of upset and frustration. You also seem less helpful. That increases the possibility of violence.

12. *Finally, and perhaps most importantly, look for indications the employee wants retribution.*

   If the person threatens or hints at "getting even," respond to that in a neutral way using empathy. For example: "It's easy to understand that you're really upset about this." That's it. Don't focus on it. After the person has left, consult security, law enforcement, or other experts to determine what to do to ensure safety. If you are concerned the employee may do damage on the way out of the premises, you can arrange for a security escort, but try to make it as subtle as possible to avoid further humiliation.

Is Workplace Violence Predictable?

Let's shift gears away from the specific violence and dismissal topic to the general topic of workplace violence. Violence at work certainly isn't confined to manager targets; it also occurs between employees.

Here are the most common questions I receive in my defusing hostility workshop:

➤ Is workplace violence predictable?

➤ How can I be sure a particular person won't attack someone?

First, our ability to predict who will commit workplace violence is quite poor. The best information around on the subject still will lead us to more prediction errors than prediction hits. Given that the ability to predict is poor, is the prediction information useful? Yes. Knowing the violence indicators may give us advance warning of a potential problem so we can prepare for it in advance. For example, if you suspect someone may be potentially violent, you might offer supportive counseling. You might take any threats more seriously than if they came from someone who didn't fit the indicators.

Insider Secrets

We aren't very good at predicting violence, but that doesn't mean you are helpless to prevent it. We know that certain things can set off violent reactions. One of the easiest is to eliminate action that humiliates an employee: public criticism, demeaning comments, or ignoring positive contributions while criticizing poor performance.

But let's be clear. Some people turn violent without any indicators, or you may not be aware of them given the employee's behavior on the job. The fact no indicators are present doesn't mean there will be no violence. And where there are indicators, it may mean nothing at all.

So, I guess that answers the second question: You can't be sure a particular person won't turn violent, not with any degree of certainty. However, the following indicators may provide advance warning, and may help save a life.

Personal Indicators

Workplace violence perpetrators (particularly murderers) tend to be males over 35 years old. The person may have a history of mental difficulties, but often the problems have gone unnoticed. The perpetrator may believe that violence and aggression are legitimate ways to solve problems. He may also have a history of violence outside the workplace, particularly domestic violence. Look for a pattern of behavior that suggests the person is disgruntled and has a disdain for authority. Also, there is a tendency for perpetrators of workplace violence to be loners or socially isolated.

Two additional personal patterns: Is the person a substance abuser? That's an indicator. So is being a part of an extremist group (that is, the person is a bit of a zealot, be it about politics, religion, or race).

From the Manager's Desk

Indicators of potential violence are just that: indicators. Someone who fits some of the items may never be violent. Also, someone who fits none of them or few may very well commit a violent act. The purpose is to provide some early warning so you can try to get the person help before it's too late.

Finally, people who commit violent acts at work tend to externalize blame. That means they don't own up to their own errors and will often place the blame on others.

Workplace Behavior

There are some predictors of violence related to work behavior. Often the perpetrator has a track record or pattern of being involved in workplace violence or verbal violence previously. The person may have uttered threats and have a hair-trigger temper. Does the person seem to hold grudges way beyond what would be considered normal?

How does the person react to criticism from the boss or others? Is the reaction way out of proportion to the issue? That may be an indicator.

Obsessions

Obsessions seem to be fairly typical of violence perpetrators. Perhaps the most important one is an obsession with violent issues, news, or weapons and firearms. Does the person talk a lot about those things? That's a prime indicator.

Also, is the person obsessed with the job? Is it the main or only focal point for his life?

Another indicator is compulsive behavior in general. For example, is the person obsessed with neatness or cleanliness?

Finally, does the person have intense romantic obsessions that are unwarranted, or has the person talked about stalking or been accused of stalking in the past?

Action Changes and Behavior

Our last set of indicators has to do with specific changes in behavior. Be aware of newly acquired negative traits or peculiar behavior that emerges. That may signify that the person is "losing his grip."

Has the person withdrawn from his normal social circle? That can be an indicator of increased isolation and mental difficulty.

There are a few others, and we'll list them. Most of these are indicators of increased emotional distress or illness that might presage a violent incident:

➤ Inability to concentrate

➤ Suddenly lowered productivity that can't be explained

➤ A sudden inattention to personal hygiene

➤ Increased absenteeism or lateness

➤ Inappropriate emotional responses

➤ Inability to control anger

➤ Getting rid of personal property

➤ Any indicators of depression

➤ Experiencing personal, family, or financial problems

Preventative Steps for All Workplace Violence

Now it's time to look at actions you and your company can take to reduce the possibility of violence and reduce personal injury if it occurs.

This Won't Work!

You don't need to be a psychologist or pry into the personal affairs of someone to identify changes in work behavior or actions on the job. However, managers who are detached or uninvolved with employees may miss the signs. Get to know your employees. It's worthwhile.

Corporate Initiatives

Have a policy on workplace conduct that specifies what kinds of interpersonal behavior are inappropriate. Such a policy should include things like verbal abuse and sexual harassment. Keep it simple, short, and readable. The policy should spell out the consequences of unacceptable behavior and procedures to lodge a complaint. Then each manager should be responsible for ensuring that employees understand it and for enforcing it.

Insider Secrets

Corporate initiatives to improve safety have some pleasant side effects besides improving safety. Policies and support show the company cares about its employees. They also help reduce stress and uncertainty in difficult situations by providing clear instructions about how such situations should be handled.

From the Manager's Desk

Law-enforcement officials in your area may be willing to design an action plan to guide you if workplace violence occurs. If that option is not available, there are private security firms that can come in. Get an expert to help.

From the Manager's Desk

A crisis can occur anytime and anywhere. Your ability to respond to an emotionally distressed employee might mean the difference between life and death. Keep a list of help resources (crisis lines, substance abuse agencies) with you at all times. Don't just have it in your office.

Have a workplace-violence action plan. Most companies have procedures mapped out in the event of a fire. Now companies need the same thing for a workplace-violence incident. Such a plan can include who to contact and under what circumstances legal authorities should be contacted. It should address the use of "panic buttons"(call buttons) if they are available. It should specify what people should do if they're threatened or attacked. The best way to design such a plan is to involve the experts, usually law-enforcement professionals. Many police forces have officers who will help you get this done.

Do a safety audit. A safety audit is an examination of both the physical space of a company and its policies to determine whether optimal safety is provided for. For example, you'd be amazed at how many individual offices place the owner away from the door, or have easy access to the door blocked by furniture or any visitor. In the event of a potentially violent situation, the office owner can't get out without going past the potential attacker.

Provide support services for those in distress. Most larger companies provide such support services, often packaged as part of an Employee Assistance Program (EAP), but such services may also be a part of health-care benefits. While these benefits and programs do add cost, what's a life worth? By having support programs and resources available, it allows each manager to use them as needed. Often the need comes up unexpectedly.

Initiatives You Can Take

We'll end this chapter with things you, as the manager, can do to prevent violence or reduce the potential damage.

Keep a list of emergency resources with you and at your desk. It should include crisis lines and contacts for substance abuse agencies and domestic violence groups. It's very important to connect a distressed individual with help as soon as a potential crisis emerges.

Model correct behavior, and don't ignore abusive or uncontrolled behavior in the workplace. Don't set a violent tone.

Be alert to the presence of the indicators we have presented. If you are concerned, don't keep it to yourself. Talk to your boss or the human resource department, and if you are really concerned contact the experts: law enforcement.

Threats should never be taken lightly. While most threats go unfulfilled, you never know which one is real. And it only takes one. Follow your company's policy, assuming it is one that's well thought out.

Never attempt to humiliate someone in private or publicly. That can provoke even normal people to violence.

Do a common-sense safety audit of your office (although it's better to have it audited professionally). Do you have access to a door, or are you blocked? If a potential attacker enters, do you have a way out?

Ensure you and your staff know what to do in emergency situations. It's your responsibility.

Follow the progressive discipline steps, and always deal with poor performance with the least possible pressure and force.

The Least You Need to Know

➤ Violence in the workplace is worth serious attention, but it isn't as prevalent as it seems from media reports.

➤ If you follow sensible procedures when dismissing an employee, you should be able to reduce the risk of violence.

➤ There are indicators of potential violence that can provide you with an early warning system, but they are not completely reliable.

➤ Both the company and managers can take positive steps to reduce violence in the workplace.

Part 4

When The Difficult Person Is Your Boss

Almost everyone has a boss. And bosses can be difficult, too. From the credit-stealers to the bosses who pile on more and more work, the difficult boss can make your life truly miserable.

Is your boss "nutso"? We'll help you find out. Are there ways to deal with the difficult boss? Sure there are.

We'll also look at ways you can get through to any boss so your ideas get a fair hearing. We'll talk about some tough situations where your boss may be doing something illegal. And we'll give you specific tips to deal with the credit-stealer and the boss who makes unreasonable demands.

Chapter 15

The Nutso Boss

> ### In This Chapter
>
> ➤ Some bosses really are nuts
>
> ➤ The different breeds of nutso–ness
>
> ➤ Basic tricks to survive a nutty boss
>
> ➤ The basic survival mind–set
>
> ➤ Getting through to your boss with benign trickery

Unless you own the company, you have a boss. Aren't you lucky? Not only do you deal with difficult employees and difficult peers (we'll discuss them later in this book), but you also have to deal with the peculiarities and oddities of *your* boss. Unfortunately, you're in a less-influential position with respect to your boss then you would be with your employees. Your boss has enough power to make your life miserable and significantly affect the path of your career.

That's OK if you have a great boss. It's even OK if you have an average boss. It's a bit scary if you have a difficult boss, and it's out-and-out frightening if you have a completely nutso, maladjusted, irrational, or disturbed boss.

In this chapter we'll look at difficult bosses so you understand them better. As with difficult employees, we'll talk about getting the right mind-set so you can deal with your boss more effectively. Then we'll talk about an important part of dealing with anyone in command—communicating with him or her so your ideas and concerns are heard.

Some Bosses Really Are Nuts

Is your boss just plain nuts or is your boss just normally difficult? This is an important question. Why? Because if you work for a crazy, maladjusted boss, it's not likely he or she is going to change. While you can try to make the best of the situation, if this person is an egomaniac, a career destroyer, or a legitimately nasty human being, eventually you have to make a serious choice. Do you want to continue to suffer career-wise and health-wise by staying? Or perhaps it's time to consider other options, such as trying to get transferred or preparing yourself for a job search.

From the Manager's Desk

If you work for a nutty boss, realize that the boss isn't likely to change. Weigh the effects of a lousy boss on your health and future. Is it worth staying? If not, look at options and draw up a contingency plan if you decide to leave.

If your boss is nutso, you'll face that bottom-line decision of going or staying much faster than if you work for the average difficult (but human) boss. So, what are the indications that your boss isn't going to change no matter what you or anyone else does?

A definition might help here. The *nutso boss* is a person who has certain characteristics and/or personal issues that cause him or her to treat other people in destructive, unpleasant ways. The nutso boss can't change because the reasons he or she acts badly are within. Whether it's a result of severe personality flaws, a lack of integrity or ethics, or other things, it isn't likely anything you do will make the nutso boss a better person.

How can you tell whether your boss is beyond redemption? Let's look at some of the nutso-boss types. Keep in mind that your boss must consistently follow one or more of these patterns to be considered nutso; occasional lapses don't count.

Employee Handbook

The **nutso boss** is a person who has certain characteristics and/or personal issues that cause him or her to treat other people in destructive, unpleasant ways. Nutso bosses don't usually change. That's because nutso bosses aren't very nice people, or hold values and beliefs that are hard to change.

Jelly-Fished Out

The jelly-fished out boss is the person who can't take a stand, can't make decisions, and worse, won't allow anyone else to make decisions either. This kind of boss, while not intentionally harmful to others, makes other people look bad through inaction. Delegation of responsibility is a stranger to ol' jelly guy. And Jelly's motto is: "Why make a decision today if you can wait a year until it's too late?" If you are a dedicated manager, Jelly will drive you nuts, because it's almost impossible to do a good job when you can't get decisions made or are not allowed to make them yourself.

Egomaniac Puppeteer

Sad! The puppeteer is a controlling egomaniac who exhibits a number of really horrible characteristics. The egomaniac won't allow others to make decisions, because he mistrusts everyone or has a desire to control everything and everyone. The egomaniac meddles or micromanages with a finger in everything.

This is a person who doesn't allow you to do your job because half the time you're on the phone or in a meeting with him. And that conversation consists of edicts, orders, or just plain rambling. Some egomaniacs have a knack for acting as if they want to hear your views and ideas but never pay attention to them. Often this boss is abusive in some way, or certainly abrupt. You get the impression you and your employees are irrelevant, and you're right. This person is selfish, self-centered, and damages productivity. Sometimes it seems like the puppeteer issues orders and edicts just to throw his weight around, because the next day he changes his mind.

This Won't Work!

The egomaniac is so nasty and aggressive that he creates aggression in others. If you blow up at an egomaniac, you may be in big trouble. You've just given the puppeteer legitimate ammunition to make your life miserable. And this guy loves to use ammunition.

The Substance Abuser

This one's sad, too. And we don't need to go much into it. The substance abuser is most likely a person who has an alcohol problem but may be dependent on drugs. This person, like many people who are addicted, is unpredictable, unreliable, and tends towards dishonesty.

The Paranoid Empire Builder

This creature is also often an egomaniac. You can recognize this hopeless case by her lack of communication and withholding of information. The "builder" is out to win at all costs in the world of corporate or company politics. She sees things as "me against the world," so understandably doesn't trust anyone. Given the lack of trust, she controls things by keeping her cards close to the vest. You never know what's going on. Everything is hush-hush. So the result is you are paralyzed—you can't make decisions because you don't have information.

The paranoid empire builder also has a habit of taking credit for everything good and never shouldering the blame for anything. She spends time playing back-office politics and lobbying for position within the company rather than doing something really useful.

The Totally Incompetent Nice Addict

The motto of the nice addict is: "Love me, love me, love me." A compelling need to be liked (rather than respected) makes this person weak and incompetent. The nice addict likely has very few management skills, since he hasn't taken the time to learn any. Most of his time is spent learning how to be nice. The nice addict never makes hard decisions and appears to be interested in others' opinions but doesn't want to offend anyone. Like Jelly, he prefers to do nothing rather than annoy someone. The nice addict isn't able to put distance between himself and his employees. To him, you are all friends who must love him.

This Won't Work!

If the empire builder is a better politicker then you and you go head-to-head on her playing field, you'll end up dead meat. These folks are dangerous to your career.

Let's pull together the common threads from the nutso boss categories:

➤ Nutso bosses aren't likely to change their behavior because they can't change their personalities.

➤ Most nutsos are either overbearing and obnoxious or totally uninvolved and passive.

➤ Nutso bosses make their employees (that's you) look bad.

➤ Nutso bosses have two horrible effects. They drive you crazy because they make it impossible for you to do your job properly. They also are horrible to deal with, because it's clear you and the nutso aren't on the same side.

So, what's the bottom line with nutso bosses? You can't count on them to change, and it's unlikely anything you can do will cause them to become more competent, or better bosses.

Tricks to Survive a Nutty Boss

Because nutty bosses aren't going to change, you have to figure out how to survive these people. Their personal agendas are so strong (and often so self-centered) that you can't work with them in any meaningful way, and you can't really discuss the problems you have in a forum where there is true communication.

Insider Secrets

You get to define what "surviving a nutty boss" means for you. It could mean winning (but you have got to recognize that this isn't likely). It could mean just getting out of the situation in one piece. It could be keeping a positive attitude and not allowing the boss to wreck your emotional life. Figure out what it means to you to survive and make choices that will get you there. For example, Erica worked for a nutso boss, but the boss was mentoring Erica in her position. After weighing the options and plusses and minuses, she decided she should stay as she was building her skills and her career. She felt the op–portunity to learn and the good salary made it worthwhile.

If you work for one of these folks, you have to recognize that the boss does not have the best interests of you or your staff at heart, and may not really care about work getting done. That's the starting point.

Get Connected

If you work for a nutso boss, are you prepared to become a difficult employee? That is, are you comfortable entering into the back-channel world of the selfish nutso boss? It's important to decide because the ways we manage nutty bosses will involve some back-room politicking. If you aren't comfortable doing this and living with the consequences, it may be time to consider finding another position in order to save your sanity.

OK, so your answer is, "Yes, I'm willing to enter into the dark realm of internal politics." Your first task is to get connected. Cultivate the ears of your boss's peers and other important leaders in your company.

How do you use these connections if you have them? Your hope is that your nutty boss will come to the attention of people above him or her and some decisions will be made to remedy the problem. The way to push this along is to make information available to your connections.

From the Manager's Desk

One way of managing a difficult boss is to try and win at the boss's game. You may find that process unpalatable (I do). You can be open and honest, or you can use the same dirty tactics some bosses use and try to win. It really is up to you.

It's important to understand that you aren't launching a personal assassination attempt here, and you must stay away from revenge or any deliberate attempt to harm your bozo boss. First, it's wrong. Second, if you enter in that dirty world, you will lose all credibility with the good, sane people who can help you.

Insider Secrets

People with titles and formal power aren't the only ones you need to connect to. Sometimes the most influential people aren't those with formal power but are influential because they are productive and respected. Identify who these people are and cultivate them. For example, Joanne worked for a very difficult boss and had difficulty communicating with him. All her ideas were rejected. She decided to spend time socializing with and helping some of the other managers reporting to the difficult boss, occasionally making suggestions to them. The idea was that her ideas would be better received coming from others, and she was right.

The information you need to deliver to your connections has to do with the bottom line: how the nutso boss is causing problems with productivity.

You don't say: "My boss is a complete idiot and jellyfish."

You say: "It's getting more and more difficult to hit the work quotas because I can't get George to authorize the overtime."

You don't say: "George is a stark-raving empire builder.

You say: "It would help us get things done faster if I had more authority to make decisions."

See how it works? You are making basic information available to others. Notice what you are doing here. You aren't complaining endlessly. You aren't telling people what they should do with the information. What you hope will happen is that others will have the same experiences and be in a better position to exert some positive influence.

Conduct Business Publicly

Many of the nutso-boss types thrive on concealing their bad behavior from others. It's kinda like hiding under a rock with the other crawling beings, but we don't want to insult innocent insects here. Also, because nutso bosses are unpredictable, dishonest, forgetful, and even devious, it's best to conduct as much business as possible with other people present.

OK, let's be blunt here. This is CYA (cover your ass). You want to survive without being blamed for things you aren't responsible for. Witnesses are very handy.

Here's an example:

> You need a decision from a nutso boss. You can try to get that decision from him or her in a private meeting, or you can wait until there's a management meeting and ask there. Which is better?

Probably the second. If you can get a decision stated publicly in front of other people, your boss is less likely to change the decision or pretend the decision was different. And if it ever comes down to push versus shove, then at least you have other witnesses.

The Written Word Is Gold

If you've figured out that nutso bosses aren't trustworthy, you're catching on. You have to be prepared to protect yourself by having some documentation about your interactions with the nutso boss. That happens two ways.

1. **Record important incidents.** When the actions of your boss have contributed to some failure in work output or productivity, jot down some notes about times and dates and any conversations that might be useful in protecting yourself from crazy boss tricks.

2. **Ask your boss to put it in writing.** If you feel you are being asked to do something really dumb, ask for a written request. The same for things like inane policy decisions. You can't force your boss to do that, but it's worth a try. If the boss refuses, document that action.

Get Small, Get Invisible, Be Sneaky

This approach is one I've used with crazy bosses and is my favorite. The general idea is to take oneself out of the crosshairs of the difficult boss by keeping a low profile, not making waves, and appearing to go along. But you don't.

From the Manager's Desk

One motto of the invisible, sneaky, hard-to-find survivor is: "It's easier to do something, then ask permission, than to ask permission first." This frequently applies with a nutso boss.

You don't ask permission. You don't go to the boss for decisions. You work around him or her. You do things the right way and try to minimize your boss's effect on your work unit. You stonewall. You withhold information when possible. You work in the shadows.

When you have to, you nod a lot when speaking to the nutso boss, then forget what it's safe to forget. You claim misunderstandings if confronted. You never argue.

With a savvy crazy boss this is obviously risky, as are most tactics you might use to survive a nutso boss. Then again, if your boss is driving you crazy, maybe being sneaky is the way to go. You have to decide what you're willing to do and what you are willing to risk. Consider how your particular boss will react to these techniques. How might the boss react and what effects will those reactions have on your job, your career, and your reputation?

Developing a Productive Mind-set

Dealing with any kind of difficult person requires the right mind-set. Dealing with a crazy boss is no different. You can adopt a mind-set that will contribute to going nuts yourself, or you can adopt one that helps you stay sane and focused on what you can control. Here are three elements of the productive mind-set.

Focus on the Work

If you spend most of your time thinking and reacting emotionally to a nutty boss, you're going to damage your mental health. If you can't change your boss, you need to focus as best you can on what you get paid for. That's getting the work done, creating results, and succeeding. If you're good enough at creating results for your company, there's an added benefit. You get more informal clout and leverage that can come in handy later.

One of my favorite sayings fits here: "Living well is the best revenge." Or to change that, "Succeeding on the job is the best revenge."

Even if you get no formal credit from your boss, at least you have the satisfaction of knowing you are contributing as well as you can. And you know what? Almost always, other people in the organization will recognize your success despite any efforts by your nutty boss to disguise it.

Don't Expect Squat

I figure you're pretty smart. You bought this book, didn't you? I also figure that if you've worked for a nutty boss, you know you can't expect much of anything good from him or her. So get used to it. Get comfortable with it.

If your boss never gives you credit for good work and you've decided to continue working for that person, then you can wait for some magical change to occur or you can be smart and realize that's just the way it is. Which makes more sense? To live in some imaginary world that doesn't exist, or deal with the real situation you have in front of you? It's a no-brainer.

Be Prepared for Surprises

One characteristic of most of the nutty-boss types is that they are unreliable and unpredictable. So, you cover your butt. Anticipate shifts in direction, and don't let those shifts get to you in an emotional way.

Explore Alternatives

The worst situation you can put yourself in is to feel you are helpless, desperate, and lack options. So think about some of the options available to you in terms of your career. Perhaps it's time to quietly prepare to find a job without a nutty boss. Look at transfer options. Knowing you have options helps keep things in perspective.

So You Want to Try Getting Through to Your Boss?

How do you feel about the options presented so far? Are you saying, "Hey, I don't want to play those games," or "If that's what I need to survive, I'd rather just move on"?

From the Manager's Desk

Remember this? What you focus on, you get more of. If you focus on how evil your boss is, you will get more disturbance, more anger, and more frustration. If you focus on dealing with the situation and getting work done, you're likely to get more success and a greater sense of accomplishment.

This Won't Work!

If you expect too much from your nutty boss, are unprepared for the many surprises nutty bosses throw at you, or expect your nutty boss to change his spots, you are going to be more and more frustrated. It's often the mismatch between your expectations and reality that is so frustrating. Because you can't always change the reality, you need to change your own perceptions and expectations.

Those are both reasonable reactions. If your boss plays hardball, it's difficult to survive without also playing hardball, and that's not for everyone. Although crazy bosses aren't likely to change, it's possible to manage them a little bit. And the things you do to get through to your nutty boss are the same things you do to get through to any boss. We are going to talk about these techniques. Although there is still an element of game playing involved, you'll find it much more palatable.

From the Manager's Desk

The techniques you use to get through to a nutty boss are the same as one would use with any boss, even a really good one. They are useful for getting heard. Don't use them only with the nutty bosses.

What Drives Your Boss?

Here's your starting point. Take some time to answer these questions:

➤ What drives my boss crazy or keeps him or her up at night?

➤ What turns the boss's crank? What gets him or her excited?

Have you figured out why these are important? Think about a really good salesperson. What do they do? They identify the needs and wants of the buyer, then link their product to those needs and wants. In other words, a good salesperson solves a potential buyer's problems, and then the potential buyer becomes a buyer.

It's no different with a boss. Even twisted bosses have problems, ambitions, and things that drive them crazy. Link what you're after to solving those problems and you just might get the attention and help of even the nuttiest boss. And if your boss isn't nutty, the approach still helps you get heard.

Link Your Goals to the Boss's Problems

First, figure out what you need from your boss in a given situation. Is it a specific decision? Increased budget? Perhaps it's more autonomy. Whatever it is, look for the selling points from the boss's point of view—even if the boss's point of view is nutso, twisted, and bent.

If your nutty boss isn't much interested in productivity but is into politics and empire building, it will be pointless to highlight the productivity increases of your request. It's far more useful to highlight the political benefits that will come to your boss for making "such a wise, insightful decision."

If your boss is one of those jelly types and hates making any decisions, how can you get more autonomy and authority? Simple. Link the autonomy and increased authority with reducing the workload of the jelly person or with reducing his or her stress. Link it to what drives the person crazy or what excites the person.

Do the Pitch

Now you are prepared to pitch your idea. Again, appeal to the weak, crazy parts of a crazy boss. If your boss is an egomaniac, frame what you want as his or her idea in the first place. Here's an example:

> "You know, last week, I think you had a great idea about how to look really good to the board. And I think we can do that if [make your request]."

Insider Secrets

Here's a secret about bosses in general. Want to get covered in glory and get promoted? Make your boss's life easier from his or her point of view. Try this with your boss, and the next boss up as high as you can go, and you'll be amazed what happens.

If you have a boss who takes all the credit but never the blame, or one who refuses to delegate, try this one:

> "You know, I can see you're swamped with work and there's a lot of pressure. I might have something that can get that pressure off you. How about if you refer complaints and problems to me, and I'll take care of them? After all, that's what you pay me for."

See how all this works? You sell based on the needs and desires of the boss.

Here are a few other tips for making the pitch:

➤ **Pick your timing carefully.** Don't pitch a new idea or suggestion on a day where the boss is frustrated, upset, or feeling over-worked. You aren't going to get a real hearing, even with a good boss.

➤ **Be brief, concise, and concrete.** Nutty bosses may not have long attention spans. Introduce the subject (what you want to happen) by starting with the problem it will

From the Manager's Desk

Learn that less is more. When you give too much information, you actually dilute the selling points and make it harder for your boss to see the positive qualities of your idea. Keep it tight. Cut it down and don't ramble. Hit the "killer" advantage.

solve for the boss. Describe what you want only after you've listed the benefits to the boss. Don't overload on detail. When pitching, less is more because your boss won't get bogged down in the details.

➤ **Leave something in writing.** If what you need is complicated or the boss needs to have the details at his or her fingertips, prepare a one-page, bulleted summary of what you want to do. Your nutty boss probably won't read it, but it is a form of documentation. Keep a copy for yourself. For the non-nutso boss, the summary will be handy. Again, stress the benefits to the boss from the boss's point of view.

➤ **Do a no-pitch pitch.** This one's a little tricky. A no-pitch pitch is a disguised way of getting the boss to think about your idea by making it seem to come out of his or her own head. In the no-pitch pitch, you don't ask for anything. You just drop hints, like this:

> "You know, I bet I wouldn't have to take up so much of your time if I could decide on shift schedules on my own."

That's it. You drop it in, then leave it. You make it appear as if the idea just popped into your head. This can work very well with bosses who think their ideas are the only good ones. So you play along. Let the boss think she's thought up the idea and is absolutely brilliant.

Drop your idea to others, too. If you want your boss to notice your idea or need, use the no-pitch pitch to others the boss is likely to talk to—the boss's peers, his or her boss, or even other managers. They might see enough merit in the idea to present it to the boss. And that's good. If you surround your boss with an idea that seems to be in his or her interest, you are more likely to get it accepted if it comes from several people over time.

The Least You Need to Know

➤ Nutso bosses don't often change for the better.

➤ You may have to be the one to change.

➤ Your mind-set is important for survival.

➤ Decide whether you want to fight, live with your boss, or move on.

➤ Use all the techniques for getting through to your boss, even if that person isn't nuts. They apply everywhere.

Chapter 16

Fighting Fire with Water— Your Difficult-Boss Options

In This Chapter

➤ The importance of knowing what you can afford to lose

➤ Identifying your difficult-boss options

➤ The pros and cons of different options

➤ Prepare yourself and deal from strength

In Chapter 17, "Silly Boss Behaviors—Specific Situations," we'll look at what you can do to counteract defined difficult-boss behavior. But before we get to those specific situations, you should know your options, and the pluses and minuses attached to each course of action.

In this chapter we're going to start with what has to be a fundamental question. Before deciding how to deal with your difficult boss, what are you prepared to lose? We'll help you come at that question intelligently, because the answer determines how firm or aggressive you can be.

Consider the Consequences

In earlier chapters we talked about the importance of doing a reality check as part of deciding what to do with difficult employees. You may recall that the reality check principle involves asking several questions to determine how difficult the employee is, and the objective consequences of those difficult behaviors.

From the Manager's Desk

If you have a difficult boss and need to decide what to do, your first step is to determine what you are prepared to lose and what you can afford to lose.

Identifying what you can live with and what you are willing to sacrifice allows you to negotiate from a position of strength and sureness.

If you have a difficult boss and must decide what to do next, the reality check is even more important than with employees. Why? It's your butt on the line. Your boss has something your individual employees don't have, and that's power over you. He or she can do things your employees can't. Make your life miserable so you'll quit? Sure. Have you transferred to a janitorial position? Pass me the broom! Fire you outright? Quite possibly.

There's an added irony. As a manager, you may have less protection from retribution from the boss, particularly in union shops, than your employees. Managers are often excluded from collective bargaining agreements and grievance procedures. You may not have the backing of a union to counteract any actions your boss takes against you.

Your reality check has to address the same things you look at with an employee. For example, what are the effects of your difficult boss's behavior? What will happen if you do nothing? Can you live with that, or if you do nothing will it get worse?

But there's an added consideration, and that's deciding what you are prepared to lose and what you can afford to lose. After all, we're talking about your career, your livelihood, and possibly your ability to feed your family. Standing up to a difficult boss when you can't afford the consequences can be gratifying morally but debilitating financially. You may see yourself as doing the right thing and standing up for principles, and we all respect that. But if standing up for your principles results in your starving and living on the street, you have to think twice.

Let's not forget that by standing up for principles and getting yourself fired, you lose any ability to make things better in your workplace.

So, let's walk you through the process of answering some very important questions.

Start with the Effects and Outcomes

You start by assessing the effects and consequences of your difficult boss's actions and behaviors. What do you need to consider?

1. First, how is your boss affecting the productivity of your work unit? Is there interference? Do you feel you can't get the job done?

   This is an interesting one, because you may have more ammunition to go over the boss's head if he or she is preventing you from getting work done. In this situation, you have evidence. The flip side is if you do nothing, you may be held accountable for your work unit's failures, even if those failures are a result of the actions of your boss.

Insider Secrets

What's easier? Dealing with a boss whose quirks are annoying but don't affect productivity, or a boss who does affect productivity? The second is easier because you can find more allies to help you with a problem that affects the bottom line.

2. Second, does the behavior of your difficult boss damage or hurt people, particularly your employees? If so, in what ways? And here's an additional question: Can you live with that? Some managers can, some can't.

3. Third, how is your boss affecting your career—your chances of promotion or future employment? A boss who makes you look bad affects not only the present but the future. If you do nothing, you may end up losing more than you can afford. A supplementary question: Do you care? Some managers aren't worried about promotion or career. Are you? If so, then a boss who interferes with your career is of greater concern.

4. Fourth, what about your mental health? Is your boss the main reason you're experiencing high stress levels connected to work? Do you dread going to work because your boss drives you crazy? Are you experiencing high levels of anxiety or depression because of your boss? Sometimes it's hard to tell exactly why those things occur, but if you have a really terrible boss, you'll be able to connect the dots.

5. Fifth, are you sailing on a sinking ship? Occasionally, a boss can be so destructive that he or she ends up destroying a work unit through things like layoffs or damaging its functionality. There's little point trying to bail out a swamped boat with a small cup. Is the writing on the wall, either for your work unit or you, personally?

So let's say you've evaluated the situation and decide that you really can't sit back and do nothing, because the consequences of doing nothing are too severe. Let's take a look at the effects on you personally.

What's Your Personal Situation?

Let's make this simple. What happens to you if you lose a battle with your boss and end up quitting or getting fired? What are the practical circumstances? Here are a few things to consider:

➤ Do you have sufficient savings to survive without a job for a year? (That's a conservative estimate of how long it might take until you find a suitable position.)

➤ Are you employable elsewhere? How quickly are other people in your field finding employment?

➤ What's your current debt load?

➤ Mentally, are you able to be unemployed for an extended period without going crazy?

➤ Will your spouse support your leaving or losing your job?

This Won't Work!

In a perfect world, everyone should be able to stand up for what's right. Unfortunately, in our less-than-perfect world doing so has consequences, so you need to examine your personal situation before acting.

The answers to these questions tell you what you can afford to lose. If you can't afford to lose your job and the consequences of living with a difficult boss are palatable, then weigh your options carefully. It may be you need to bide your time until you are better positioned to accept the risks involved in going head-to-head with a difficult boss.

Here are more questions, not related directly to economics but to how important your current job is to you:

➤ If you leave your current job, will it impact negatively on your future?

➤ Can you handle losing your social support group from work?

➤ Do you really love your job (except for your boss)?

➤ How important are principles to you—important enough to lose your job?

From the Manager's Desk

Think first before deciding how to deal with a difficult boss. Don't ever let your difficult boss cause you to react without thinking it through. Forget "take this job and shove it." That only works in country music songs.

By answering these questions honestly, you help yourself by figuring out where you stand. I can't stress how important this is. Going off half-cocked and doing something that gets you fired when you aren't ready for those consequences is just plain dumb.

Remember this: How you respond to a difficult boss should not be spur of the moment. It should be thought out and planned. It's your livelihood. Don't lose out on a particular future unless it's absolutely necessary.

What Are Your Options?

Now it's time to consider the options available to you. We'll go through these one by one, indicating when each is desirable and when each is not. Here is the quick list:

➤ Quit immediately.

➤ Lay the groundwork for moving on.

➤ Present an ultimatum.

➤ Appeal to your boss's boss.

➤ Appeal to the human resources department and grievances committee.

➤ Get sneaky.

➤ Work it out.

➤ Live with it.

Look at the list and you will see it starts with the most drastic options and moves to more cooperative and constructive behavior. In an ideal world you would never want to get sneaky or appeal to your boss's boss. But we don't live in that ideal world (or at least most of us don't). Still, we want to try to work things out before we escalate into a confrontational process that might make things worse.

Quitting Immediately

Quitting immediately is the most drastic step you can take. It has the advantage of bringing fast closure and ending any suffering on your part, at least in one area. If you quit you don't have to deal with the things that drive you crazy. Your nutty boss becomes a footnote in your personal life history. However, quitting immediately brings with it a whole host of other possible sufferings. If you quit you need a way to support yourself and your family. You have to deal with that situation, and it could last some time.

Here's a question to ask: Which will be more stressful, being out of work and searching for a job, or living with the situation you have now with a nutty boss?

Only you can answer that for you. Some people bring new hope and revitalization into their lives by entering the job market and accepting a newer and healthier challenge. Others don't.

I don't recommend quitting immediately because I think the next option, laying the groundwork for moving on, is a more rational and planned way to accomplish the

same thing. However, I can envision situations where immediate resignation may be necessary. In fact, I did it once myself. If you're in a situation where your company or your boss asks you to do something you can't live with and there is no hope of getting the decision reversed, it may be in your best interests to leave. After all, you have to live with yourself, and sometimes having a secure paycheck means nothing if you can't stand the person that stares back at you from your mirror every morning.

Here's an example of a senior executive who gave up a $100,000 government position of great prestige. During a series of layoffs and downsizing, he was asked to compile a list of people to get rid of. His department was already quite small. His view was that if he went along with his superiors, his department would be unable to do what it was supposed to do. He also held the view that getting rid of employees was a last option, and in this case, one that had been used far too often. So he quit. He preferred to be able to live with himself. By the way, his integrity and knowledge stood him in good stead, and he is now doing well, both economically and life-wise. I would guess if you asked him, he would say leaving was the best thing he had ever done.

So, is your boss (or your company) asking you to do something you can't live with? Is it against your principles? Will you regret going along with it? If so, then a fast resignation may be the path for you.

One thing to consider, if you are asked to do something you can't live with and you quit, is whether you are, in essence, giving up and letting the bad guys win. By not fighting first to change the decisions or actions being imposed, you may be leaving others in your organization unprotected. Can you live with that?

Lots to consider, huh? But that's the point. Think before you leap. Consider where you're at and what you can live with. That's so important because many quick resignations are executed on the spur of the moment, without thought. Then the poor soul who quit has to figure out what to do with the rest of his or her life.

Laying Down the Groundwork for Leaving

If your boss or company is making you miserable and you can hold on for at least a little while, this is a better strategy than quitting immediately. Really, all we're talking about here is preparing to leave by quietly exploring other job opportunities or transfers, networking (again, quietly), sprucing up the old resume, and mapping out your potential job market.

I think every employee should go through this process once every five years at a minimum. I'll tell you why. It strengthens you and reduces fear by reducing the uncertainty associated with moving on. Is that important? Yes. It's amazing how much easier it is to protect your mental health and act with integrity when you have in place some plan of action to deal with the consequences of speaking up, or speaking out. Even if you end up realizing you aren't that employable elsewhere, at least you know where you stand, and any reduction of uncertainty is good.

From the Manager's Desk

Having a contingency plan to go to if the "stuff hits the fan" allows you to act according to your principles. It's always a good thing to stay prepared for job searching and create options for yourself. Call it a safety net that gives you confidence.

So, when you realize your situation is unpleasant, then start preparing that backup plan. Here are some things to do:

➤ Update your resume-writing skills. Read a book or two.

➤ Redo your resumé.

➤ Think about possible job markets and positions you might want.

➤ Decide what's important for your next job (money, status, responsibility, a normal boss).

➤ Upgrade your interviewing skills.

➤ Network by joining associations and making some social calls.

➤ Read a few current books on management (if only to know the current buzzwords to use).

➤ Quietly explore transfer options in your firm (but be aware that it's hard to keep such things quiet).

➤ Do a skill assessment—what are your strengths and skills?

➤ Get a feel for your job market possibilities. Are there jobs open? Are there fields related to what you do now where you could make use of your skills?

You can do these things over time. After you have positioned yourself to move on, it makes using other options much easier. Knowing you have other employment options gives you strength to stand up to that bully of a boss, or the boss that asks you to act dishonestly. And you can continue to try to change things within your company while you are there, secure in the knowledge that if you get your bottom booted out you will survive and even excel.

Preparing to move on is a good holding action. It leaves you with the most flexibility, and can be used with many of the other options available to you. In fact, it *should* be used with the other options.

Laying Down an Ultimatum

Here's a fantasy for you. Mary works for a nutty boss. One day Mary goes to the CEO and says, "Get this guy off my back *now* or I'm out the door." The CEO shudders with horror (Mary is his best manager), immediately fires the nutty boss, and promotes Mary to the vacant position. Nice, huh? I guess there may be a few people who have brought this fantasy to reality. Heck, it's a weird, unpredictable world. But by and large it *is* a fantasy. Companies (and life in general) don't often work this way.

This Won't Work!

A common error people make is to overestimate their own value or think they are irreplaceable. If you deliver an ultimatum, even your expertise may not save you. My motto is: Never issue an ultimatum unless you've already decided to leave!

You can use an ultimatum to stand up for a principle you feel is good and right, or even for your own sanity, but chances are your ultimatum is going to get your rear end escorted out of the building even faster than if you quit immediately. Yes, even if you're extremely competent.

The reality is people get really pissed off when you threaten them, and an ultimatum is basically a threat. People take it personally.

So, the rule is never lay down an ultimatum unless you are prepared to leave and can live with leaving more quickly than you had planned.

If this action has such a low probability of success, why do people use it? They get fed up. Or they don't want to give up just yet. They want to give things one final try to see whether something gets better. So they give it a shot.

Laying down an ultimatum is a reasonable course of action if you've decided you can afford to leave but you want to give the company one more chance to rectify what you see as an impossible situation.

Something else you should know about ultimatums. They are power plays. Do you have enough power, pull, or influence to make it work out OK? Here's some advice. Far too many people think they are indispensable or irreplaceable. Perhaps there are some situations where that is true, but you'd be amazed how replaceable you will become if you drop an ultimatum bomb on a nutty boss. Don't overestimate your position and always be prepared to lose.

Insider Secrets

Never, ever use an ultimatum as a bluff. Don't say you will leave when you aren't prepared to leave. I guarantee you that if you give an ultimatum, someone will call you on it.

I once worked with a woman who had actually quit her high-paying job seven times and withdrew her resignation seven times. Unfortunately for her (but great for everyone else), the seventh time was the charm. Upper management refused to ignore her resignation. She got her bluff called.

Appeals

It's the old "go-over-the-head" approach to boss problems. There are actually two forms of this.

1. The first is the out-in-the-open attempt to involve the boss's boss to fix a difficult situation. The intent is to solve a problem, not get your boss.
2. The second attempt falls under the sneaky tactics because it's behind the scenes, really involving the backroom politicking techniques you no doubt hate when they're used on you.

Let's take a look at these options.

Appeals to the Boss's Boss

First, let's look at involving your boss's boss in the spirit of help and cooperation. There are two ways of doing this.

The first is with the involvement of your boss. You approach your difficult boss, lay out the problem(s) you're having with his or her behavior and decisions, and ask the person whether he or she is willing to involve the boss up one notch. The idea is to get your boss's cooperation to enlist the help of the senior boss, and *not* to go around your boss without his or her involvement or knowledge.

From the Manager's Desk

Going over your boss's head is always a sticky situation. That's why it's always good to include your boss in the process and do it in the open. That way you'll be less likely to be perceived as backstabbing.

This is often a good starting point because it portrays you as a problem solver rather than a backstabber. There's another reason. Some bosses will refuse to intervene in a problem situation unless both parties are involved in designing a solution.

What do you do if your difficult boss refuses? That brings you to a fork in the road. If you go over your boss's head, that will be seen as confrontational and dirty pool. It's really a form of backroom politicking. You need to decide whether you are comfortable with that, and the probable consequences.

There is a middle ground. You can let your difficult boss know you're going ahead anyway and that you will be talking to the next boss up. Or you can do it without informing your boss. The first is more fair but allows your difficult boss to get there first. However, it looks better.

In the spirit of cooperation, when you speak to the difficult boss's boss, you must stress that you only wish to solve a problem that affects productivity. If you come across as having an ax to grind, or worse, want your boss's job, you're not likely to get any support at all.

Here's a little trick if you decide to go to your boss's boss. Present the problem and its effects on things like productivity or the bottom line. Do so fairly. Then ask for advice and suggestions as to how to handle the situation. This shows deference and respect. It paints you as willing to listen and is far better than providing the solution yourself. Think of it as managing the boss's boss.

Appeals to the Human Resource Department

You can give a call for help to a third party. Sometimes the human resources department can be helpful in either intervening as a neutral third party or helping you find another position in the company. However, unless your boss is acting contrary to specific company policy or is doing something illegal, the human resources department may be impotent. Usually human resource departments don't have formal authority over a manager without some violation of the rules.

One other thing you should know. It isn't uncommon for human resources departments (or any department) to be what we might call "leaky." Things get around even if there are confidentiality rules. Assess whether you can trust the third party you approach for help. And assess any potential damages if someone leaks information that eventually gets to your boss.

Insider Secrets

Human resource departments ... OK, I don't live in a barrel. I know that many human resource departments are unable to help with difficult bosses (or anything else). Before you go off on your boss, consider that it is very rare for a human resources department to have any real power at all. They may want to help but are often not in a position to do so unless your boss has committed a violation of some sort. It's still worth finding out what your human resources department can do with your problem, but be understanding. If your human resources department can't help, don't vilify the people there. The last thing you need is human resources personnel who think you are the problem.

Getting Sneaky

Getting sneaky includes indirect attempts to rally support to your side of the issue and organizing others whom your difficult boss manages, and can include things like boss sabotage (making your difficult boss look bad). I consider most of these practices unethical, although some informal lobbying or organizing people to improve the health of the company might be reasonable. Or, if there is illegality, then the stakes are higher.

One problem with getting sneaky is that you drop to your difficult boss's level of scuzziness—or even below your boss. You sacrifice integrity and doing-the-right-thing thinking in order to win. So it darn well better be an important game to win.

This Won't Work!

Most sneaky things actually erode your status in a company unless you are truly good at being sneaky. That's because you get labeled as the difficult person, and you lose much of your credibility. People reap what they sow.

Consider this. Do you want to go home every night plotting the downfall of your boss? Or scheming about that meeting coming up? Don't you have better things to do with your time than damage or manipulate people? If you don't mind the plotting and scheming, then you have a chance of pulling it off. If you DO mind, then you probably aren't going to be any good at it, so don't try.

If you do go this route, you must have a power base or sphere of influence you can use to apply back-channel pressure. You need to be comfortable using people. You need to know when to push and when to back off, and when to stop. And you need to keep in mind that you are doing all these nasty things to make the workplace a better place, rather than for your own vengeance.

It's a dirty game. But sometimes business is a dirty game. I'd pass on this approach if I were you.

Working It Out

The most productive option you have is to try to work out your problems with the difficult boss. That means sitting down, negotiating, listening, compromising, and finding some common ground. It means finding some solution both of you can live with.

From the Manager's Desk

You never know whether working it out will work in advance. Sometimes the most difficult-appearing bosses can turn easy if approached expertly and in a way that gets through to him or her. Sometimes you may be pleasantly surprised.

It's almost always the first step you try after you have determined you can't ignore the situation. If it doesn't work, you still have the more heavy-handed options.

Here are some suggestions for you. Before you approach your boss to initiate a discussion, plan out your course of action. Decide the facts of the situation and try to be objective. Figure out what is important to the boss, and how you might sell some specific solution or suggestion. Decide beforehand what you will do if the negotiations fail, and how much you can bend.

During the actual discussions or negotiations, keep your cool. You're dealing with a difficult boss here, so be alert to any attempts to manipulate your emotions. Enter into the negotiations with a positive attitude and express that openly. Saying something like:

> "I'm sure we can work this out between us if we work at it, and I think it's worth it."

Try to keep the ball in the boss's court if you can. Ask the boss for potential solutions, and press a little bit. Also, try to listen as much as possible to determine what the boss needs to make a solution work. Use "we" as much as possible. Use "I" as sparingly as possible.

If you come to a successful resolution, decide whether you need something in writing or not. Often it depends on the issue. Is it possible this will become a legal issue or a company policy? Then you politely request something in writing. Or, as an option (this often works better), draft a brief memo outlining the agreement made and ask your boss to sign it. Keep in mind that some people are hesitant to commit anything to paper. Getting a written commitment isn't always possible with a difficult boss.

The challenge of working it out is that it takes two. You may be willing, but your boss, being difficult, may not be willing. Still, it's an almost mandatory starting point when dealing with a difficult boss. If it doesn't work, at least you tried, and you will be able to prove you tried.

Living With It

This brings us to the last option. Whatever the issue, you can just plain suck it up, keep your mouth shut, and live with it. That sounds terribly wimpy, right? But even hard-nosed negotiators know when it's time to fold 'em. Fighting losing battles is a waste of time.

Living with it may be a viable option if …

➤ You can truly live with it without suffering damage to your health and/or career.

➤ The difficult boss behavior is annoying but not critical.

➤ Any stronger action is liable to be more damaging than doing nothing.

➤ You are financially unstable.

➤ You have other personal or family problems and cannot deal with yet another set of problems.

Apart from your own feelings about doing nothing, there are some situations where doing nothing is not an option. If your boss is doing something illegal or something that puts your company or others at risk, you might *have* to do something. Here's why. If you're aware of illegal or improper acts but do nothing, you may be held accountable.

From the Manager's Desk

Whether you come to a successful solution or not, keep some notes about any attempts you make to work it out with your boss. Record times, dates, and the gist of the discussion. The documentation is useful if something goes awry. It's also useful if you decide to use stronger techniques later, such as going to the boss's boss, because you can document that you have tried to work this out quietly, but to no avail.

This Won't Work!

Sometimes people "live with" something far too long and pay a price in terms of their careers or physical and mental health. It's often a fear of change or the unknown. Don't allow anyone to be a part of damaging your health or your future.

For example, let's say John, your boss, does things that could be construed as sexual harassment. The behavior is consistent over time. You know about it. You do nothing. As a manager (particularly with respect to your own staff), you might be included in any legal action launched as a result of John's illegal behaviors.

You get the idea. Management comes with some ethical responsibilities, but also with some legal ones. Sometimes the consequences of doing nothing are so severe that it isn't an option. Again, it's your call.

Wrapping It Up

The options we've set forth here aren't mutually exclusive. You can, for example, prepare to leave your position (quietly) while trying to work it out with your boss. You can try to work it out with your boss while including your boss's boss. However, remember that you should start with the least possible force. You can always escalate if you feel it's worth the risk. And no matter what, you have to present the appearance of working in the interests of your company. You must never appear to be trying to destroy your boss for your own personal gain. It usually backfires.

The bottom line here? Decide what you are willing to lose and what you are willing to accept, and consider the costs of any actions you might take. Evaluate yourself first.

The Least You Need to Know

➤ Know your options from strongest to weakest.

➤ Be clear about what you can afford to lose before doing anything.

➤ Always begin with the gentle techniques.

➤ Never bluff (or at least not unless you can afford to lose).

Chapter 17

Silly Boss Behaviors— Specific Situations

In This Chapter

➤ Step-by-step options for the credit-stealing boss

➤ Basic steps of working it out

➤ Preparations before going into battle

➤ How to deal with a demanding boss

Well, we've mapped out your options and explained when different approaches are appropriate or not. Now it's time to get really specific. What do you do when your boss never gives you credit for your work, or worse yet, takes all the credit? How about the boss who gives you impossible deadlines and sets you up for failure?

We'll go through these situations in detail using specific examples of what you can do and say to survive them—or even excel on the job.

The Credit-Stealing Boss

Few of us in the working world have missed out on this boss behavior. Mercifully, in most bosses it's an occasional behavior, but unfortunately, some bosses do it chronically and consistently. The *credit-stealing boss* doesn't miss an opportunity to take credit for any good idea you or other employees come up with. It's never "We came up with this," or "Freddy had a great idea." It's always "I came up with it." Oh, yeah, when it comes to taking responsibility for failures, this boss is Teflon. *Then* it's your fault.

So, how do you deal with this? Let's walk you through an example. We'll see how Mary, a manager, deals with Dirk, the credit-stealing boss. Let's set the stage and the characters.

Mary is at the bottom of the management heap. She has 12 people reporting to her. In turn, she reports to Dirk. Dirk's boss is Eileen, who happens to be one of six vice presidents in the company.

Employee Handbook

The **credit-stealing boss** usually takes credit for work done by those working for him and places the blame on staff when things go wrong.

Through hard work and a lot of smarts, Mary has assembled a top-notch team whose strength is generating new product ideas. Every year her team develops some of the best ideas in the company—and occasionally her team comes up with some clunkers. Mary notices that her team gets little credit or congratulations for the best ideas but does catch the heat when an idea fails. She recognizes Dirk as a classic credit stealer. He takes the ideas of Mary's team and presents them to the other vice presidents and the CEO as his own. And, of course, when something goes wrong, he suggests people talk to Mary, because that's where the poor idea came from.

Mary's First Step: Some Objective Thinking

Mary is far from naive. She likes her job and is proud of her team. She is also concerned about the welfare of her team. Her first step is to think before reacting in any way. The first question she asks is part of her reality check. Is this a problem serious enough to warrant any action? Can she do nothing? She looks at the possible outcomes. This is what she comes up with. Mary decides that if she does nothing, there is a risk she may lose some of her best people. They might move on to work for more appreciative executives elsewhere. She's also concerned the lack of recognition will fester and damage morale.

Then she considers her own position. Her ambition is to move up to be in charge of all product development. In other words, she has some higher career aspirations. Her own personal concern is she will be buried under the blame for the failed ideas. She considers the possibility that her boss is attempting to keep her down by stealing the credit for the good ideas. She must decide whether she can live with the possibility that her difficult boss may make it impossible to gain a promotion she wants and deserves. In her mind, that's a serious issue.

On the flip side, Mary knows she is well respected. Most people in the organization know where the brains lie—with Mary and her team.

Insider Secrets

Want to hear a wonderful thing? Credit-stealing bosses can fool some of the people some of the time. But the rest of the time, people know what's going on. So, while a credit-stealing boss can sometimes get accolades from his superiors for an idea, it's usually only temporary and limited. People know. Take a longer term approach and have faith that people in your organization know who is good at generating great ideas, and who is not. If you are good at it, people will start to recognize your unique personal style in generating ideas.

What does Mary decide? She isn't comfortable ignoring the problem or living with it. Neither is she prepared to go to the wall and risk being fired. At least not yet. When and if it's clear she has little future, then that could change.

Trying to Work It Out

Because Mary wants to try to work things out with Dirk, and hopefully improve their relationship, she sets up a meeting with him. In a flash of brilliance she doesn't want to give Dirk time to prepare arguments, so she's a bit vague about the topic of the meeting when she sets up the appointment.

Mary must prepare for the meeting, so she asks herself these questions:

➤ How can I sell the idea of sharing credit in terms of Dirk's point of view?

➤ Is there a minimum I will settle for before I decide to take stronger action?

➤ How can I introduce the issue of credit so I don't sound petty or self-serving?

From the Manager's Desk

Despite the fact you are trying to work with a difficult boss, you need to plan out your approach. Always know your position, what you can settle for, and how you will approach the boss.

Let's fast-forward to the meeting with Dirk. After a few pleasantries and discussion of a few other topics, Mary decides it's time. This is what she says:

"Dirk, I'm concerned about the possibility of losing some of our most productive staff. I'm sure you'd agree that we need the best

211

people to develop new ideas, and that both you and I benefit when we come up with ideas that make money. Heck, we both look good when we hit the jackpot.

"Some of my team members are wondering why they aren't getting recognized for their contributions to our division. I'm worried that a few of our best people might jump to our competition if they don't feel valued. We really can't afford that, because we won't have those new products coming out. Is there any way that we can recognize the contributions of the idea people?"

In these two short paragraphs Mary shows a considerable amount of artistry and application of what we've talked about so far. First, she makes the point that good ideas make everyone, including Dirk, look good. That's the selling point. She hits the downside for Dirk by noting that employees might leave because they aren't being recognized, and that would lead to lower sales. Why? Because she knows that Dirk is difficult because he craves looking good, and lowered sales would definitely not look good. So she's turned his weakness into a way of getting through to him.

This Won't Work!

It's almost never a good idea to use blaming language that targets the boss. There is always better language to use that deflects blame and focuses on problem solving.

Take a look at Mary's introduction again. Notice the slant. She could have said:

"I'm fed up with not getting credit for ideas my people come up with,"

but that would make her look really petty and selfish. She comes at the topic indirectly by explaining the effects of a lack of recognition—the potential loss of good ideas. And here's the key point. She says nothing, absolutely nothing, about Dirk being the problem. No accusations here. No blaming. And no putting Dirk on the defensive.

After laying out the issue to Dirk, rather than presenting a possible solution herself, she kicks the ball into Dirk's court by asking *him* for some suggestions. By doing so, she shows deference and respect, and again appeals to Dirk's sense of vanity. Mary knows that if Dirk comes up with a good way to solve the problem, he is more likely to follow through on it.

One of two things will happen. Dirk may enter into the discussion in the spirit of working together, and they can hammer out some sort of agreement. Or Dirk may respond by saying, "Hey, we pay these people big money. If that's not enough for them, let 'em leave." Regardless of the outcome, Mary documents their discussion. You'll see why in a moment.

Let's assume Dirk blocks any attempts to address the credit issue even when it's dressed up in a nonconfrontational way and sold well. What then? Let's look at other things Mary can do.

Turning Up the Heat

Because Dirk is so difficult, Mary figures she needs to turn up the heat a bit. But how? She doesn't want to lose her job over the issue. So, she decides a little sneakiness might be in order. If she can get Eileen, Dirk's boss, to begin an initiative to recognize contributions, she will achieve what she wants. The right people will get credit, not the wrong ones. First, she tries the informal approach with Eileen. Over coffee, she drops a "by-the-way" thought. This is what she says to Eileen:

> "I'm wondering whether we can do something to recognize the contributions of our staff. It's one area we haven't addressed, and I think it would be good for morale. Do you have any thoughts on how we could do something?"

Notice again the backdoor approach. And no mention of Dirk and his low-down credit-stealing ways.

If Eileen gets the hint, they might end up initiating a recognition program that will ensure that the credit goes to the originators of the ideas and not the executive in charge. And then Eileen can use her influence as vice president to motivate Dirk to be part of the new recognition program.

What if the informal whisper in the ear doesn't work? Then Mary can use the same strategy she tried with Dirk. She sets up a formal meeting and says much the same thing to Eileen that she said to Dirk. Same tact. Same gentleness. Except she adds one thing. She tells Eileen that she talked to Dirk about it but didn't seem to get anything accomplished. She can do that because she's kept her notes from the meeting with Dirk. That's her backup.

From the Manager's Desk

Moving around your boss or turning up the heat through other people has to be done subtly and artistically. Direct crude attempts to apply pressure often backfire. Be as subtle as you can. Often a whisper is better than a shout.

Eileen will either buy into solving the problem or not. If not, Mary needs to reexamine her position and decide whether she can live with the present situation, and whether she is prepared to be more aggressive.

Last Resorts

Let's say Mary has struck out so far. No luck with Dirk, no luck with Eileen. That changes the face of the issue. Given the lack of support from the two managers above her, Mary has to decide what's worthwhile. Push the point? Give it up? Bide her time? If Mary cannot live with or tolerate the situation, then she can lay her position on the line and issue an ultimatum. And lest we forget, any aggressive ways of dealing with the problem are accompanied by preparations to look for another position.

The Unreasonable-Demands Boss

Unreasonably demanding bosses tend to wear out the troops. They don't just overwhelm you with real, necessary work. Unfortunately, demanding bosses create more work than is actually required because they tend to be …

➤ disorganized.

➤ impulsive (don't think things through).

➤ out of touch with the nature of the work.

➤ poor planners and time managers.

How can you recognize this boss?

The obvious point is that the demanding boss expects more work than is reasonable for a particular period of time. Typically, every request you get will be urgent, and your boss will continually be changing deadlines (usually earlier, sometimes delayed).

It's not that demanding bosses are intentionally nasty, although a few are. They often lack (or have forgotten) the reality of getting work done. Perhaps your demanding boss has never had the chance to actually do the kind of work he expects "yesterday." Tie that in with a lack of organizational skills, and the demanding boss actually creates huge amounts of work through failures to communicate and plan. The disorganization results in inefficiency and crisis after crisis.

From the Manager's Desk

When you don't get help and support from your boss, your boss's boss, and so on, you need to weigh the pros and cons of staying and leaving. Without the support of management, you may experience huge amounts of frustration.

Employee Handbook

The **unreasonably demanding boss** is someone who, through cluelessness or inefficiency, makes impossible demands to get work done in an unrealistic time frame.

Let's Put You in the Driver's Seat

Let's say you work for Bob, who fits this profile. It's not that he's stupid—quite the contrary. He's an otherwise reasonable guy, not difficult in a nasty way, but he's got a tendency to run you off your feet. Every day Bob asks for something "right away." And he shows another characteristic of many demanding bosses. He's frenetic, appears stressed out, and is always in a rush. Because he's always rushing around, he misses details, and that's part of the reason he needs to demand so much. He messes up and creates more work, often work that is done two and three times as his needs change.

So, where do you start? *Think.* You need to get a feel for the situation. First, you decide whether this is a situation serious enough to warrant attention. Of course it is. If demands increase, you and your employees get set up for failure, which affects how you are perceived by others within the company as well as customers. There's a second reason. Bob's style of creating crisis and unnecessary work is expensive. It's not good for you, your employees, or the company to run things this way.

So, you have to do something. As with all these situations, you begin with techniques that require the least possible force and promote an attitude of working together. Start by asking the question: Is it possible that the unreasonable demands are the result of a lack of understanding of the work or a lack of skill in some areas? Given this scenario, the answer is yes.

So, you need to manage and educate Bob. If you can do that and Bob is well meaning, you may be able to stop or at least reduce the unreasonable demands.

This Won't Work!

Working with a boss who is difficult in only one way is much easier than working with one who is difficult in multiple ways. A multiply difficult boss is unlikely to change. Can you spell RESUMÉ?

Do you tramp into Bob's office and say: "Bob-O, you stupid twit. You haven't a clue about how we get our work done, and that's why you overwork us. Get a clue, buddy!"

No, of course not (you do realize why not, right?). Here's a better indirect way to start educating your boss.

> "Bob, you know I think the staff would love to have you come visit for ten or fifteen minutes a week to see what we do and talk informally. It would really help everyone if you could fit that into your schedule. In fact, why don't you come down for lunch tomorrow?"

Why would you do this? Because you want Bob to get to know the team and their jobs. You educate, little by little, so Bob understands the complexity of the jobs you do. Bob gets exposed to explanations of the work process. And chances are, he's going to learn that what you do isn't easy and that it takes time to do it correctly.

Educating the boss about the work you do is a great tactic, regardless of whether you have a difficult boss or not. It's much easier to work with a boss who understands what you do. But there's another step. Somehow you need to get this guy organized; he has to understand that it might be possible to do more with less flailing in all directions. He can conduct business with fewer crises and greater efficiency.

Take a moment to think about how you might do this. There's the direct approach, which involves trying to get Bob some help in the areas of organization and time management. Consider bringing in a time-management trainer to work with everyone, and lean on Bob to visit. Or pass him some really good articles that point out the value of better efficiency and the cost of being inefficient, or articles on workplace stress, that kind of thing.

Insider Secrets

I once worked as a trainer and my boss's boss had no direct understanding of what was involved in designing and delivering training. My direct boss did a great job of educating him by getting him to design and do training. She was able to rope him into doing it by appealing to his rather large-sized ego.

The difficulty with this approach is that Bob might be offended if you get too direct. After all, constantly suggesting time-management courses implies, to most people, that you believe they are lacking in those skills. That can cause resentment.

There's an indirect approach that takes the focus away from how Bob behaves and aims attention at how the *work* gets done. Here's what you do. Sit down by yourself and figure out what you might need to reduce unnecessary work caused by Bob's bad habits. Let's say you come up with the following list:

➤ Greater advance warning of work

➤ Fewer surprises

➤ More regular (but brief) communication between the two of you

➤ Clear, stable priorities

Then work out a plan that includes Bob as an actor. Lay out a better way of processing work, setting priorities, and improving work planning. Perhaps that plan might include you (a good planner) being more active in the work process. Or it might involve more regular meetings.

Then you pitch it to Bob.

The Pitch

Again, we come down to a pitch. You have a plan that benefits you, your team, and Bob. You have to convince Bob that it is in his interest to change his behavior or allow you to help him out. It's back to that sales thing. Figure out the benefits to him, from his point of view, and tout the idea as a solution to his problems. For the demanding, frenetic boss, it could be the bottom line, less work, less fuss, more efficiency, less stress, or more time to play golf (just kidding). Then you pitch it. Here's an example:

"Bob, I know we're all under the gun here and feel overwhelmed, including you. I've been thinking about how we might reduce some of the load by becoming more efficient. Can I tell you about it? I'm not sure if it will solve all our work problems, but I think it's a start."

After you have Bob's attention, explain some of the details.

Your Other "Working With" Options

Here's a nifty option for dealing with a demanding boss who's not very efficient. First, I need to mention a universal rule about work success. The best way to do well at work and get promoted is to do your boss's job, or at least make his or her job easier to do.

How does this relate? Well, Bob's not very good at his job and feels stressed out. By offering to do more, you get to use your expertise in organizing things. In essence, you replace what he lacks with your ability. It might seem odd to talk about offering to do more when you and your staff are already overwhelmed, but if you can gain control over a task that Bob has loused up, you may be able to fix the process. For example, offer to take on the job-scheduling role for Bob. Then do it a better way.

Here's another interesting option. You can attack the too-much-work syndrome in several ways. You can try to reduce the work by educating your boss, or by adopting a better process that is more efficient. Or, you can get more hands involved— in other words, share the work with other parties or more people. Lobby your boss for more resources, using the selling tactics we've talked about in this and the other chapters. Make it appear to be in Bob's interest to get more resources.

From the Manager's Desk

Believe it or not, one of the best ways to get through to a difficult boss is to offer your help and offer to do more. Sometimes your doing more can result in actually doing less if you're more efficient than your boss.

Finally, there's a way to combine these tricks. Get Bob to hire someone to help him, or offer to lend him an additional assistant to help him get organized. Can't do that? OK, just keep dropping hints that maybe good old Bob is looking tired and might need more help.

If None of That Works ...

By now you've probably caught on that in working with a difficult boss, some indirect (benevolent) sneakiness is often the best way to attack problems. However, without some cooperation from Bob, none of that works. Then the other options kick in, much as we've already described.

You can arrange to talk to Bob's boss, presenting the appearance (and reality) of being concerned about the company's welfare and customers. You can try to sit down with Bob and his boss to work things out together and come up with some solutions.

If nothing changes after that, you have to decide what it's all worth. Can you live with the present situation? Is it affecting your health? An overly demanding boss can create havoc with your stress levels and even your health. Are you prepared to move on if things don't change?

If so, then that enables the more extreme courses of action. You can present that ultimatum in a polite form. You can push harder and be more aggressive in going over Bob's head. Always be prepared for the worst if you follow that path.

A Sobering Thought

Here's something you need to consider. Sometimes it appears that your boss is acting unreasonably. From where you sit, you see the chaos that comes from a disorganized and ineffective boss—the unreasonable demands, the rush, rush, rush mentality. But here's a thought. What if your boss is as much a victim as you are? Maybe his boss is completely impossible. Or maybe he doesn't have the information he needs from his superiors.

From the Manager's Desk

You will be much more successful educating and managing your boss if you first educate yourself about your boss's job and constraints.

If that's the case, all the educating and boss management is going to be wasted, because you're educating the wrong person. That's why it's good to get the difficult boss talking about what is restricting him in his job. While we talk about educating the boss, you can also educate yourself about the boss's job. That positions you to be of more help—and the more help you are, the more you can help yourself and your team.

If you discover that the problem isn't your boss but the system in which you all work, then you are up against a very difficult challenge. If you do not have access to the people you need to deal with to solve the problem, it's not likely you can solve it.

I know several managers who have looked around them, seen that the problem isn't one person but a set of people who don't manage well, and decided the company was a lost cause.

It comes down to this: You try to change what is in your power to change. If you can't change something important, then you need to decide whether you can live with the status quo.

The Least You Need to Know

➤ Credit-stealing bosses can't fool all of the people all of the time.

➤ Credit-stealing bosses are infuriating, but if you stay cool and work with the boss, you can succeed.

➤ The overly demanding boss often creates unnecessary work by being disorganized.

➤ Managing your difficult boss involves educating him or her about what you do. You also need to educate yourself about the boss's job.

Chapter 18

Is Your Boss Doing Something Illegal?

In This Chapter

➤ What to do if your boss acts illegally

➤ Ways to approach authorities

➤ Three options if your boss is doing something wrong

➤ What if the boss violates corporate policy?

It's one thing to deal with an annoying boss. It's another to work for a really difficult boss. But perhaps the most trying and upsetting situation you can face occurs when the boss is doing something outright illegal, possibly illegal, or counter to the policies of your company or organization. Frankly, these situations can be agonizing. Do you blow the whistle? Do you keep your mouth shut? Who do you contact? And what protection exists for you?

I don't envy anyone in this situation. In this chapter we will do our best to present your options, along with cautions. But often the choice you make when your boss is doing really serious bad things depends on your own moral and ethical fiber. Ultimately, what you do depends on what you are willing to sacrifice.

Clearly Illegal Acts

Bosses aren't perfect. Some are less perfect than others. Some are so imperfect they commit crimes. The range of criminal activity for bosses is probably the same as for any other occupation. Criminals can wear three-piece suits and be well manicured, or they can have spiked hair and listen to odd music.

It's important to realize this. We develop our perceptions of people in a number of ways. One of these is whether they are educated, dress well, and can communicate well. Often bosses fare well on all of these, so we tend to think they are not prone to the same human foibles that less-presentable people have.

Let's define what we're talking about here when we use the term "clearly illegal." We are talking about actions that, if proven, are against federal, state, or local laws and would be punishable by the legal system if the person is found guilty. That could include any of the following:

➤ Theft

➤ Assault (sexual or otherwise)

➤ Fraud

➤ Embezzlement

➤ Bribery

➤ Uttering threats

➤ Illegal drug use or distribution

➤ Driving under the influence

➤ Workplace safety violations

➤ Obstruction of justice (destroying evidence)

➤ Insider trading and stock manipulation

Clearly all of these are serious crimes, which is why we have laws against them.

This Won't Work!

Don't assume that because someone is well dressed, well spoken, or educated, they aren't capable of a wide range of criminal behavior. They are.

Rumor Versus Fact

There are two ways you might discover your boss may be doing something illegal. You may actually observe illegal behavior, or have access to documentation or a paper trail that indicates illegal actions are talking place. For example, while you might not actually see a manager "cook the books" to cover up theft, you might have access to the physical evidence that shows this is going on. Both direct observation or having documentation (proof) about the wrongdoing constitute hard evidence.

But a more likely situation is that you don't have that hard evidence. You might hear that your boss is cutting corners that put employees at risk. You might hear a rumor that your boss pushed an employee (that is, assaulted someone). Or you might hear rumors of certain files being destroyed. You may even know that those documents disappeared, but you have no first-hand knowledge or proof of what happened to them.

There are a few reasons why we highlight the differences. With people we don't like, we have a tendency to accept rumor or third-party accusations as fact when we have no actual proof of the accusations. Not separating what we observe or know from what we suspect is a bad idea. Confusing the two puts us at risk. If you use rumor to identify wrong-doing, you may find yourself in an impossible situation—making a charge without really having proof or documentation. If you do that, you will put yourself in an impossible situation with respect to continued employment.

This Won't Work!

Don't confuse direct observation and proof with rumor and third-party reports. Sometimes things aren't what they appear, and if you take action on the basis of rumor, you put yourself at risk.

Here's another reason to make the fact/rumor distinction. Illegal acts involve the legal system, whether it be law enforcement or the courts. The legal system requires that there be some basis for investigation, and rumors aren't usually sufficient. In fact, if you approach a law enforcement agency with a rumor, probably nothing at all is going to happen. If anything, you will lose credibility.

Here's yet another reason to make the distinction, and it has to do with fairness and equity. While the legal system assumes a person is innocent until proven guilty, office politics often assume a person is guilty until proven innocent. Many an innocent person has had a career ruined because of unsubstantiated accusations. That's because people often remember the accusation of wrongdoing but forget when a person is completely absolved. Making an accusation that might be true, or even is probably true, may end up ruining an innocent person. Frankly, that's not something I could live with.

And, just in case you need yet another reason to make the fact/rumor distinction, consider this. While there is some legal protection for whistle-blowers in some jurisdictions, the reality is that if you point out illegal activities, you're still at some risk. If you choose to take action, then at least you want to put yourself on the line for something that you're sure is occurring, not something that is rumored.

Three Options

There are three options for dealing with illegal activities. You can ignore it. You can work through internal company channels. Or you can go to law enforcement. Let's look at each of these.

Ignoring It

Our society has adopted an unfortunate propensity to not get involved. We often shy away from dealing with wrongdoing, rationalizing inaction by labeling it as someone else's problem or out of concern for ourselves. We make excuses to do nothing.

I'm not going to preach to you that you should get a backbone, because frankly it won't do any good. But let's look at the consequences of inaction:

➤ The obvious one is that in all probability the illegal acts are doing harm to someone, or perhaps many people. Are you willing to allow that damage to continue, whether it's damage to an employee, the company, or the company's shareholders?

➤ Consider the consequences if you do nothing, knowing there is illegal activity taking place. What happens if you choose to do nothing and it comes out later that you knew? Sometimes you put yourself at risk by keeping your mouth shut.

➤ By keeping information under wraps, you may also be committing a crime. It's not likely, of course, unless you lie to law enforcement, but again, different jurisdictions have different laws.

From the Manager's Desk

If you're in doubt about the laws pertaining to not reporting a crime, it's best to consult a lawyer in your area or contact law enforcement anonymously to ask for clarification. Different laws apply in different places.

Is inaction in the face of illegal acts ever justified? The most obvious situation where doing nothing is a viable option is when you have no proof and no documentation, but have heard rumors. Even here, it depends on the nature of the crime. It may be appropriate to provide information about your suspicions if the crime is exceedingly serious.

I understand that trying to stop illegal activity is a scary enterprise, because your job—and perhaps your entire career—can be at stake. Ultimately, regardless of what anyone says to you, you will make your decision based on your own morals, ethics, and principles. Just be aware of the consequences of doing nothing and of taking action, so you can make as informed a choice as possible.

Try Company Channels

The second option is probably the most advisable in most situations. You can work through existing company channels to share the load and the responsibility of any actions.

What might that involve? In part it depends on who you have access to in your company and the severity of the situation. The most common ways to use existing company channels include going through the human resources department, or approaching someone much higher up on the management power structure. Sometimes that might be the CEO.

As we've said earlier, human resource departments may have limited power and influence, so you need to be aware of that. However, they're more likely to take action if the situation is very serious. By the way, in large companies you may have other options. For example, if you are aware of fraud or embezzlement, then you might be able to approach the auditing department or even the accounting department.

In the face of blatant illegal activity that you can prove, consider going as high as you can as quickly as possible. If you can access the CEO, do so. Management lower down may be hesitant to follow up on your concerns because they lack sufficient clout. It's less likely the CEO will feel so constrained.

Insider Secrets

Sometimes making an anonymous complaint is a possible option. However, keep in mind that anonymous complaints are often taken much less seriously than when the complainant is identified. While anonymity can offer some protection, it may result in the issue being ignored. Also keep in mind that anonymous complaints may be traceable for contacts made via e–mail. For issues of interest to law enforcement agencies, consider using the anonymous tip lines that have become popular (Crimestoppers programs). To notify someone in your company of wrongdoing, you can use a letter or suggestion box. Always be aware, however, that the facts you provide often will indicate who you are.

Here are the advantages of working through company channels:

➤ It allows you to share the load in a legal situation. Because it is often (but not always) in the interests of your company to stop illegal activity, you will hopefully have allies to deal with someone who has an established power base (your boss).

➤ In cases where you don't have proof of illegal acts, working within company channels can mobilize resources to obtain that proof. After all, you aren't a professional investigator. In cases where you lack proof, always consider what we talked about regarding the guilty-until-proven-innocent syndrome that occurs in companies. Be very careful when making accusations when you lack proof.

➤ Going through company channels allows some protection for the company. Few companies want their dirty laundry displayed in public and prefer to handle things internally. Going through company channels shows that you are a loyal employee who has consideration for the company's reputation.

So, in short, you may get more support by at least starting with internal channels.

When going through internal company channels, consider the possibility that your company will do nothing, or that you'll end up being labeled as a troublemaker. It's sad, but sometimes that happens.

Do you have any protection? Maybe. Maybe not. As we've said, there are some parts of the world with whistle-blower statutes that can provide some protection against retribution. That's in theory. But regardless, there is no guarantee. And often any legal guarantees require long, drawn-out legal proceedings that can wear out your resources. Again, consult a lawyer beforehand.

From the Manager's Desk

If you use internal company channels, get some independent legal advice about any whistle-blower laws you may have as protection. We suggest you do that first, before taking action.

The Long Arm of the Law

Your third option is to deal directly with law enforcement. This option may be the only one available to you if your company refuses to take a complaint seriously. It's probably appropriate to try internal channels first, unless the crime is serious or if you feel there is conspiracy to protect a person committing illegal acts.

As with all the options, I suggest you consult a lawyer first, for several reasons. Again, this route offers self-protection. Also, an attorney can find out the best way of getting your information to the proper authorities. There is actually a wide range of agencies beyond the police, and determining which one is the right one may require some expertise. For example, you might need to contact the workplace safety and health regulatory body in your area for safety issues. You might need to contact the securities commission if you discover stock manipulation or insider trading. It gets pretty complicated.

To reiterate, if you take this step, it's best to have some documentation and to make the rumors/fact distinction we talked about earlier. And never make frivolous complaints.

How to Pass Along Information

Regardless of who you approach to address an illegal situation, it's important to carry out the approach correctly. There is a good way and a bad way to do it. The good way is emotionally neutral and well thought out. The bad way makes you appear vindictive and out to get someone. Here are some suggestions about what to do and what not to do.

1. When communicating with company officials or law enforcement, make the distinction between what you know and what you suspect. There may be some situations where it may be appropriate to present suspicions, but never, ever present those unsubstantiated suspicions as facts. That immediately marks you as lacking credibility.

2. When approaching the company internally, be clear that you're doing so because of concern about the company and its employees and not out of spite or vindictiveness. Lay out the consequences of the illegal actions, just in case they aren't easily understood. Stay away from personal remarks about the person. The facts are important, not whether you like or respect the person.

3. Focus on facts, proof, and documentation. The more you know and can prove, the better a hearing you will get. The less information you provide, the more likely you will be perceived as a troublemaker.

4. Let the company or law enforcement decide what action is necessary. In other words, don't insist on what you think the next step should be. You don't want to be overbearing, and truth be told, the authorities should be better positioned to decide what to do next. At minimum, even if nothing happens you will have discharged your moral and legal obligations by providing the information.

And maybe you will sleep better.

This Won't Work!

You aren't a detective and don't even play one on TV. Don't get suckered into investigating when you lack the skills to do so. Leave it to the experts. Bottom line: It can be a safety issue if laws have been broken. On very rare occasions corporate criminals may attempt to stop your investigation or threaten you. Leave it to the pros.

Gray-Area Illegal Acts

Some activities may or may not be illegal, and it isn't always easy to tell. Yes, there are gray areas in the law, particularly because courts are often responsible for interpreting law, and they can act somewhat unpredictably.

What are some of these areas? Sexual harassment is the most obvious. Discriminatory practices against members of protected minority groups can fall into this area. Even things like theft could be a bit gray.

Let's start with what you need to know about sexual harassment, and we can talk about the other gray areas later.

This Won't Work!

Be aware that what you think is harmless behavior may in fact be illegal if the person exposed to that behavior does not want the attention or advances. The fact you do not believe it is illegal does not diminish any legal obligations you might have.

If I haul off and smack you in the nose, the law calls that an illegal act. It is the act itself that makes it illegal, and that act is called an assault. Sure, there might be circumstances like self-defense that make it a tiny bit gray, but generally it's fairly clear. I hit you. I assaulted you. Assault is illegal.

With sexual harassment it gets more complex.

If I make some off-color remarks to a female employee, that might or might not be harassment. If the female employee does not want those advances, it probably is. If the advances are welcome, it might not be harassment.

So the definition of what's illegal harassment depends in part on the perceptions of the person targeted by the behavior. Does that have a practical impact on you if you witness harassment?

Yes, it does. In all likelihood, you will not want to be directly involved (that is, lodge a complaint with the authorities) unless you're the victim of the harassment. Ultimately, the victim must be actively involved.

What you can do is support and advocate for the victim. Generally that would mean helping her (or him) determine options, untangling the mechanics of legal action, and doing your best to protect the person from the wrath of the harasser. This is particularly true if your boss is the person committing the harassing acts.

You may choose to bring the circumstances to the attention of the human resources department or similar internal agency, but again, you must have the cooperation of the victim to do so.

What about other gray areas—for example, discrimination on the basis of characteristics like race, gender, and disability? Again, these are best dealt with by discussing the situation with internal company staff responsible for your company's adherence to employment equity laws. They presumably have more expertise. As with the harassment issue, unless you're the victim in question, you'll probably need the cooperation and involvement of those victimized by discriminatory practices.

If the discrimination is a systematic process going on throughout your company (rather than isolated to your boss), then you can consider more direct action. As always, get legal advice.

Finally, in the gray areas, some actions, while technically illegal, may be so trivial that pursuing them may be pointless and leave you looking silly—theft, for example. Let's say our boss is in the habit of pocketing a pencil or two from the company supply room. Maybe it's for his kids. Well, I guess if you want to be a stickler for the law, this could be theft.

Do you have any idea how you will look if you pursue this? Like a complete fool. If you complain about this "theft," you'll immediately be considered as mentally strange or as having a hidden agenda or ax to grind. So use your common sense here.

When the Boss Violates Policy

Probably the most prevalent serious difficult be-havior bosses engage in is cutting corners or vio-lating internal corporate policy. It's not generally illegal, although it can be. Here are some exam-ples:

➤ Hiring unqualified relatives

➤ Violating conflict of interest guidelines

➤ Treating people badly (when that is a policy issue)

➤ Not following standard procedures

➤ Juggling budget figures

➤ Some kinds of lying

From the Manager's Desk

Conduct a reality check if your boss appears to violate corporate policy. Do that by considering the damage done to real people, customers, or the company as a result of the violation. Is there any damage?

There're probably a few more you could add to the list. Notice that the some of the ones we've listed can be fairly serious and some are not. Often it depends on the cir-cumstances. Before we talk about how to handle these, let's consider the issue of cor-porate policy.

I'm not a great fan of red tape and unnecessary corporate procedures, rules and such things. I understand why they are there, but to be perfectly honest, a lot of time those corporate policies can interfere with actually getting things done.

Some bosses are quite adept at getting around corporate policies. That's because skirt-ing some policies isn't harmful (or doesn't appear to be) and it gets things done. In fact, some of the best managers I've worked for have had the ability to get things done by tiptoeing around policy.

Also, consider the positive benefits of your boss's actions. Is moving around the pol-icy allowing you to become more productive, provide better service, and contribute to the company?

Whether you are considering the damage or the pluses, consider the long-term effects also. For example, let's say your boss hires Timmy, his son, to fill a position he isn't very qualified for. While this isn't a horrible transgression, it may affect the morale and perceptions of other staff about the company, and about the honesty or fairness of management.

So, you need to determine whether the violation is a significant one. If it puts people or the company at risk, then that's significant. If it has the capability of affecting staff morale and the perception of management, that's significant. If it's taking a pencil or two, that's probably not significant.

Insider Secrets

Violating corporate policy is a weird thing. On one hand, it's a characteristic of many very good managers because they know when to go around rules and when not to. On the other hand, some managers edge into destructive violations over time. Many of our recent political scandals have started off as a little harmless avoidance of procedure under the guise of getting things done.

Because we consider violations of corporate policy as different from contravening the laws, your options are more limited. You don't have the ability to take this to an independent agency. You do have the option of going directly to your boss to discuss it. You have the option of using other internal channels.

Like all the situations we've talked about in this chapter, how you approach the boss or others in your organization is important. Again, present your information within the context of the facts and the effects of the violation on the company. Make sure the issue is important enough so you won't sound like a fool. Present information in an impersonal way. Make sure you aren't motivated by "getting someone." That attitude always comes through.

Basically, use your common sense. Pick your battles.

The Least You Need to Know

➤ People have a tendency to not want to get involved.

➤ Sometimes by doing nothing in the face of illegal activity, you put yourself at more risk.

➤ Make the distinction between rumor and fact.

➤ You may have some protection under whistle-blower statutes, but consult a lawyer.

➤ Some activities fall into the gray areas of court judgment.

➤ Sometimes sneaking around corporate policy can be harmless or even beneficial.

Part 5

If It Wasn't For My Difficult Co-Workers

We've talked about dealing with difficult employees and difficult bosses. Co-workers can also be difficult and aggravating—the insensitive folks who never take responsibility for anything, the backstabbers and gossips, and the turf-warriors. These people can also interfere with getting the work done and drive you to the rubber room.

We'll look at different kinds of conflict and at the five major strategies for managing it. We'll also look at how you can mobilize support from the rest of your organization to address the difficult co-worker.

Chapter 19

Difficult Colleagues

In This Chapter

➤ Distinguish between annoying and work-killing colleagues

➤ How to use self-talk to chill out

➤ How to mobilize team resources to help

➤ Get better at specific co-worker situations

So far we've talked about managing difficult employees and managing difficult bosses. But what about your difficult colleagues or peers? You know the ones. They're at the same level as you in your organization. Their difficult behaviors range from the annoying and aggravating to more serious behaviors that affect your ability to do your job and manage your employees.

As with most difficult people, the difficult behaviors of your colleagues take on two basic forms. Drawing a distinction between the two is important because knowing what you are dealing with helps you decide what you can do (or should do) about the particular difficult solution. The two basic categories are the annoying and frustrating peers and the work-killers.

In this chapter we'll go through some of the common difficult tactics your co-workers use, and present some ways of managing them effectively.

The Annoying and Frustrating

Do you have a co-worker who drives you crazy? Perhaps it's someone who is consistently rude. Never admits to being wrong. Argues about every little thing. Do you know this guy? Or maybe it's someone who has some personal habits that get on your

This Won't Work!

If you've been using the term "personality conflict" to describe a difficult person, stop now. By using this label, you give up control and give up on the situation. You don't have difficulties with someone because of their personality; you have problems with someone because of his or her behavior and your reactions.

nerves: the pencil tapper, the fidgeter, or the deadly knuckle-cracker. Maybe it's someone who talks constantly and doesn't listen. Or wears ugly ties!

These are examples of annoying and frustrating behavior. Often this kind of behavior doesn't really interfere with getting work done—or at least it doesn't interfere unless you allow it to get to you. But dagnabbit, it's annoying.

Often people label this kind of behavior as a personality conflict, but that's misleading. That's just a convenient way to say, "I can't stand this person," or "She gets on my nerves." It's often a cop-out on your part, because it really amounts to giving up.

We're going to deal with the frustrating and annoying situations differently. And I'm not sure you're going to like it much. The in-a-nutshell comment is this: First, look closely at your own reactions, and second, chill out.

It's Your Annoyance

Why do people get on our nerves? Well, there are two parts to the equation—assuming their behavior is relatively harmless. First, annoying people do things you don't like. It's really not more complicated than that, whether it's the ugly tie, a lack of listening, burping a lot, or anything else. That, however, is the minor part of the equation.

Ever wonder how someone you find so annoying can be liked and admired by the person next to you? I mean, how could someone soooo obnoxious or difficult (in your view) be liked by anyone? It's really simple. Annoying and frustrating behavior is almost always in the eyes of the beholder. Yes, that's you, buddy. So that's the second part of the annoyance equation. Being annoyed is a combination of what the person does and your own perceptions.

That gabby person who talks your ear off is probably someone's best friend (hard to believe, I know). The person who is never wrong probably has someone who admires his or her confidence. Go figure.

Now, I know that the fact that someone else actually likes someone who drives you crazy isn't very helpful to you. But it does point out the fact that many of your reactions to people come from within you. While these reactions have something to do with the other person's behavior, they are also based on *your* perceptions. Essentially what you're doing is saying to yourself, "If I was that person in that situation, I wouldn't behave like that." In other words, the other person's behavior isn't consistent with what you'd do, and you don't like that.

Insider Secrets

Here's a common stupid human trick. When people are annoyed with someone else's trivial behavior, they tend to try to rationalize their own negative reaction by searching for apparently objective reasons for it. This amounts to making a mountain out of a molehill. We should all try to stop building cases to justify our annoyances about unimportant issues. Take Paul. He gets annoyed because Mary interrupts him occasionally. He rationalizes his own reaction by saying to himself: "How can she expect to have a reasonable conversation this way?", or "Everyone knows you should never interrupt someone." In fact, those "reasons" have little to do with Paul's annoyance.

While you might not like to hear that your perception of another person is the cause of your negative reactions, it's not a completely bad state of affairs. Here's why. It's difficult to change people's behavior, particularly when you have no formal authority over them. It's a loser's game.

What you can do is work on yourself to alter your reactions to those annoying and difficult people. That is something that's under your control.

You might ask: "Why should I? This guy's a bozo. *He* should change, not me." Well, I suppose in an ideal world, that might be true. Why should you accommodate some idiot who drives you up the wall?

From the Manager's Desk

It isn't usually possible to "fix" another person. It is easier (but not easy) to work at changing your own reactions to someone who annoys or frustrates you.

Let's put it this way. It isn't Bob or Mary or Freddy that is driving you crazy. It's your *reaction* to Bob or Mary or Freddy. With a lot of annoying behavior, it's you doing it to yourself. So the first answer to your "Why should I" question is that you're making yourself miserable. Do you want to continue to be miserable, since it's unlikely that annoying Bob is going away? If your answer is "No, I don't," then start with yourself.

Besides your mental health and well-being, there is an even more practical reason to change your reactions. When you deal with someone you find annoying, eventually your annoyance and frustration come through. This happens to the best of us.

Despite your best efforts to control your behavior, sooner or later you'll do things to make your annoyance public or, worse, blurt out things that will completely poison your relationship with the annoying co-worker. And then you don't just have an annoying co-worker; you have a real live enemy. And you look bad in the eyes of those around you.

So, the reason to address your own inner reactions is that you're the one who pays the price for being annoyed. It isn't the bad-tie guy who has his blood pressure skyrocket. It's you.

OK, Wise Guy, How Do I Change My Perceptions?

So, you're tired of letting a bunch of little things get to you. You don't want to allow that annoying colleague to get under your skin. And you recognize you can't control the behavior of everyone around you, but you can start thinking and reacting differently. We're going to go through some techniques to help you modify what may be an overreaction to annoying behavior.

Employee Handbook

Self-talk refers to what we say to ourselves, in our heads. We know that self–talk influences our reactions in many situations.

The principle behind changing our own reactions has to do with what we call *self-talk*. Simply, self-talk refers to what we say to ourselves, in our heads. We know that self-talk influences our reactions in many situations. Some kinds of self-talk result in increased anger and frustration, while other kinds help us keep things in perspective. Self-talk either feeds negative emotions or helps us reduce them.

Let me give you an extreme example.

> Sam has a phobia about elevators. Whenever possible, Sam avoids using them and uses the stairs.

What drives this phobia? Whenever Sam thinks he may have to ride an elevator, he starts with the negative self-talk. He thinks (talks to himself internally) about getting stuck, about dying in a crash, about the last time when he freaked out, or about how stupid he'll look if he takes the stairs. All this negative self-talk actually creates the extreme fear and results in a self-fulfilling prophecy. Is it no wonder that by the time Sam actually gets in the elevator, he's close to a panic attack?

That's the power of self-talk as it affects negative emotions. By the way, therapy for such phobias often involves changing the self-talk (among a few other techniques), and there is a considerable success rate in curing phobias via these methods.

The following techniques to reduce your reactions to annoying people come from this basic principle:

1. Recognize that when you get annoyed, you experience the high blood pressure, increased heart rate, and other physical reactions. Getting annoyed doesn't harm the annoying person. It harms *you*. You are the one who feels miserable. And you have it in your power to sit back and become more tolerant of annoying behavior.

   When faced with that annoying behavior, remind yourself that you are allowing the person to harm you. Ask yourself whether it's truly worth it to allow someone you don't particularly care for to stress out your blood vessels and churn your stomach.

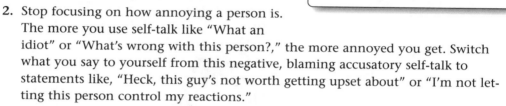

From the Manager's Desk

Recognize that annoying behavior doesn't have to annoy you. *You* are in control (or can learn to be in control) of your reactions. And doing so may add a few more happy years to your life. Sounds good to me!

2. Stop focusing on how annoying a person is. The more you use self-talk like "What an idiot" or "What's wrong with this person?," the more annoyed you get. Switch what you say to yourself from this negative, blaming accusatory self-talk to statements like, "Heck, this guy's not worth getting upset about" or "I'm not letting this person control my reactions."

3. Use reality check self-talk. Ask yourself whether this person is legitimately harmful or just annoying. Talk to yourself and get things in perspective. Is that knuckle-cracking person really destructive? No. Very annoying, yes, but in the grand scheme of our short lives, why allow something unimportant to affect us? Life is too short. Remind yourself of that.

4. What about rude people, or verbally nasty people? Here's a great self-talk method to avoid responding in kind. Remind yourself that you are the better person and you will prove it by not descending to the level of the rude or nasty person. You aren't going to soil yourself or roll in the muck with that nasty person. Say to yourself, "I will not get suckered into acting badly."

5. What about group situations where someone is annoying or nasty? Understand that groups usually recognize when someone is acting stupidly or unfairly. If you are the target, you gain the support of the group by acting with dignity and control. Say to yourself, "This nasty person is just making himself look stupid. I'm not going to join him."

6. Let's talk about a more general issue. When you are stressed out, tired, and ill fed, you are much more likely to be react in extreme ways to annoyances. It's kind of a vicious circle. When you get stressed you react more emotionally to tough situations. That in turn increases your stress levels. And that's one road to a bad case of burnout.

This Won't Work!

Negative, blaming, or aggressive thinking and self-talk is liable to kill you, or at least reduce your quality of life. Don't do this to yourself. Take control of your own reactions by talking to yourself differently.

So, one of the best ways to increase your ability to stay cool under fire is to do the standard stress management things. Keep yourself de-stressed as well as you can. That includes regular exercise (even walking everyday for 20 minutes is good), eating properly (three meals a day, low fat, less sugar, reducing caffeine and nicotine intake—both are stimulants, you know), and balancing your life. Work at leaving your work in your office. When you take those business clothes off at the end of the day, imagine you are shedding your job for the day.

Now, I'm not going to snow you here. These kinds of techniques need to be practiced consistently, but if you can modify your lifestyle and self-talk style, you will make a huge leap towards making yourself almost invulnerable to your annoying, frustrating, and obnoxious co-workers.

Insider Secrets

We have a rough idea of how long it takes to learn and stabilize new behaviors, habits, and self-talk. Generally, it will take at least six weeks of working at it to succeed, and you have to work at it consistently. Then you will probably find that your new way of self-talk becomes more of a habit. Monitor your self-talk as often as you can. Identify the kinds of ineffective self-talk you use. Every day remind yourself to use more constructive self-talk that will help you stay calm.

Consider writing some key positive self-talk phrases out and putting them where you can see them. Some people actually incorporate them into their computer screen savers. Remind yourself to use those key phrases.

You *can* do it. The results may extend beyond your work life over time.

The Work Killers

The *work-killer colleagues* are different from the annoying ones. Their difficult behaviors actually interfere with your ability to get work done, so it's a double whammy.

238

Not only are they annoying and frustrating, but they cause real concrete problems for you and your work unit.

We have a two-pronged approach. The first is the things we mentioned in becoming less reactive. You must control your annoyance and frustrations first before you deal with the concrete problems these people create.

Employee Handbook

Work-killer colleagues inter-fere with your ability to get work done. They aren't just annoying.

Here's why. When you get annoyed and frustrated you're less likely to see the issues clearly. There's a tendency to make things personal and to forget you aren't out to "get the person" but to solve a work problem. So you do things to make a bad situation worse. But there's a more important reason. It has to do with the perceptions of others. When people around you see you are bent out of shape and venting about a co-worker in an emotional way, they presume that you're probably a problem, too. So the use of positive self-talk helps you avoid looking bad and actually helps you maintain credibility with the people you may need to help you deal with that problem co-worker (for example, your boss, other staff, or managers).

The Resource Hog

Here's the deal with the resource hog. She or he is not much of a team player and is so focused on his or her own work unit that it can actually reduce the effectiveness of the company. It's a weird thought that you can have a situation where one work unit improves its productivity but damages the productivity of other units, and the company as a whole gets a negative return. But it does happen. And if you're the manager of one of those work units damaged for the benefit of the resource hog, it's a problem.

This Won't Work!

Resource hogs often do what they do because they really want to do a good job. It's just their focus is too narrow. Don't assume they're evil. First, approach them as committed people trying to do a good job—they just don't understand how they're affecting the rest of the organization.

Here are a few examples of resource-hogging behavior.

> Resource hoggers often go for the budget jugular. They try to get more money to play with, and because the money pie is finite, it has to come from somewhere. And maybe it's *your* budget that gets reduced. If the resource hog is good at it, things can end up out of whack.

Another area resource hoggers focus on is staff levels.

> Hoggers who want to increase their staffing complement lobby and present apparently reasonable explanations for why they need those extra people. And again, because salary and staffing resources are limited, you may end up short-staffed while the hogger ends up with people just sitting around. Good resource hoggers on this grand corporate scale usually succeed when they have the ear of a senior executive.

There are some other, more local kinds of hogging behavior.

> Ever go to your resource library to get that book or video and find that a hogger seems to have *all* the resources? Or you find that the hogger's work unit has all the files on projects you're involved in? It happens. In these cases, it's not likely there is any intent to damage you or interfere with your work, but that's hardly comforting when you have to spend two hours tracking down the location of something you need, is it?

So, what are your tactics? First, use positive self-talk to keep the situation as unemotional and calm as possible. Don't approach the resource hogger when you're angry because that's likely to create a much worse situation. Wait until you've settled down and have some perspective.

Then approach the resource hogger and lay out the issue on a factual basis. Explain what resources you need and have lacked, and the effect that not having them is having on you and your work unit. Assume the best at first. Assume the person is simply oblivious to these things and not deliberately malicious. Try to negotiate some agreement, and stay focused on the issue: an allocation of resources so you both have what you need when you need it.

This straight and honest approach will work for good managers or reasonable managers. Mostly their resource hogging is a case of not having thought about the effects of their behavior on others. However, it won't always work. Then what?

The other options you have involve other people, either other members of your management team (at the same level), your mutual boss, or someone who might be able to institute a more team-oriented program to help *all* of the managers share resources more effectively.

We'll talk about boss involvement in the next chapter. Let's focus on working with the general management team. If there is a resource hogger on the management

From the Manager's Desk

First, use positive self-talk, then approach the hogger directly in a nonemotional way. Many resource hoggers aren't aware of how they affect their co-workers. A quick, nonthreatening direct approach may be enough to solve the problem.

team, it's likely the hogger is also affecting other managers in negative ways. They should be prime participants in the process of negotiating with the hogger.

The idea is to create a discussion focus about the general issue of resource sharing and resource hogging that doesn't single out any particular manager. This is best done at general management team meetings where you can bring up the subject. Here's a good way to phrase it:

> "How can we share resources to become more productive in all our work units?"

There are two reasons to present it this way. We want to make the resource hogger aware that he may be doing things that cause problems for others on the team, but we don't want to single the hogger out. Sometimes by broaching the subject in a nonthreatening way, the oblivious hogger becomes an unoblivious non-hogger. The second reason is to apply some group pressure on the individual in a subtle way that will allow the hogger to feel the pressure but not feel personally attacked.

If you want to introduce the topic at a team meeting, here's one way you could do it.

> "You know, in the past few months I've been having more and more trouble getting or finding the files I need to get our work done. I'm wondering whether I'm the only one facing that problem and whether we can figure out some ways to ensure that all of us have what we need when we need it. That way all of us can benefit. Have others here hit this issue?"

The example above is positive, constructive and non-blaming, which opens the door for others, or even the resource hogger to suggest a solution.

> **From the Manager's Desk**
>
> There are two reasons to involve other team members in dealing with a resource hogger: to come up with a group solution everyone buys into, and to apply some subtle indirect pressure on a resource hogger without mentioning him or her specifically.

Just Insensitive

The insensitive colleague can fall in the annoying and frustrating category or in the work-killer group. It depends, so we'll have to do a reality check on the insensitive. Step back and examine the person's behavior. Is it affecting getting work done in your work unit? Is it having a clear-cut effect on your other peers and team members? And is that effect just in the form of aggravation, or is the work actually suffering?

Insensitivity can be very mild to quite extreme, ranging from occasional rudeness and interrupting to consistent use of bad language, sexist remarks, and generally unpleasant interpersonal behavior. Whether you need to take any action at all depends on whether it is causing a threat to getting work done.

Insider Secrets

Some insensitive behavior is illegal. For example, sexual remarks are certainly insensitive, but they may well be illegal and subject your company to legal action. In situations like this, look for advice from your human resources department, legal department, or, if you have neither, contact the appropriate government agencies for advice.

Apart from the techniques in the next chapter (getting help from others), you have two options here. One is to attempt to deal directly with the person, much as we described previously—that is, sticking to facts, keeping it cool, and approaching the person when you aren't angry.

Unfortunately, with some insensitive people all that does is expose you to more insensitivity when you try to address the problem and, yes, on occasion, more abuse. That's the thing with insensitive people. When you try to discuss their insensitivity, they treat you in a callous and insensitive way. It's worth a try, though.

Another less direct way is to put these issues on the table for the entire peer group. You do that in much the same way you would do it for the resource hog—indirectly, as a general issue about how you treat each other in the workplace.

As with the resource hog, it's likely that you aren't the only one affected by an insensitive peer, so others will be interested in solving the problem. Schedule a discussion at a team meeting if you can. Keep the issue general, and try to keep the discussion positive, specific, and non-blaming. Here's one way to present the issue to the group.

> I know we've all been under a lot of stress lately, and maybe we've been a bit short with each other. I think it's important for all of us to work well as a team, so maybe we should revisit how we want to be treated and how we should be treating each other. After all, we can't afford to be arguing among ourselves all the time, and we can't expect to treat our customers and employees any better than we treat ourselves. Do you folks think this is something worth talking about?"

Notice the tone. Nobody is singled out. And it's phrased in a helpful, positive way.

No-Fault Teflon Co-workers

I just hate these folks. The no-fault Teflon co-worker is the person who is never responsible when things go wrong. It's always someone else or some other part of the organization that's screwed up. Or maybe it's you. Teflon people have no problem accepting praise, though.

Apart from being annoying, the Teflon co-worker interferes with solving problems. Let's say the Teflon manager's work unit has screwed up on something, but he or she completely denies any responsibility for the screw-up. How are you ever going to make sure that the problem doesn't occur again? You can't, unless the person needed to solve the problem at least admits he or she is part of the problem.

From the Manager's Desk

Don't go after the Teflon co-worker on principle. Only make it an issue if you see it having a specific damaging effect. Keep in mind that most people can see through the Teflon co-worker's smoke.

Dealing with a Teflon co-worker is difficult at the best of times. All the usual rules apply if you want to try a direct approach: calm, not blaming, problem-solving focus, good timing, and so on. Frankly, I'm not sure that's going to work. And the indirect approach (using other team members to develop solutions or apply some subtle pressure) isn't likely to work either. Teflon people really don't believe they're at fault. So whether you talk to the person directly or more subtly, the teflon person won't recognize that the problem relates to him, or will deny it and do the teflon thing once again.

I think the main tactic here is to involve your boss (presumably the same boss as your co-worker). We'll come back to that in the next chapter. Before we leave this, again, always separate the annoying frustrating part from the actual factual problem. You're going to need to be calm and problem-focused when you approach the boss.

Backstabbers and Gossips

These are the folks who, either maliciously or out of habit, like to gossip or talk behind other people's backs. More often than not their intent is *not* malicious (at least for gossips). They just like to appear to be in the know. It enhances a false sense of worth on their part. Let's look at the backstabbers' situation, because it is more likely to be intentionally malicious.

This goes beyond annoying. So while you can use the other techniques we've described in this chapter, probably your first action needs to be to calm down. Do the positive self-talk. When you feel you're ready to make a direct approach, do it. This requires more firmness than some of the other situations, and it's likely going to end in a heated discussion. But let's face it: If you find that one of your fellow managers is running you down behind your back, you can't really allow this behavior to continue. So in you go. Your direct approach will contain any evidence you have regarding specific things the backstabber has said; dates and times are good. Then you give a firm request to stop right away. And couple that with any actions you'll take if it continues.

Here's how it might sound.

"Tom, I understand that you've been making some comments about my management ability to other people. While the information I have might not be completely accurate, that's not an acceptable way to do things around here. I would like you to stop making remarks about me to third parties and come directly to me if you have a problem, and maybe we can work it out. However, if I do hear that this is continuing, I'm going to have to bring this up with the vice president because it makes us all look bad."

This Won't Work!

Two things make situations worse with backstabbers: being aggressive and shouting or losing your temper, and arguing. Say what you have to say, and leave. The longer an argument goes on, the worse things will get.

This is assertive and relatively nonaggressive. It's not inviting argument, but if the person does argue, you have the choice to continue the discussion or end it, saying "OK, well, I've said what I needed to say, so there's no point continuing."

One important note to remember: It is possible your information isn't accurate. If you aren't sure it's true, then you have to check it out first with the alleged backstabber.

If that doesn't work, I think you need to go up higher in the hierarchy, although again, you can try the group pressure approach with the rest of the management team.

Gossips are usually not malicious and may not be aware that gossiping is actually harmful. If the gossip is about you, then you can request that it stop. You can provide real factual information about rumors. That tends to make gossip less satisfying.

If people want to gossip with you about other people, turn it off right away. Send the message that you don't engage in discussing rumors or gossip because it doesn't interest you. If it occurs at a social setting (like lunch or coffee), here's what you can say:

"If you guys want to talk about this, I think I'm going to excuse myself. I'm not really comfortable talking about others without them being here."

If they continue, then leave politely. Don't make a big deal out of it. Don't try to force them to stop. Just lead by example, and don't play the gossip, rumor, or backstabbing game.

Insider Secrets

Gossip and rumors tend to thrive in organizations that don't communicate information well internally. In an information vacuum, people create rumors and gossip to fill the void. If you see a good deal of rumormongering or gossip, see whether you can help create a system where communication is more open. When real information is available, there is less need to create false information.

You know what, though? That's easier said than done. Many of us really do like a good rumor or good gossip. But remember that when you condone gossip or rumor, you also condone gossip and rumor about *you* when you aren't around.

The Authority Underminers

Colleagues who undermine your authority tend to communicate with your staff and go around you. In most organizations, it's expected that if another manager needs to talk to someone in a different work unit, he or she goes through the manager of that unit. It's a courtesy, but it has a practical dimension. Managers need to know what goes on in their bailiwick, and when there is conversation going in all directions at different levels, it means you may not have the information you need.

From the Manager's Desk

If the issue is your manager's co-workers going around you, it's best handled through negotiating either one-on-one or in a group to come up with a flexible and practical solution about how to handle communication.

The drawback of having a rigid policy is that it slows things down and can make for less-efficient communication. It may eat away at your time. Maybe it isn't necessary that you be involved in such communication.

Some organizations set up very rigid communication rules. For example, in an information technology setting, employees were instructed that any requests for service, no matter how small, had to be directed to the manager, so he or she could decide whether to schedule the service. The result of that was that employees couldn't ever act directly, even if meeting another department's request would take only five minutes of time. The result was the information technology group became known for its lousy service, and other managers simply tried to get things done without their involvement.

Because this is mostly about communication and common understanding (as well as common sense) of how things should be done, it's best handled in the management team. Most of the time the kinds of communication that appear to undermine your authority with staff are not meant maliciously at all. They come from not thinking or wanting to get something done quickly. So first, don't assume it is nasty.

So, bring up the subject with all the managers at your level. Develop some guidelines that each of you agree to follow, and allow managers to have slightly different policies. It's perfectly OK for one manager to want to have things routed through her, while another manager may say "Heck, on these subjects, just go to my staff directly, but notify me after." Different managers need or want different things.

When all managers understand what each needs, then the potential for problems is dramatically reduced, as is the level of inter-manager conflict.

The Turf Warriors

The turf warriors are often referred to as empire builders. They grab projects, claim credit, and try to expand their staff and influence. They definitely aren't fun because

From the Manager's Desk

If you are around a turf builder, keep your eyes and ears open. Knowing what the turf builder is doing and trying to grab will at least help you make sure there aren't any surprises if the turf-builder targets you or your work unit.

they play internal politics constantly. Perhaps they're ambitious for promotion. Maybe it's just always trying to prove they're important. Who knows?

You have two major strategies to deal with turf warriors. One is to enter the game of turf fighting—that is, you use the same politicking and tactics of the turf warrior. Now, that's fine if you enjoy that kind of thing, but generally it's not good for the company. And if the other person is better at it than you (that's likely), then who knows what will happen? The truth is, you may lose and lose badly.

Your second option is to do the minimum required to protect yourself and your work unit but without entering into the turf warrior game. In other words, you ignore it to the extent you can. You work it another way. You protect yourself and your staff by getting the work done, and by making sure people know you are doing a good job by showing results. You win by being as good as you can be, and that's where you put

your effort. Spend less time worrying about that competitive S.O.B. turf warrior and more time getting better and making results happen.

Trying to approach turf warriors directly isn't likely to succeed. Turf warriors tend to be rather manipulative in nature, and covert in what they do. They aren't often going to admit to what they're doing. You do have the option of involving your common boss, however, which we'll talk about in the next chapter.

The Least You Need to Know

➤ Your first line of defense against annoying behavior is addressing your own re-actions.

➤ You can change your reactions and reduce stress by working to change your self-talk.

➤ Take responsibility for your emotional reactions.

➤ You can approach work-killers directly or indirectly via group pressure.

➤ Whatever your approach to work-killers, you must not personalize the prob-lem or get into blaming. Focus on problem solving.

Chapter 20

Real Conflict and What to Do About It

In This Chapter

➤ Two different kinds of conflict

➤ Is all conflict bad?

➤ The five ways to address conflict

➤ When different methods are best

➤ Disadvantages of various approaches

So far we've written about difficult people and difficult behavior as being bad, something we want to eliminate if possible. It's pretty obvious why. Difficult behavior in the workplace is aggravating and frustrating, and can affect things like employee morale, job satisfaction, productivity, and even employee health.

But there's something more here. Certain kinds of conflict can actually be healthy for organizations. Some conflict can improve productivity and job satisfaction. So we need to address a number of issues about conflict—the good, the bad, and even the ugly.

In this chapter we're going to talk about conflict, how to use conflict for good purposes, and the different methods available to you when you're faced with conflict with your coworkers or even your employees or boss.

Two Kinds of Conflicts

There are really two distinct types of conflict. The effects of each "flavor" are quite different. One can be used to improve the organization. The other rarely is useful for anything.

Substantive Conflict

Substantive conflict is conflict that occurs as a result of a real (or apparent) disagreement about how things should be done, who should do it, or similar areas. Its roots are based in the premise that two well-meaning people can sincerely disagree about something.

Employee Handbook

Substantive conflict is conflict that happens because there is a very real(or apparent) difference of opinion between two people. Two well-meaning people can sincerely disagree about what should be done or about how something should be done.

Let's take an example.

You and George are both managers at the same level. You've been asked to develop a computer system to automate order processing. Because you and George will both be using the system when it's complete, the idea is that you should *both* be major players in its development. Unfortunately, you hit a disagreement. You feel your company has the in-house ability to develop the computer system without going outside the company. George, however, is concerned that doing it internally will delay what is a high-priority solution, and wants to hire an outside computer company to get the work done quickly.

In fact, there are pros and cons to both strategies. Your major disagreement is about what constitutes the best course of action.

In a pure substantive conflict, you can have a complete lack of difficult behavior on both sides. In other words, neither side plays games or uses sneaky tactics to win. There is no dislike of the other person. If both parties are legitimately concerned with achieving the same goals, there need be no difficult behavior at all.

Personalized Conflict

Personalized conflict refers to conflict that has become focused on the other person's behavior, difficulty, personality, style, or other things that are not directly linked to a disagreement about business or task issues. The parties entertain a dislike and lack of respect for each other.

If you observe how parties in a personalized conflict behave, you'll see that they spend almost no time actually solving the original problem, but a lot of time rubbing each other the wrong way. In fact, it often appears that both parties have completely forgotten whatever issues need to be solved as they lobby for position, make destructive remarks, and generally run each other down. Usually personalized conflicts are more emotional than substantive conflicts.

You might be wondering how this kind of conflict relates to the theme of this book, difficult people. While substantive conflict, with two mature, sincere parties, can occur without difficult behavior, personalized conflict always involves difficult behavior. Because the parties forget they are there to solve real problems and not run each other down, they tend to both use difficult behaviors.

It's probably obvious to you that personalized conflict is often destructive, wastes time, and can have a negative impact in the workplace. After all, we have talked about many of the difficult tactics people use.

Employee Handbook

Personalized conflict refers to conflict that has little to do with a specific disagreement and almost everything to do with personality, style, or the way people see themselves being treated. In personalized conflict, the parties generally dislike each other or lack respect for each other as people.

Is Conflict Always Bad?

No, conflict is not always bad. In fact, I'll make the case that some conflict is actually beneficial to an organization. When we talk about the effects of conflict there are three categories. There's good conflict, bad conflict, and … well, there's ugly conflict. The behavior of the parties involves determines what you get: good, bad, or ugly. One other factor is the length of time the conflict continues. The longer the conflict continues, the more likely it will go from bad to ugly.

Conflict: The Good

So, how can conflict be good? Successful organizations (and successful managers) are always looking for ways to improve. One way to describe this is as a quest for continuous improvement. In today's markets, where change is so fast, an organization that doesn't move quickly and innovate is more likely to fall by the wayside. It's no longer possible to succeed over decades doing the same things in the same way. In case it hasn't occurred to you, the same applies to managers. Managers who do the same old thing over and over again often find they are doing the same old wrong things.

That means you need ideas. You need ways of doing things better or faster. Good conflict is handled in such a way that it creates new and better ideas through the process of resolving differences of opinion.

From the Manager's Desk

To create a situation where conflict will yield good results and great solutions, you need to assume the other person will discuss things in good faith and play fair. You might not be correct, but you *must* begin with that assumption.

251

Let's go back to our example of the computer system we described earlier. You believe the development should be in-house. George wants to go outside. In your discussions with George, you discover both of you have the same concerns: quality, speed of development, and cost. If you are both open and not being difficult about this conflict, you might find that neither of your initial opinions is perfect. If you can work together you might find that taking bits and pieces of each of the solutions and pulling them together gives you a much better solution.

So, in this case, you might decide to do the system development in-house but hire outside expertise on an as-needed basis. It's cheaper. It makes use of internal resources, but it also allows for adding some manpower and expertise when it's needed. So the conflict and disagreement has actually resulted in a better solution.

Insider Secrets

While substantive conflict and disagreements aren't always easy, they are often the raw materials from which new and better ideas emerge. An organization that has little substantive conflict is likely to be one that is uncreative, and not changing or adapting. For example, I was involved in a loud disagreement with a co-worker about the use of a parking space. He thought he should have it. I though I should. When things calmed down, we both realized that the system for allocating parking spots was faulty and needed to be made more specific and fairer. Everyone benefited when we changed the parking system.

Generally, the positive aspects of conflict can only occur when both parties stop using difficult behavior to win and people listen to each other and share the same underlying goals. If George wants to do the job in-house because he wants to create a personal empire and isn't concerned about cost or quality, then it will be difficult to have a positive outcome to the conflict. The same is true if either you or George starts backroom politicking to win. In a well-handled substantive conflict, everyone wins.

Conflict: The Bad

So, if good conflict is conflict where both parties keep sight of the objective—finding the best solution—and act in un-difficult ways, what is bad conflict?

Usually bad conflict emerges out of the potential for constructive conflict. It involves one or both parties acting difficult and obstructive but not in an extreme, all-out-war way. And generally, it occurs when a particular area or conflict issue has not been resolved. In other words, it's a running conflict.

Through lack of attention or other reasons, the conflict issues have nagged at both parties, so they get frustrated and begin to dislike each other, or at least behave like they dislike each other. There's more of an emphasis on trying to win, or perhaps giving up on the whole thing.

Apart from the frustration, this kind of long-term conflict doesn't add value for anyone, because it doesn't usually result in any creative solutions. Sometimes it never results in *any* solution.

This Won't Work!

Even with conflict that has gone down the bad path, you'd be amazed at how the situation can still be turned around if you keep focused on the issues, and don't get pulled into using any difficult tactics.

There are a few things to consider here. First, if bad conflict can emerge from good conflict situations over time, it's important to address substantive conflict as early as possible. Don't let the issue become a nagging one. Second, bad conflict can escalate into ugly conflict, which we will discuss in the next section. Third, it takes only one person to move a good conflict into a bad one or worse. That means it's absolutely essential you don't start acting difficult as you get frustrated. Keep your eye on the prize; work towards the best solution possible rather than acting out your frustrations.

Conflict: The Ugly

Ugly conflict is really personalized conflict. The issues have been lost. So much junk has occurred that whatever the original issue was, the parties are no longer looking to solve it, but to get back at each other or to win at all costs. The agenda has shifted.

We don't need to discuss this in much depth because we've already outlined many of the difficult behaviors people use, and boy, do they use them in a personalized, ugly-conflict situation. There's game playing. There's personal attacks and politicking. There's a lack of listening, and on and on. You don't want to go there.

From the Manager's Desk

With an ugly personalized conflict involving a co-worker, it may be necessary to look for some outside assistance. You might ask someone to mediate or even decide the issue. Often your boss is a good resource if he or she is willing and able.

As with the bad conflict situations, it takes only one person to push a conflict into this arena. So, make sure it's not you. Stay focused on the problem issue. Don't let your frustration turn you into a difficult person, because if you do, you can pretty much bet the other person is going to escalate and get more difficult.

Five Different Ways to Manage Conflict

Before we move onto talk about the different methods you can use to manage conflict with your co-workers, let's point out the difference between managing conflict and resolving conflict. Resolving a conflict refers to a situation where you have solved the damn thing once and for all. It's done, finito ... resolved. In our example with George, resolving the conflict might involve coming up with a solution both of you really like. Or it might involve George quitting and no longer being a party to the conflict. In either case, it's done.

Employee Handbook

Managing conflict is a process to reduce the negative outcomes of conflict and improve the chances that something good will come out of the conflict. Its purpose is not to make a conflict go away, but to improve the results.

Unfortunately, many conflicts can't be permanently and finally resolved. That's because it takes two to resolve something for good, and that willingness may not exist. So we talk about managing conflict. *Managing conflict* is a process we use to minimize the negative aspects and effects of the conflict and maximize the positive aspects and effects.

So, let's look at your conflict management options.

1: Avoidance and/or Denial

You can always choose to pretend there is no conflict occurring or to simply ignore it. We call the decision to ignore dealing with a conflict head on *avoidance*. We call pretending it doesn't exist *denial*. They aren't the same thing.

Denial is an approach a lot of people use when faced with conflict. Because some people are uncomfortable with any form of conflict, they choose to pretend everything is fine. They may actually believe there is no conflict situation. This is rarely smart. When you deny you are in a conflict situation and choose not to acknowledge it even to yourself, it's likely going to get worse. These things don't go away on their own. Also, not acknowledging there is a conflict going on means you can't think it through to pick the best course of action. Denial is never a good thing.

Avoidance is different, though. Some conflicts will go away if you just let the situation be.

Let's say that George, your co-worker, is going to be transferred to Australia in two weeks. Both you and George disagree about that old computer-system deal.

It doesn't take a rocket scientist to realize that the conflict with George is no longer going to be an issue. You won't be dealing with George again. So, why put in the time to use other techniques if there is no compelling need?

The difference between denial and avoidance is this: When you deny a conflict situation exists, you are doing so because of your discomfort dealing with it. When you make a deliberate decision to avoid taking action about the conflict, you do so because you have analyzed the situation, used your brain, and decided that on balance, it won't cost much to avoid it, and it may even be beneficial. Denial is a blind reaction, while avoidance is a calculated, thought-out strategy.

So, let's say you don't want to act blindly. When is it appropriate to avoid taking action with a conflict situation?

It is more appropriate to avoid a conflict situation when ...

➤ the conflict issue is minor or inconsequential.

➤ the conflict isn't in your bailiwick (it's really someone else's problem).

➤ the cost of taking more positive action is much higher than the cost of doing nothing.

➤ other, more active approaches aren't going to work.

➤ you aren't concerned about building a better relationship with the other party.

➤ the conflict is going to go away on its own.

This Won't Work!

Avoiding a conflict sounds so darn wimpy. John Wayne wouldn't do it. But sometimes it just makes sense. Don't let your ego stop you from backing away from a stupid, meaningless, unimportant fight. Don't you have better things to do?

You can see there is a lot of judgment involved here. You have to analyze the situation and decide what will be best for you and the company both in the short and long terms.

Are there situations where you should not avoid the conflict situation? Yes. These tend to be the flip sides of the factors above, but let's look at them.

It is not appropriate to avoid a conflict when ...

➤ the conflict issue is a serious or important one.

➤ you need to establish a better relationship with the other party.

➤ doing nothing is too costly or damaging.

➤ there are time constraints that push you to manage the conflict issue quickly.

➤ there is potential for the conflict to get ugly if ignored.

➤ the other party is constantly forcing the issue.

What's the bottom line? When you decide to avoid a conflict situation, make your decision based on thought. Consider the results of avoiding the situation with respect to the preceding list.

2: Giving In or Yielding

Giving in is another conflict-management option. It means going along with the other person's viewpoint, even though you may not agree with it. Sounds pretty weak, right? So let's think of it as yielding. You're driving along. You are about to merge onto a highway, and you see a huge semitrailer approaching. Forget who has the right of way ... you know this guy ain't stopping. Do you yield to the truck or do you force the issue?

If you have any brains, you'll yield. This isn't an ego thing, and it's not about winning. It's about getting the best result you can. In this case, you don't want to get mashed into little pieces.

Insider Secrets

It's amazing how much time people spend on arguing about conflict issues that have no particular significance whatsoever. Sometimes it seems like the less important the issue, the more intense the argument. If you really don't care about an issue, consider just yielding. Pick and choose your battles.

It's no different with conflict. Sometimes it just makes sense to go along. When?

It may be appropriate to give in or yield to another person when ...

➤ the other person is likely to get his or her way anyway.

➤ the other person has more formal or informal power.

➤ the conflict issue is not important to you.

➤ it's someone else's conflict (that is, something your boss should be dealing with anyway).

You'd be surprised at how many conflicts aren't worth a lot of your time. Giving in doesn't mean you are necessarily weak. It means that the issue just isn't important to you.

When is yielding not a good approach? It may not be appropriate to yield when ...

➤ the conflict issue is important.

➤ the other person's position is damaging to you, the company, or other people.

➤ you feel other methods may be workable.

When there are other alternatives, the issues are too important to just give in, or there is damage taking place, it's best to hold your ground or at least try to work out a solution together.

3: Compromise: Give a Little, Take a Little

Compromise is a strategy that is more active and involved than our previous methods. It involves some negotiating with the other party. It involves being prepared to give up a little bit of what you want in exchange for things the other party gives up.

Essentially, *compromise* means that neither of you will get all of what you want, but both of you will get something of what you want. During a compromise negotiation, the two parties are still working in adversarial mode—that is, each person is trying to get the best deal. So in this sense it isn't a completely cooperative process. It's an "I'll-give-you-this-if-you-give-me-that" kind of thing.

Employee Handbook

Essentially, **compromise** refers to a give-and-take process. You give up something, and the other person gives up something, until you hit a solution that both can live with. Neither of you will get all of what you want, but both of you will get something of what you want. In compromise mode, the two parties are still working in adversarial mode.

Here's something you should know. Because the process is still adversarial, new creative solutions aren't likely to come out of compromising. Also, while you can unilaterally avoid a conflict situation or unilaterally yield in a conflict situation, compromise takes two. If one person gives up stuff and the other person refuses, well, it's not really compromise, is it?

Compromise is appropriate when ...

➤ you don't really need a creative solution but simply *a* solution.

➤ the other person shows a willingness to give up some things in exchange for you doing the same.

➤ the cost of compromise isn't too high.

It is unlikely to be a wise choice if ...

➤ you need a creative or innovative situation.

➤ it makes no sense to implement a partial solution.

➤ the other party refuses to give away anything.

➤ the issue is just too important.

You can see that no approach to conflict fits all situations. Compromise is used often because most people have some sense of how to negotiate this kind of solution.

4: Competition or Power-Based

One of the more commonly used methods of addressing conflict is to try to convince the other person you are right or use a power-based approach. While avoidance and compromise sound wimpy, competing or using power to get one's own way sure sounds … well, manly, doesn't it?

In fact, competing or trying to create an "I win—you lose" scenario is probably way overused in the workplace. Why? Because even if you manage to win, you may alienate the other person so that you create a situation where future conflicts can quickly become personalized ones. And that's not good.

Insider Secrets

You bully someone into giving up the fight. Hurrah! You win. Or do you? What's going to happen the next time? If the person has lost face or holds lasting anger about your use of a competitive or power-based approach, he's likely to be out to get you the next time. That's a huge drawback of relying on competition or power—the loser gets mad.

Competing to win or the use of power takes on several forms. The simplest one is trying to convince, argue, and assert your position. It's really trying to get your way. In competition mode, you might use other techniques if that doesn't work. For example, if you have formal authority, you might use that to make a decision, and ignore dissent. Or you may lobby, get support from others, and exert pressure on the other party to give in. For example, you might get the support of your boss.

If you are a sharp reader, you will realize that using a power-based or competitive approach can be perceived by others as being difficult or even playing dirty pool. In some situations, it is. So, you have to be careful with this one. It may be appropriate when …

➤ you need a quick decision.

➤ you have the power to make that decision.

➤ you feel strongly about the issue.

➤ you can garner support if you need it.

➤ you aren't concerned about having a good relationship with the other party.

It's really not a good option if …

➤ you use it too often.

➤ you need to develop a good relationship with the other person.

➤ you don't have a hope in hell of succeeding.

If you have enough power and clout, a power-based solution can be the fastest way to move past the conflict or get things in motion. However, the use of power generally creates other long-term fallout and bad feelings.

5: Collaborative Win-Win Method

The conflict-management methods we have presented are designed to help you live with a conflict situation, minimize the downside, and increase the upside. However, they aren't the tools most likely to create new innovation, new ideas, and a higher level of productivity.

A collaborative approach is designed to achieve these goals. What is a collaborative approach?

A *collaborative approach* is often called a win-win situation because the parties look for and achieve a solution that may exceed the expectations of both of the parties. They work towards that by defining the problem, negotiating, and generally working together towards a set of stated common goals.

You might wonder why a collaborative approach isn't used more often because it can yield such wonderful results. There are a lot of reasons.

1. Collaboration takes longer than, let's say, using a power-based approach. It requires an investment of time and a dollop of patience.

2. Of all the methods, collaboration is the most demanding in terms of interpersonal skills and use of analysis to solve problems. Because many people lack these skills, it's not surprising the method doesn't come to mind.

3. Collaboration requires a great deal of self-discipline. The collaborative process requires the ability to see things from another person's perspective and to cope with the frustration that can arise from the process. It means *not* venting out those frustrations, and staying focused on the problem, not the actions or style of the other person.

Employee Handbook

A **collaborative approach** is often called a win–win situation because the parties look for and achieve a solution that may exceed the expectations of both of the parties. By being creative, defining the real problem, and by negotiating and working together, the parties may come up with a brand-new approach to the problem that neither, by themselves, would have developed.

4. It takes two. You can avoid a conflict on your own by simply doing nothing. You can impose your preferred solution using a power-based approach, provided you have enough clout. But with collaboration, and to a lesser degree, compromise, both parties need to be able to move off their original positions. Both need some degree of openness.

From the Manager's Desk

After you and the other party in the conflict have agreed about the ultimate goals or results you want to achieve, the task is really well on its way to success. That's a starting point: Find the points of agreement.

So, when is a collaborative approach appropriate? It fits when …

➤ the company needs to find new solutions to problems, and not Band-Aid solutions.

➤ both parties are willing to define and work towards achieving common goals.

➤ both parties are not so angry they can't work together to develop new solutions.

➤ both parties have the needed skills.

➤ there is sufficient time to collaborate, because it tends to take a while.

➤ the problem issue is important enough to warrant a significant degree of time investment.

It's probably not a good fit when …

➤ the problem isn't very important.

➤ one or both parties lacks willingness or skill.

➤ there is a significant lack of respect or dislike on one side or the other.

Want to learn a bit more about collaborating? Here are some tips and suggestions.

Keep in mind that your goal is not to win, and the other person needn't lose. To achieve that, you must work together. There are two steps to start with.

First, define what it is you are trying to achieve by addressing the problem at the root of the conflict. De-cide that for yourself, independent of the other party. Be prepared to put that information on the table, so there are no hidden agendas operating from your side.

The second opening step is to listen. To collaborate, both people need to understand each other. The only way you are going to understand what the other person wants or needs is to listen carefully, and to verify you understand through a reflective listening or rephrasing process. If the other person has difficulty articulating his or her position and needs, then use questions to tease that information out.

If your positions are very different, work backwards until you find at least one principle or goal you can both agree on. Focus on hitting that agreed-upon goal.

For example:

> In a dispute about whether to outsource or use in-house resources for a computer system, the two parties may disagree on the method, but agree that the priorities are to get the job done on time, and do it as cheaply as possible. After it's established the solution has to address these needs, then the creative work can begin. It can work.

The best collaborative efforts tend to be wide-open efforts to generate as many ideas as possible. After you have some common goals agreed upon and you've waded through any bad feelings that might crop up, it's time to get those ideas popping. Try making a list of ideas together. Don't rule out or evaluate any of them until later. Just get them out on the table. Then, when you can't think of any other ways that might solve the problem, go through them one by one to see whether each one is reasonable or not.

Remember, it doesn't matter whose idea ends up getting implemented. Your goal is to find the best solution possible.

The Least You Need to Know

➤ Substantive conflict is about issues, while personalized conflict has lost its way in personalities.

➤ Conflict can be a good thing and revitalize companies and organizations if handled well.

➤ Avoiding a conflict can work if the issue isn't very important.

➤ Compromise involves both parties giving up things, so neither will get everything they want.

➤ Competitive or power-based approaches often leave one party much angrier than before.

➤ Collaboration is the best way to use conflict to maximum benefit, but it isn't always the best path.

Chapter 21

Getting Help from Others, Including the Boss

In This Chapter

➤ The importance of long-term boss cultivation

➤ How do you cultivate the boss?

➤ How to approach the boss for help

➤ When should you involve the boss?

➤ Other resources

➤ How to mobilize other managers

Whatever the difficult situation, your boss can be your biggest help and ally—or your biggest problem. Nowhere is that more true than in dealing with difficult co-workers at the same level as you in the hierarchy. That's because you have no formal authority over your co-workers, and if negotiation and attempts to directly work out problems fail, your boss may be the only one who can really help out. He or she may have enough authority to bring about a solution. Or destroy you.

In this chapter we're going to talk about how you involve your boss in a problem with a co-worker (or for that matter, an employee). But apart from those tactics, we're going to talk about something much more important—creating a permanent relationship with your boss so he or she will be there to help when you need it. I call it *boss cultivation*.

Boss Cultivation—The Long Approach

If you have a problem that requires the assistance of your boss, which of the following situations will be the most beneficial?

This Won't Work!

Your boss will be a poor ally if he or she doesn't know you well or doesn't have a positive relationship with you. Cultivating the boss is necessary. It's like putting money in the bank so it will be there when you need it.

From the Manager's Desk

Boss cultivation means having the boss get to know you and develop respect for your contributions, integrity, and character. It is a long-term process.

You have established a long-term positive relationship with your boss so the boss respects your work, values your judgment and integrity, and knows your value.

or

The boss doesn't really know you very well, perceives you as just another employee, or hasn't had much personal contact with you.

I know which one of these bosses I want at the plate when I'm stuck or can't solve a problem by myself. I want the person who knows me, respects me, and values my work—not because he or she is necessarily going to take my side in a dispute, but because the boss who respects me will know I'm looking for help for the right reasons. The boss who knows me knows I don't hold grudges. He knows I have the company's interests at heart. He knows me as a straight shooter. That's what I want.

Of course, if you're a sneaky, manipulative scuzzball, then maybe you *don't* want your boss to know you very well. But this book isn't written for you (fine time to tell you that).

So how do you place yourself so that your boss can help when it's needed?

Boss-Cultivation Principles

Imagine you feel hungry … really, really hungry. But hey, there's no food in the refrigerator and all the stores are closed. What can you do? You go out to your garden and plant some seeds for some vegetables—a few tomato plants, six or seven potatoes. Then you stand there waiting so you can eat.

This is obviously really silly. You know you have to plant your garden way in advance of the time you'll be hungry. You have to water it and take care of the plants and you have to fertilize the garden if you want the food when you need it. It's no different with your boss.

1. The first principle of boss cultivation is that you have to plant early and nurture the relationship so when you really need help, it's there. Maybe even a little fertilizer, but you don't want to shovel … er, cover the boss in … well, you understand.

2. You will get more help if you have a track record of making the boss look good. That is, you do your job with a minimum of fuss. You don't whine. You don't complain. You just get things done. You cause little trouble and add lots of value.

3. If you have a poor relationship with your boss and have to deal with a co-worker problem, you may be faced with a situation where the co-worker has a better relationship with the boss than you do. And that spells serious trouble for you.

4. While some people can succeed in creating relationships with the boss through things like flattery, butt kissing, and other unpleasant techniques, generally those things don't create respect. People eventually see through this stuff and are less likely to help when they feel someone is not very genuine or tries to curry favor. So you're going to build your relationship over time by acting with integrity, not playing games or sucking up, but by being helpful, useful, and an upright corporate citizen.

5. Bosses don't want to intervene in all kinds of problems they feel you should be able to handle. After all, you were promoted to manager so you would manage, not weasel out of difficult situations. You only want to involve your boss when it's absolutely necessary. If you look for help infrequently, it will probably be there when you really need it.

From the Manager's Desk

Your boss will be more prepared to support you if you have built a strong, solid relationship over time, based on respect and the fact that you are a valued employee who makes good things happen.

This Won't Work!

There is a limit to how often you go to the boss for help with problems you should be able to deal with yourself. Think of your boss as a bank of goodwill. You can only withdraw so much before the account is empty. Don't overdraw your account.

OK, so it's pretty clear, isn't it? If you need to involve your boss, you'd better have a good relationship based on respect. And that comes from doing a good job, showing you have integrity and that you aren't trying to manipulate or profit at the expense of others.

Is it possible to build a relationship with your boss in other ways? Sadly, yes. Some bosses aren't very bright or very effective, so they are vulnerable to flattery or may be convinced to conspire with you to get "even" with someone. Am I going to tell you how to build these false relationships? No. If you want to build relationships using deviousness rather than integrity, you'll have to figure it out without me. Because, to be blunt, those who fight with the sword die by it. Sooner or later, if you fight dirty, you'll come across someone who is better at it and more devious, and then you'll get what you deserve.

When to Involve the Boss

Keeping in mind we don't want to overdraw our "account" with the boss, when does it make sense to involve him or her? It comes down to a general rule. You only involve the boss (and take up his or her valuable time) when it's absolutely necessary to resolve a problem. If your co-worker (or employee) is late for meetings a few times, should you involve the boss? Probably not. If you're just annoyed with a co-worker about his difficult behavior and it isn't affecting anything seriously, what then? No. The expectation is you should handle these things yourself.

If you go to the boss with trivial stuff or even just to vent, you'll look foolish and overdraw your account.

What if a co-worker commits an illegal act—maybe theft or some form of harassment? You're in your boss's office like a flash. In fact, that's the first place you go. You don't try and work it out with a criminal. You lay the responsibility where it belongs, and that would be with your boss.

Unfortunately, like most things, it's not black and white. There are lots of shades of gray.

There is another factor you need to consider. Bosses differ in terms of when they want to be involved in problems. Some like to be informed of almost everything. Some are indeed flattered if you come for help. But some are the exact opposite. They don't want to see you unless absolutely necessary because they are already overworked. They expect you to do your job without help.

Forget trying to classify everything as right or wrong here. You have to know your boss well enough to figure out whether or not to ask for help or to keep him or her informed. That's part of the long-term relationship thing. If you establish a good long-term relationship with your boss, either you already know or you can just ask, "Do you want to be involved in this situation?"

This Won't Work!

Some managers have good relationships with the boss and feel comfortable venting their frustrations about a specific situation. That may overdraw the account. Vent to your wife, your friends if you have to. Don't vent to the boss.

From the Manager's Desk

There's no substitute for knowing and understanding your boss, because each person is different. Figure out what your boss needs and wants, and you'll do much better when you need help.

Here are some things to ask yourself before seeking help from the boss:

➤ Have I tried to work with the problem co-worker and hit a brick wall?

➤ Do I need the authority and clout of my boss to solve this problem?

➤ Is the problem associated with some bottom-line result? Can I demonstrate that the problem is important?

➤ Is my boss likely to perceive my request for help positively or negatively? Will it overdraw my account?

Approaching Smart—Involving Smart

Let's say you've tried to work out a problem with a co-worker, a serious problem, and you need the involvement of the boss because your co-worker won't listen to anyone else. You feel your boss will be predisposed to help because you can demonstrate that the co-worker is causing significant bottom-line damage.

So, how do you involve the boss in a smart way? How do you approach the boss?

The Approach Process

While bosses differ in how they can be best approached, we can make at least a few generalizations here. If you follow these principles and tactics you are far more likely to succeed.

First, your approach needs to involve laying out the facts of the issue or problem and how the situation is having a clear and obvious effect on things that may be important to the boss. Usually bottom-line impacts or impacts on the quality of work or customer service work well. But there may be other effects you might want to use. For example, if you know your boss has a thing for teamwork and harmony, you can use that. If your boss doesn't give a rat's butt about teamwork, then it's not something you should mention.

From the Manager's Desk

First things first: Explain the facts of the issue and the consequences of the problem in ways your boss will understand and value. Don't count on the consequences being obvious.

There's no substitute for knowing your boss.

You need to stick to the facts and focus on the effects in terms of what the boss values so that it's clear that you aren't asking for help to "get" the other person. Your motivation should never appear to be revenge or personal dislike. It should be about the company's success, getting work done, and even your boss's success.

If you cut corners, don't present a fair factual account of the problem, and appear vindictive, you have about a 50–50 chance of turning your boss against you.

Second, after you have presented the basic information, do not provide the solution to the boss unless you are asked for it or you are sure that's what the boss wants (again, know thy boss). Why? If you say, "Boss, fire this guy" or "Please go read the riot act," you'll appear to be using the boss as an instrument under your control. That's not a good thing. If your boss feels manipulated, then you end up worse off than when you started.

The trick here is to lay it out and ask for advice rather than immediately offer a course of action you want the boss to take.

Here's an example of an approach.

> Here are the players. Liz is the V.P. to whom Jack and Jill report. Jill has been having trouble getting information from Jack about their joint project, and from what Jill can figure, Jack is behind schedule and stonewalling. She's talked to Jack, but Jack turned really nasty in the private meeting.

> After considering whether this was worth involving Liz, she decides the project was too important to allow the problem to continue. So she arranges a meeting with Liz.

> After the usual pleasantries, Jill begins:

> "Liz, I've hit a problem on the XYZ project, which I know you've said is really important. I'm not sure what to do here and need some advice. Last Monday I tried to get a status update from Jack about his end and couldn't get much concrete information. I don't know where we're at. I've having some trouble getting along with him, in any event, but my concern is we get this done on time because if we don't, we're going to be at a competitive disadvantage."

This Won't Work!

If you make a request that sounds as if you're spiteful or vengeful and your boss doesn't share your desire to "get" the other party, you're probably in real trouble.

At this point Jill stops, to permit Liz to think and to comment or offer help. Let's say Liz asks what Jill needs. Jill continues:

"I need the status information, target dates, that kind of thing. The sooner, the better. And I need some regular communication."

Then if things go well, Liz provides the needed help. Liz says:

"OK, I'll get the information from Jack before lunch, and then we'll set up a regular status meeting with the three of us, OK?"

That's how it works when it works well.

So, let's see what Jill did:

➤ She focused on the problem, not the interpersonal conflict.

➤ She presented the basic facts without embellishment.

➤ She referenced the consequences (competitive disadvantage).

➤ She left room for the boss to offer the help and to come up with solutions.

➤ Although she's frustrated, she remained calm and objective.

That's what works.

Smart Involvement

Well, we've mapped out an ideal scenario. But what happens if your boss doesn't offer to help or says, "Work it out. That's what we pay you for." That does happen.

Insider Secrets

Bosses don't always bite on the first approach. Don't give up just because you didn't get an immediate offer of help. Sometimes boss intervention can be more complicated to the boss than it appears to you (oh, those internal politics). Some managers also need to think it through.

At the initial meeting you can offer additional reasons why it's best if the boss helps out, but don't push it. Now's not the time if you have hit the wall. What you can do is let it go for a few days and try again later. Who knows? You might find the boss in a more receptive mood, or the first meeting might have seeped into his skull over time.

Be a little more forceful in the second meeting. Make the consequences of inaction clear and obvious. If the boss still doesn't want to get involved, ask for advice. "What would you do?" you might ask, or "How would you handle this?"

There are several reasons for this. You may get some good advice. And if you follow it, you're really doing what the boss suggests. That gives you more leverage. Second, it kicks the problem back into the boss's lap for at least a moment. And finally, it encourages the boss to think.

You may suggest some specific action you think the boss might be willing to take. If the boss doesn't come up with solutions, then you need to suggest a few. Usually your suggestions need to involve minimal time, effort, and complication for your boss.

Beyond that, it's not likely you'll get much farther if you are refused twice.

Just for your information, here are some of the things bosses can do:

➤ Have an informal word with an employee

➤ Get information you can't get

➤ Host a meeting with all parties attending

➤ Start a formal mediation process

➤ Make an executive binding decision

➤ Help to set ground rules

Don't count on your boss to think up these things. If your boss can't see how he or she can intervene, you might want to offer several options.

Help from Other Sources

I wish I could give you a foolproof solution to deal with difficult colleague situations when your boss opts out of the process or otherwise refuses to help. I can't, because so much depends on your circumstances.

However, there may be other sources you can access, but generally the more outsiders you involve, the more you put yourself at risk.

How you approach other resources will be virtually identical to the way you might approach your boss. The process and principles are similar whether you're going to the human resources department or up the ladder to the boss's boss. Just be aware that if you do so, you will probably fracture any trust you have with your current boss. Is it worth it?

Let's talk about the use of other peers or managers. That's a bit safer than going outside or going over your boss's head. Ideally, you want to mobilize the support of other managers so they might put a word in with the other difficult party, most likely in an informal way. And sometimes a person who is difficult with you may be more receptive to an approach from another uninvolved and neutral colleague.

In approaching other managers, don't ask them to intervene. Don't push them. Just lay out the facts and the consequences calmly and ask for advice. Otherwise you're likely to set up two camps that may engage in guerrilla warfare, and nobody benefits.

If they choose to speak informally to the other colleague, that's their decision. You didn't put them up to it or lobby them. If they help, it will be because they see it's in everyone's best interest to solve the problem and get the job done.

If the situation with your difficult colleague has become intolerable and must be addressed somehow, then you can look at the mediation process, which we talked about earlier in the book. What you'll need is an experienced mediator who can help both parties identify and clarify the problem and solve it together.

There are two ways to do this. If your boss doesn't want to be directly involved, see whether you can get the boss to at least authorize such a process and put some pressure on the difficult colleague to enter into it. That's not perfect, but it can work.

This Won't Work!

When trying to get help from other peers or comanagers, don't push and don't try to get them on your side. Taking sides is the last thing you want unless you want to fight. And this kind of fight tends to make losers of everyone.

Or you can approach the difficult colleague on your own. Here's what you might say:

> "Jack, it seems like whenever we work together we somehow rub each other the wrong way and end up arguing. I know it's uncomfortable for me, and it's certainly making things difficult for both of us. I have an idea. What do you think about meeting with a mediator to help us unravel this so we can at least work together without being at each other's throats?"

You may have to explain the process and identify someone who can play the mediation role.

One thing to remember: Mediation is most useful when the investment of time is worth it for both of you. If it's a single minor issue, mediation probably isn't merited. If you've had a long-running feud with a colleague and you have to work together in the future, then it makes much more sense.

Where do you find mediators? Your human resources department may be able to help. Or, if you have an employee assistance program (EAP) in place, a counselor may either offer mediation services directly or be able to suggest someone.

Knowing When You Are in Big Trouble

What if you can't get support from anywhere? First, answer these questions: Is the issue trivial? Have you overreacted and made a mountain out of a molehill? Is this problem with your colleague really a serious one?

Insider Secrets

If you're looking for a professional to help you in a mediation situation, you can check your area to see whether there are any experts in Alternate Dispute Resolution techniques. It's called ADR for short and is becoming more available and more common. Outside mediators bring a lot to the table. They are objective and uninvolved, have highly developed facilitation skills that most of us lack, and don't have any baggage that can interfere with finding a good solution.

This Won't Work!

When you have a serious situation and can get no commitment from your boss to help you resolve it, you may have to face the fact that you may never get what you need from your boss. Simply, you may be in big trouble over the long term at your job.

If it is a serious issue and you haven't overreacted, then you have to face facts. For whatever reason, you are in a situation where you lack the support and the supporting cast you need to do a good job. Maybe your boss thinks you're a troublemaker or incompetent, or just doesn't like you.

If you consistently lack the support of your boss regarding difficult colleagues and in other areas (resources, scheduling, and so on), not only do you have a difficult colleague but probably a difficult boss.

If you are in this unfortunate situation, you have to consider the obvious. Can you live with this if it is a permanent state of affairs? Is it worth fighting your boss in the future? Is it worth putting your job on the line by going up the hierarchy, and do you have the stomach for it?

It really comes down to being realistic, deciding what you can live with and what you can't live with, and preparing for the future.

Sometimes working for a boss who won't support you in getting your job done just isn't worth it. Maybe it's time to do some career planning. You need to decide.

The Least You Need to Know

➤ You can't get help from a boss who doesn't know you very well.

➤ Cultivate the boss. Build a bank balance of good will.

➤ Use the boss resource only if absolutely necessary.

➤ The approach is critical. Facts and consequences need to be presented, not emotions.

➤ Stay away from personal attacks. Stay focused.

➤ You can mobilize other managers to help if you are subtle.

Chapter 22

Knowing Your Communication Media

In This Chapter

➤ How different communication media work

➤ When you need to work face-to-face

➤ The limitations of e-mail

➤ How to use e-mail more effectively

➤ Can e-mail cause conflict?

Think for a moment about the communication delivery methods you have at your disposal. You can write a letter or a shorter memo to a colleague or your boss. You can pick up the phone and you can talk in person. You can communicate within a group context or one on one. You can fax or you can use e-mail. There are a lot of choices.

Most people use a variety of methods without realizing that each media type works differently. The dynamics of e-mail communication are quite different from, let's say, a telephone conversation or a face-to-face conversation. Each medium has different pros and cons.

It's good to know these differences and how to use each medium when it is appropriate. It's probably even more important to understand the differences when dealing with difficult colleagues or, for that matter, when you're communicating about any difficult conflict situation. So that's what this chapter is about. We'll talk briefly about the pros and cons of letters, e-mail, and face-to-face communication. We'll focus on the newest method of communication, e-mail or electronic communication.

How Communication Media Differ

Here's a test. You're in a conflict situation with a colleague. You can communicate via letter, on the phone, or via e-mail. Of these three, which is most likely to result in someone saying something that is likely to escalate the conflict?

If you chose e-mail, you are correct. People tend to say things in e-mail that they wouldn't put down on paper or say on the phone or to one's face.

Let's try another. In a disagreement situation, which media are most likely to make it easier to come up with some kind of win-win solution? Face-to-face communication, phone conversation, a letter, or e-mail? Which is worst?

Did you choose either face-to-face or the phone? Either of those is probably correct, although face-to-face is probably a bit better. What about the worst? If you choose either a letter or e-mail, those are good answers.

The point here is that different media are good for different things. The medium actually affects how communication works. It's not that there are good media or bad, but some communication methods are better than others for a specific purpose.

But how do different communication methods differ? Let's look.

This Won't Work!

Ignore how different communication media work, and you're likely to increase the frequency and intensity of difficult situations with your colleagues, boss, and even total strangers.

Speed of Communication

Communication methods differ in terms of speed, but it's more complicated than you think. Some methods, like e-mail, have fast delivery—that is, after you send the communication, it gets to the recipient very quickly. Letters, on the other hand, are slow. A fax would be considered fast.

But there are two more components to the rate of communication. One is the speed at which people create the message. E-mail is a fast creation medium—that is, people tend to write e-mail very quickly. On the other hand, people create material written on regular paper much more slowly. They tend to edit and try to get just the right phrasing before they send it. Face-to-face and telephone communication are the fastest.

Finally, there is the speed at which people read the communication. Do they take their time understanding the message, or do they dash through it? Face-to-face communication generally involves less absorption, because real-time conversation happens so fast. E-mail is next. People don't read e-mail received on a screen like they would read a letter. They read much more quickly and often don't take the time to absorb it all. Letters and written communication are the slowest. People tend to read letters more carefully, think about the content, and reread if it's necessary.

Insider Secrets

Although we live in a fast-food world, fast communication is often not good communication. With that speed comes a higher likelihood that the message will be misunderstood. The faster messages are created and the faster they are received, the more likely there will be miscommunication. And that means more conflict. Why? Because speed means less thought. The faster the communication, the less people think about what they communicate, and the less people read carefully. That results in misunderstandings.

Interactivity of Communication

Interactivity refers to the degree to which two people can interact in real time. For example, sitting in the same room talking, both people can communicate with each other immediately. There isn't much of a time gap between what one person says and the other person says. People respond to each other immediately. Telephones are similar. Letters are the least interactive. One person sends the letter. There's a gap of time for delivery. Then the other person reads and responds. The process can take several days.

E-mail is somewhere in the middle. It's like a fast exchange of letters, but sometimes it can be just as slow, depending on how quickly each party responds. That actually can be a problem if each person in an e-mail conversation participates at a different pace. When one person wants it to go fast and the other wants it to go slow, conflict results.

Employee Handbook

Interactivity refers to the degree to which two people can interact in real time. A highly interactive process allows both parties to communicate information to each other at the same time, as in a face-to-face situation. A less-interactive process only allows communication in sequence, one at a time. That's the case with e-mail.

Spontaneity and Formality

Some communication methods encourage spontaneity in communication. For example, when you talk face-to-face, you don't spend a great deal of time planning out what you're saying. You say what pops into your head. Same with the phone. When you write a letter or a memo, you tend to think it out.

E-mail is kind of the oddball here. While it might seem logical that it would be like writing a letter, it's not. It's a far more spontaneous medium than letter writing. In fact, most people treat e-mail like a real-time conversation.

This Won't Work!

Don't expect e-mail communication to be like written communication. Most people write e-mails like they speak—informally, complete with grammar mistakes, slang, and misspelling. Don't criticize their grammar and spelling, any more than you would criticize someone's spoken English over a beer at the bar.

Formality has to do with the language we use. Generally we don't write the way we speak. We write far more formally than we speak, using less slang and paying more attention to correct sentence structures and such. Letters tend to be more formal. E-mail can be either, but is usually much closer to spoken speech than written communication. Most unrehearsed talking communication tends to be informal. The exception would be formal presentations that are written out. So, why am I telling you all this? Because these differences affect which communication method is best for what circumstances. For example, because e-mail is fast and tends to be informal and spontaneous, it's useful for the exchange of information but not very good for resolving emotional issues or creating good solutions to complex problems.

Next, we're going to look at the different communication media and map out when they are best used in dealing with difficult situations.

From the Manager's Desk

Face-to-face communication is the best way to deal with complex problem solving or emotionally laden issues, although it can be uncomfortable.

Face-to-Face and Telephone Communication

Face-to-face communication is fast in all respects. Messages are delivered immediately, and people speak quickly and often understand badly. However, face-to-face is also highly interactive. It's also usually informal.

So, what's it good for? And are there situations where it isn't so good?

Face-to-face communication is probably the best choice for figuring out how to solve a problem or disagreement. If, for example, you have a disagreement with a colleague and you wish to come up with a win-win solution, then face-to-face is the best method (telephones are OK, also). Why? Because problem solving works best when you can interact.

You aren't bound by formal communication rules, and you can work quickly provided both parties are willing and able to communicate positively. Also, because both parties are physically able to see each other, that helps develop understanding about emotional states, because body language (smiles, frowns, and so on) can be seen immediately.

However, with those advantages come some problems. When emotions run high and people aren't in control of their expressions and behavior, there is a tendency to have very heated and emotional conversations because face-to-face communication is so fast and so spontaneous. That's both a good thing and a bad thing. It means some face-to-face conversations can be uncomfortable, until the emotions cool down. The good thing is that the release of that emotion can be worked through. Very few highly charged emotional situations are resolved via an exchange of letters, but they can be resolved face-to-face.

Also, because of the fast pace of face-to-face communication, people don't always hear everything that's said, so understanding can be a problem. You can't re-hear something the other person said. It's said, then it's gone.

So, when is face-to-face a good choice?

When issues are very complex and understanding of details is critical, face-to-face should be augmented by some written material. Ideally, precede the conversation with a written document that contains an agenda. Both parties should prepare by reading the document (when that's possible).

When you need a quick resolution, face-to-face is the most productive method of communication, provided you don't get bogged down in negative conversations. That's because it's interactive and misunderstandings can be clarified immediately. That's especially important when you are negotiating in a give-and-take situation.

When you have a highly sensitive situation where emotions are high, face-to-face conversation is a good idea because it is less cold. For example, it is best to notify people of a layoff in person and not through a letter or e-mail.

From the Manager's Desk

Consider using multiple communication methods. For example, negotiations generally use a combination of face-to-face and written communication. Face-to-face allows good problem solving, but points might get lost or forgotten. Get the conclusions written down.

Written Communication

Written communication (stuff on paper) is probably the opposite of face-to-face communication in most respects. It takes longer to create the message. Its delivery is delayed. And it's slower when the other person receives the message. It's also more formal and less spontaneous.

From the Manager's Desk

When there *is* little urgency and it is important that each party understand details and complexities of an issue, the written word (on paper) is probably a good choice. Sometimes speed is *not* a good thing.

So what are the pluses? Because it's slower, it's a better way to communicate details than other media. People take their time reading and understanding, and they can reread. Provided the message is well written and complete, it should be easy to interpret. If my goal is to tell someone how to design a bridge or a nuclear reactor, then I'd better include paper communication, rather than to rely only on face-to-face conversation!

Written communication is also the recognized way to keep records of conversations. If you need to document what you've said and what the other person has said, the on-paper process allows you to do that in a way that is official and legal.

Because written communication is slower and more formal, people tend to be less abusive when they write. People know a letter or memo is a permanent record, so they are less willing to say really nasty things.

On the minus side, it's really hard to solve complex problems via letters because the process is so slow. You can't brainstorm or throw around a bunch of ideas or interact.

Written communication is also a kind of arm's-length communication. It's hard to use the written word to create great relationships or convey emotion. So if the issue is to build relationships, then other forms of communication are better. That's why it isn't a good idea to fire someone via letter. Because it's perceived as arm's length, such an action would be seen as cold, heartless, and even cowardly.

So, when is the written (on paper) method useful and when is it not?

When you have complicated details, paper is still the best method to use. There's no need to restrict yourself to the written word only, of course, but the more complicated the issue, the more important the on-paper stuff becomes.

When you have worked through a conflict with other methods (like face-to-face) and want to make sure that both sides understand and agree with the conclusions or solutions, then include a written component. It's like a letter of understanding.

Written communication is also important if there is some legal or other need to have a formal record or documentation of the communication between you and the other person. For example, if you want to reprimand an employee, then you would do so face-to-face, but you would also want to document the conversation on paper.

When is it not so useful? As the primary method to solve a complex problem, it is lacking—too slow, too formal. As a means to build better relationships, it's weak. And of course, if there is a need to solve issues right away, it takes too long.

From the Manager's Desk

Written communication, because it does not involve face-to-face contact, can be perceived as a cowardly way to communicate about issues that may be emotional. That's why it shouldn't be used alone when emotions may run high.

E-mail Communication—A Brave New World

Now we get to the most interesting of communication media—e-mail, or communication on the Internet or via computer.

Insider Secrets

E-mail and voice mail are two newer communication methods that are both blessings and curses. Many people are finding that these technologies increase the volume of communication so it actually takes longer to get back to people and takes up more time. It's the price of technology, I suppose. Just because you can use them, doesn't mean you should.

We're going to spend the rest of the chapter on this one, for one simple reason. Most of us understand letters. We understand direct conversations and phone conversations. We've grown up with them. But few of us have grown up with e-mail, so we don't understand it as well. And we need to.

E-mail requires a different way of communicating; let's start off with how it's different.

> ➤ **E-mail is fast.** It gets delivered fast, it gets written fast, and it gets read fast. We treat it like we treat either letter writing or talking, but it's neither of those. E-mail feels like writing a letter because both letter writing and e-mail writing usually involve entry on a keyboard. It feels like talking because it's so fast.

> ➤ **E-mail feels interactive.** It appears to us that we are having a conversation, but we aren't, really. In a direct conversation we can see each other, or if it's on the phone, we can gauge a person's emotional state by his or her tone of voice. While e-mail feels like a real conversation, it lacks those features. It's a really poor way to communicate emotion accurately.

> ➤ **E-mail is easy to use on a mass scale.** Because it's so fast people tend to overuse it. Most people I know who rely on e-mail receive far more e-mails every day than letters or even phone calls. The convenience of e-mail is being destroyed by the volume of messages sent and received.

This Won't Work!

If you get easily offended or get angry when people misinterpret your communication, you may get into trouble with e-mail. People will send you things they wouldn't say to your face, and they will often misinterpret messages sent via e-mail.

Things You Need to Know About E-mail

Because e-mail is becoming so common, there are some things you need to know that will help you use it more effectively.

The Paperless Message

First, despite the fact that e-mails seem like paper messages, people don't write or read e-mails like they read paper. They read more quickly, miss a great deal of the details, and respond more quickly. What does that mean? It's easy to create misunderstandings via e-mail. This happens because you either haven't written carefully (as you would with a letter) or the other person hasn't taken the time to read the e-mail slowly.

So you need to know that e-mail can create difficulties and conflicts where none existed before. Sounds weird, I know, but it happens everyday and it's really nobody's fault. Perhaps later we'll all use e-mail more carefully, but right now it's the fast-food way of communicating.

Insider Secrets

Perhaps it will change in the future, but e-mail tends to be a conflict-provoking medium. You need to remember that and keep it in perspective. People say things in e-mail they wouldn't otherwise communicate.

This also means that e-mail is a really poor way of communicating when emotions are high. Feelings don't transfer well over computers. Or at least, they don't transfer accurately.

You can't control whether the other person reads your e-mail with care and understanding. What you can do is slow down your reading of e-mails sent to you, and slow down your responses. Many people get an e-mail, click the reply button, and start writing a reply *before* they've read the entire message. Don't do that. Make sure you read it. If it's a conflict issue or a disagreement issue, read it again. Ask yourself whether you think you understand before you respond.

"I Really Didn't Mean It"

Second, due to the speed of sending e-mail and the lack of editing and reflection, people say things they would never say to you in person or in a letter. And that tends to add fuel to conflict fires or, as I said earlier, tends to create conflicts.

So, recognize that the smokin', cussin' e-mail you just received from a colleague may not give you a true reflection of how that person feels. Perhaps he just responded too quickly while he was angry for 10 seconds. Don't assume the e-mail is a fair and accurate reflection. Clarify via e-mail or, better yet, pick up the phone and try to work out the problem that way (or in person).

"It's Lost in My To-Be-Read File"

Third, because e-mail has become so much of a volume issue, some weird things happen. For example, you send an urgent e-mail to a colleague. You wait and you wait

but you don't get a reply. So you get annoyed. You assume that the person has read it but is ignoring you. That's because you are used to the instant feel of e-mail.

But consider this. Perhaps the person receives a hundred e-mails a day, and just hasn't gotten to yours or hasn't had a chance to reply. You don't know why your message hasn't been answered. Or the e-mail might never have reached its destination. That happens, too.

E-mails can be great for getting information to places quickly, but that doesn't mean it gets handled just as quickly at the other end. Keep that in mind. If something is truly urgent, sure, go ahead and use e-mail, but don't rely on it exclusively. Use the phone, too.

Not for Your Eyes Only

While it may appear that e-mail is a private method of communication, it isn't. It feels so much like writing a letter that we think we have the same degree of privacy.

If you think your e-mail will be read only by your intended recipient, you can get into all kinds of pickles. Many a person has discovered the lack of privacy. There's the guy who wrote e-mail to a colleague about what a dirty SOB his boss was, only to find that somehow the e-mail was made available to the boss. Bye-bye. Or the person who was using corporate e-mail for sending explicit love letters. Many red faces there!

Always keep in mind that your e-mail, particularly if you are using a corporate mail system, is stored somewhere—and probably in several places. Almost always there will be others who can legally access it if they choose, and there may be people who can access it illegally. Some companies actually monitor e-mails.

Write your e-mail as if it were public. Never say anything in e-mail that you would not want people in your workplace to hear.

Some E-mail Tips

OK, e-mail isn't perfect, and the more you understand it the better you can make use of it. But here are some tips:

➤ **Keep the length short.** It's difficult for a person to read a long e-mail on a screen. It's hard to take it all in. If you have a great deal to convey, you might want to "attach" or send a document that is meant to be printed out. People can absorb detail better on paper.

Insider Secrets

Short e-mails are better. The longer the e-mail, the more likely the reader is going to miss important parts or misunderstand. After all, people often skim them anyway.

➤ **Don't fall in love with e-mail.** It can interfere with productivity. One manager I know sends five to ten e-mails a day to his staff. All of them work within 30 yards of his office. E-mail is not a toy; use it when it makes sense. Don't use it when you can get out of your chair and talk. Real people have to take real time to read what you've sent. If you send too much e-mail, it gets ignored.

➤ **Be careful with humor.** It doesn't always translate very well, and you can end up getting your tootsies roasted because someone took your joke or comment in a way you hadn't intended.

➤ **Don't draw conclusions about a person's intelligence on the basis of e-mail format, grammar, and spelling.** E-mail is not like letter writing, so take that into account.

From the Manager's Desk

The more important the content of the e-mail, the more time you should spend composing it. Help the reader understand by organizing it clearly. Reread it before sending and edit if necessary. Pay special attention to whether the tone is right for your message.

➤ **Don't rely on e-mail to communicate really important things.** For example, if you have a new safety procedure, don't use e-mail only to communicate it, because it's guaranteed that a good percentage of people will ignore it or not read it. If it's important, it's worth communicating in multiple ways and talking to people face-to-face.

➤ **E-mail is not a good way to announce new things to a bunch of people.** How come? Let's say you have 50 employees. You announce a new bonus program. But, of course, your people will have questions. So you're going to get back a whole bunch of messages that could take you hours to respond to. It's more effective to have a staff meeting when that's possible.

E-mail can be a great tool and productivity enhancer but, as with any tool, you need to learn to use it appropriately and recognize that it has limitations. We aren't at the stage yet where e-mail can replace other communication methods, although it can be a great additional communication method.

The Least You Need to Know

➤ Not all communication media are the same.

➤ Good communication means using the right medium for the right job, and knowing the pros and cons.

➤ Face-to-face conversation is best for problem solving and working through emotional situations, although it may be uncomfortable.

➤ Letters are more formal and slower than other media forms, but good for communicating detailed and complicated information.

➤ E-mail is fast but prone to miscommunication, misunderstanding, and unnecessary conflict.

Part 6

I Confess, I'm Difficult (Help for the Guilty)

OK, confess now. You aren't perfect. No doubt there are people who think you are a pain in the neck, and at least sometimes, they're probably right. We're all difficult sometimes, but it's important to look at ourselves to see whether our own quirks and habits are creating problems for ourselves.

We'll look at the possibility that you are difficult too often and at how to determine whether that's true. We'll give you specific tips and suggestions about how you can change your use of language so that people see you as easier to work with.

Chapter 23

We're All Difficult Sometimes— Are You Difficult Too Much?

In This Chapter

➤ How others see you

➤ Ways to gauge people's reactions

➤ How to ask your boss for feedback

➤ Getting information from your staff

➤ Using performance management to get information

As we inch closer to the end of this book, it's time to return to one of the themes we started with. Right at the beginning of the book we mentioned that everyone is difficult sometimes. The more difficult you are, the more you will tend to find others difficult. And round and round it goes.

So, we return to thinking about you. In this chapter you'll have a chance to assess whether you're a difficult person, and you'll learn to identify some of the difficult behaviors you use, probably unintentionally. Just like most other difficult people, you aren't malicious or hurtful. Forgetful on occasion, perhaps. Or maybe just oblivious to the glitches in your own behavior, like all of us are sometimes.

Why It's So Hard to See Our Own Difficult Behavior

No matter how mature you are and how self-aware you are, it's always hard to see the difficult behaviors you use in everyday life. There are a couple of factors that tend to make us blind to our own flaws, particularly the smaller ones.

First, you've probably been using the same difficult behaviors for many years. You use many of them automatically, whether it's interrupting someone who is speaking to you or choosing the wrong phrase and offending someone. So many of these things have become habits. You've been doing them for a long time, and you don't even think about them. The only way you can look at them is if you look *for* them. You have to hunt them down like bugs!

Insider Secrets

It's easier to recognize our really big flaws than our little ones. We take our little ones for granted, and people often don't tell us about them. Unfortunately, most average difficult people are perceived as difficult because of all the small, difficult quirks that pile up, not because of one or two major traits. So when you look at yourself, take into account that you may have a number of little quirks that add up to make you appear difficult to other people.

The second thing that makes it so hard is that we can't step out of our perceptual goggles through which we look at things. It's a challenge to see ourselves through the eyes and minds of other people. We can only use our own perceptions and our own standards Those perceptions and standards color how we see ourselves, and it's likely our "glasses" are going to be different from each of the people around us. If we want to know how other people see us, ultimately we have to involve them in the process and ask them.

To use a simple example, try imagining what it would be like to be a member of the opposite sex. You might think you can guess at what it might be like, right? But if you are a man imagining what it would be like to be a woman, you apply your male values and perceptions about women. And you're probably going to be considerably off base. It's no different if you try to imagine how you come across to Joe the deliveryman or Mary the CEO or Fred, the guy who works for you. You see yourself through *your* eyes.

The third reason we have a hard time seeing our own foibles applies more to managers than anyone else. When people feel free to be honest and straightforward with you and tell you how they see you, it's extremely helpful in identifying the ways you might be difficult. Unfortunately, because of their positions, managers tend not to receive this information, particularly from employees. Few employees feel comfortable telling their bosses they're stubborn and pig-headed or don't listen very well. That is probably the case even if you invite honest comments from your staff. Employees often fear reprisal because they might have seen in the past that honesty isn't always rewarded.

It's a real challenge to look at yourself and see what others might see. In the quest for understanding you'll never be perfect—but you can improve each and every day.

Why Looking at Yourself Is So Important

Because looking at yourself is such a challenge, you'd better have some motivation to do so. Of course, there's the abstract idea that the better you know yourself, the better human being you'll be, and while I believe that, it's kind of airy-fairy. So let's look at the payoffs for identifying and addressing the ways you might be difficult in the eyes of others.

Self-examination enables you to avoid the difficult-person vicious cycle. When you're difficult without knowing it, there is a tendency to view unpleasant situations as caused by someone else. That's because it's easier to see how another person is difficult—far easier than realizing you're also difficult.

So, let's say you're impatient and tend to interrupt people.

> Talking to George, you start finishing his sentences for him. That's annoying to George, and he starts raising his voice and ignoring you. You see that and figure, "Man, George is so difficult, I can't talk with this guy." And on and on it goes.

From the Manager's Desk

You can't succeed unless you work at it everyday. To get better, you need the help of other people. You can't improve in a vacuum. One of the keys to success is identifying how other people see you.

This isn't a big deal in a short conversation, but this is someone you have to see five days a week, and it accumulates. Both you and George think it's the other person who's behaving badly. That's often how relationships are poisoned forever and how enemies are born. Many a relationship has spoiled from a lack of self-understanding and the natural human tendency to look at the other person as the source of the problem.

So becoming aware of your own difficult behaviors and how they can trigger this vicious cycle can help you avoid escalation over time. That saves time, prevents arguments, and makes the workplace a happier place to be.

There's another payoff from identifying your own difficult behaviors. This one is simple. Difficult behavior on your part interferes with getting your job done. Again, this applies particularly to managers, who need the help of other people to complete projects and tasks. If you turn people off, they stop working hard, or worse, they become indifferent or start sabotaging you. Few managers can withstand a situation where they have alienated a number of their staff or colleagues. If you do alienate people, you may be setting yourself up for career failure, the end of promotion possibilities, and a restricted paycheck.

Another reason to take a look at yourself: People who are unaware of how their bosses perceive them can end up in very difficult situations and certainly negatively affect their own careers. A lot of promotion decisions are based on how you appear to people, particularly upper management. Yes, it does matter that you do a good job, but if you come across as an ill-mannered bore, a bull in the china shop, and so on, your career prospects are usually reduced. Even if you're a really good person but have a gruff, trouble-follows-you-anywhere exterior, you're limiting yourself.

So we have three good reasons why it's important to try to understand how others view you and to work at reducing your own difficult behavior.

This Won't Work!

Ever know someone who was shocked when his or her spouse left out of the blue? Ever know a manager who felt he or she knew everything, and didn't believe there was a need to find out the perceptions of others? Not knowing how people truly see you can yield quite surprising and horrifying results.

Some Difficulty Indicators

What kinds of cues can you use to see yourself through the eyes of other people? Are there things to look out for that might tell you something about your own difficult behaviors? Yes.

If you want to increase your sense of how other people see you, you need to pay attention to other people and how they behave with you. This isn't an exact science, but if you start observing the reactions of others, you can get some idea of how they perceive you. There are a few different sets of people to consider: your employees, your boss, your coworkers, and your personal acquaintances.

In general, regardless of the category of people, you need to notice the patterns of interaction you have with others. Let's start with a list of patterns. If a number of the following items apply to you over time and across groups of people, then you may be considered overly difficult:

➤ Are you often caught up in arguments, disputes, and disagreements, even when it doesn't seem to make sense?

➤ Are you someone who manages from crisis to crisis?

➤ Do people seem to withhold important information from you?

➤ Do you feel you're often not listened to?

➤ Do you feel people fail to appreciate you? (This has to occur across a number of situations and groups of people.)

From the Manager's Desk

When looking at patterns and how other people react, you need to think about how different people react to you in different situations. It's the patterns that count. If your boss, your employees, and your spouse have similar reactions to you, that's a warning sign.

Here's the quick explanation. The first item about arguments is a key one. If you're seen as difficult, you will tend to have your ideas challenged just because people have labeled you as difficult—even if your ideas are good. If people withhold information from you, it may be that they don't feel comfortable talking to you or harbor some degree of mistrust. The last two patterns listed are a bit different. If you feel unappreciated and not listened to, it's possible that's really happening. But why are you unappreciated or ignored? It may be because you are seen as difficult. Or it may be that your perception is inaccurate. You may have a feeling—one that difficult people often have—that you are ignored or underappreciated by those around you.

What about physical reactions from other people? Can you use them to figure out whether people see you as difficult or not? To some degree. Here's a good indicator: If you walk down the hall, do your employees all scatter as if a hand grenade is rolling at them? Just kidding—most indicators are quite subtle.

Look for nonverbal indicators and tone of voice. When you interact with your boss or your employees or pretty much anyone, their reactions to you will often be conveyed through their tone of voice and their body language.

Here are some things to watch for when you interact with people. These may indicate that others perceive you as frustrating:

➤ Aggressive tone of voice

➤ Bored look and mannerisms

➤ Frustration signals (sighing, rolling of eyes)

➤ Shutting down (getting quiet for no apparent reason)

➤ Argumentativeness

Again, keep in mind that we all get these reactions from someone now and then. If you find that a number of people react this way across situations and over time, the odds are it *does* have something to do with your behavior.

This Won't Work!

While there are lots of books on body language and reading people from their physical actions, be very careful with this stuff. Much of the material is overly simplified and can mislead you. The meaning of a lot of nonverbal behavior can be different from person to person.

Apart from trying to figure out the meaning of the actions of the people around us, there's another way to assess whether you're difficult, and that's to look at your behavior. Here are some questions to ask yourself:

➤ Do I tend to interrupt in conversations?

➤ Am I often impatient in conversation?

➤ Do I tend to talk rather than listen?

➤ Am I unreliable? Do I make promises I don't keep?

➤ Do I lose my temper easily?

➤ Am I argumentative?

➤ Do I talk at people instead of with them?

➤ Do I criticize people publicly?

➤ Do I make heavy demands on my staff?

It's not that easy to look backwards and remember your own behavior, but here's what you can do. Over the next week, pay attention to these items. Record (a little checkmark somewhere) any instance where you feel angry, interrupt, argue, and so on. Not only does that give you a very rough idea of your own behavior, but it helps you become more observant. There's no particular number of checkmarks that should concern you—the exercise is to help you become more aware of the possibility that you are being more difficult than necessary.

Sometimes You Just Have to Ask

It's an unfortunate fact of life that difficult people aren't very good at gauging the reactions of others. That's one major reason why people are difficult—they just don't notice the reactions they generate, or they misinterpret them. And that may apply to you.

So, even if you can gauge the reactions of others or are able to identify your own behaviors, you're still stuck in your perceptions, and those certainly are going to be somewhat inaccurate or biased. That's just normal. Sometimes you just have to ask people about your behavior and whether they see you as difficult or not.

There are two ways to do this. You can do it informally, or you can do it on a regular, more formal basis. We'll talk briefly about the first, and in more depth about the second.

Informal Feedback

There's no reason you can't come out and ask people directly how they see you, or how they feel you could be more helpful. If you're going to do this informally, you want to ask people with whom you have a fairly good relationship. People who can't stand you are likely to try to tear you to ribbons or will just clam up.

There's another criterion for picking people to ask. You need feedback from people who will be honest with you and people you trust and respect, otherwise you won't get good information, or you won't trust the information you get. Some people are hesitant to say anything critical about anybody. These people aren't good prospects for mining information about how you're perceived.

From the Manager's Desk

When choosing people to get feedback from, choose people you get along with, who are honest and trustworthy, and whose opinions you respect. But don't ask only those you *know* will only be positive.

Are there any tricks you can use to get the feedback you need? You bet. The key to getting good feedback is to make it easy for people to give you information without fear of hurting your feelings or putting them on the spot. So you approach people in a slightly indirect way. Let's say you have a good deal of respect for your boss and would like some sense about how she perceives you. You could ask her: "So, do you think I'm a pain in the butt?" But let's face it, that's really blunt, and I'm not sure you want to hear the truthful answer! Or you could phrase it in a less personal way, like this:

> "Mary, I'd really like to improve as a manager, and I'm always interested in ways I might do that. It would really help me if you could give me some ideas about how I might be more useful to you and the company, and be a better leader for my staff. Do you have any suggestions?"

Notice how we are staying away from asking Mary about your personal qualities, whether you're a pain or even whether you're difficult. By focusing on positive suggestions the perceptions will come out, but you won't feel like you're bending over with a big bull's eye on your behind. And not only will you get some idea about how your boss perceives you, but hopefully your boss can give you some specific suggestions about what you can do better.

Insider Secrets

Asking the boss for suggestions for improvement isn't just a good way to find out how you're perceived. It's a great way to show your willingness to learn and contribute. Bosses just eat this stuff up.

While your boss can be a great source of feedback you can use to see how you are perceived and what you can do to be less difficult, he or she isn't the only source of information. Your employees are also important. Most bosses up the chain of command don't see you very often and don't get a chance to observe how you behave everyday with your employees. And let's face it. It's important to know how your employees perceive you, because they're the ones who are going to make you look good or look really bad. And the more difficult you are, the more likely they'll be to do the latter and not the former.

This Won't Work!

If you ask for input from employees, you need to listen, not argue, and use the information you get. Otherwise you can turn a good workplace situation into a bad one—and a bad one into a disaster.

How do you get information from staff about how you're perceived? We'll talk about more formal methods, but the simplest way is to just ask them. Like asking the boss, whether you get good information or poor information depends on the way you do it.

First, keep in mind that employees, whether they like you or not, understand that you have some power and control over them. That in itself will cause them to give you less-than-honest answers. So we have to look carefully at how to approach them.

Second, you probably want to get information from staff about you in one-on-one sessions. You're likely to get more honest responses if you talk in private. And, on the off-chance that your employees really find you difficult, private discussions are less likely to turn into public hangings.

OK, so how do you do it? It could be over coffee with someone, or it could be at a meeting convened specifically for the purpose, but here's a good start:

> "Paul, although I'm the manager, I see my job as helping you and the other staff members do your jobs. That's really my most important role. So, it would really help me if you could tell me what kinds of things I could be doing to make your job easier and to make this place a better place to work. I know it's weird to have your manager ask you this kind of stuff, but the only way I can be more useful is if I know what you need from me."

Again, notice we are staying away from asking Paul to make an assessment of your personality, your degree of difficulty, or anything else that might be hard to talk about. We're also presenting the question in a way that is helpful to the employee. We're asking for specific suggestions. In the conversation that follows, you will get a good idea of how that employee sees you.

There's one other thing we have to say about this process. If you ask for information of this sort, you have an obligation to listen carefully, not argue, and make an honest attempt to use the suggestions employees make. If you aren't able to do all three, then, bingo! You *are* difficult.

In addition to your boss and your employees, you can also ask your comanagers for feedback and even ask some of your family members about what you do that drives them a bit nutso. That can be helpful. But let's focus on one more informal way to get information from your coworkers.

With this method, you ask co-workers for feedback about specific situations they might have observed. For example, at a meeting recently of the management team, you got involved in a difficult discussion with one attendee. While you believe you handled it well, you aren't sure. So you approach some of the other attendees privately and ask their opinions about whether you handled the situation as well as possible and what you might have done differently.

From the Manager's Desk

Another way to get really good feedback is to ask people who actually observed you in a difficult or challenging situation. This works particularly well with peers (other managers at your level).

As with the other methods we've discussed, we're looking for specific feedback and not general comments about personality. If you get vague comments, try to refocus the conversation about what they saw you do and what they think you might have done to handle the situation more effectively.

More Formal Ways to Get Feedback

More formal ways of getting feedback aren't that different from the informal methods. The difference is that the opportunity for feedback is scheduled at regular intervals and it's built into existing ways to communicate about performance.

The primary vehicle to get this feedback is some form of performance-management system, which we talked about in Chapter 9, "Using Performance Management to Help."

Generally, performance management includes some annual (or otherwise regular) communication process to discuss performance. Often the process happens twice a year. At the beginning of your new year you sit down and discuss performance expectations. You might recall we called that performance planning. At the end of the year, you sit down and talk about performance over the past year. That's usually called performance appraisal or performance review.

It's either your performance that is the focus (with your boss) or it's the performance of your employees (if you are doing an appraisal).

This regularly scheduled process, which should be an essential communication process in all organizations, provides a venue for the discussion of how both your boss and your employees perceive you. Yes, that's right. You can use the performance-management system to *get* information from your employees.

This Won't Work!

Some bosses aren't good at discussing performance with you. You may have to take the initiative by asking questions so you get the information you need to improve and become less difficult. Don't rely on the boss's expertise. Be prepared with questions.

From the Manager's Desk

Use performance planning and performance-appraisal meetings to both give information about your employee's performance and get information about how you can help.

Let's get the boss thing out of the way. The formal process of performance review is an ideal time to get information from your boss. In fact, that's what it's there for. We would hope that your boss would be good at running such a meeting, but often the boss isn't. So when you meet with the boss to discuss his or her expectations of you or to talk about your performance over the past year, you may need to take some initiative so you get the feedback you need.

Basically, that means coming into that meeting with some prepared questions about how your boss sees you and what you might do to perform more effectively in the next year. It's really no different than the informal process we described earlier.

OK, so what about your employees? We're going to assume that you conduct performance discussions (both performance planning and performance appraisal) with your staff. No? Well, start now.

Up until now, you've probably focused those meetings on the performance of your employees. My bet is that it hasn't occurred to you that this is an ideal time to find out how your employees see you and use the information to become a better and less-difficult manager.

There's a misconception that performance appraisals are a kind of one-way communication where the manager evaluates the employee, sort of like pouring water into a jug. In fact, the best performance discussions involve an exchange of ideas on a variety of subjects. Yes, one of those topics is your employee and his or her performance. But another one is how you can help that employee do a better job or make the workplace more enjoyable.

So, while perhaps 75 percent of the performance-appraisal discussion will be about the work of your subordinate, the remainder should be about you and your usefulness. In other words, we are going to create a forum for the employees to help you help them.

The communication process to do this is really no different than what we described earlier when we talked about informal methods of getting information. Here is an example of your phrasing which could occur at the end of a performance planning session with Mary.

"Mary, I think we've agreed that you'll be doing [insert information] in the next year. Because my job is to help you get those job tasks done, what can I do to help you get your job done or to make your life easier here? Do you anticipate any barriers to getting things done that I can help with? I may not be able to do everything, but I'll give it a shot."

Here's one way of doing it at the performance appraisal meeting.

"Mary, because my job is to make your job easier, I'd like to discuss how well I've done in helping or hindering you. Over the last year can you think of any situations where I could have been more helpful? Can you think of things I could have done differently that would have made things easier for you?"

The information you get from this regular communication process is like gold. It changes how you interact, and it can help both of you to be more successful.

The Least You Need to Know

➤ Everyone is difficult. Your goal is to become less and less difficult over time.

➤ It's hard to see yourself through the eyes of other people.

➤ You can become more observant about the reactions of other people and use that information to become less difficult.

➤ While trying to figure out what other people think, often it's good to just ask them.

➤ The best way to ask people how they see you is to phrase it in terms of how you might better help them.

Chapter 24

Getting Less Difficult—Words and Deeds

> ### In This Chapter
>
> ➤ Changing your own behavior
>
> ➤ The importance of words and deeds
>
> ➤ What it means to be congruent
>
> ➤ How can you make your decisions stick
>
> ➤ When your words and body language don't match

In the last chapter, did you discover some areas where you might appear difficult to others? Good. That means you're thinking and looking at yourself. But knowing you are at least occasionally difficult doesn't necessarily mean that you have the keys to become less difficult. That's what this chapter is about.

We're going to help you change the perceptions that people have about you. If your employees think you're difficult, we'll share some secrets about how to alter their opinions. Same for your boss. Same for your coworkers. Heck, even your spouse.

Getting Back to Behavior—the Starting Block

There are two ways to go about changing yourself. One is to try to remake your personality or alter your character so others will find you less difficult. This is the stuff that New Year's resolutions and therapy sessions are made of—"I need to become

This Won't Work!

Don't make resolutions to change your personality and expect them to work. Making those kinds of resolutions may give you a sense of self-righteousness until, of course, nothing happens. Then you feel stupid.

From the Manager's Desk

To change to less-difficult behavior, you need to know two things: what bad things you need to stop doing, and what good things you need to use to replace the bad things.

more considerate" or "patient" or "understanding." Unfortunately, those kinds of resolutions rarely bear fruit, and therapy sessions may not be that effective either (it depends).

The bottom line is that staring into your belly button and contemplating your own personality doesn't portend much chance of changing anything. I don't think there's anything bad about it, but don't deceive yourself. This kind of self-analysis is like thinking over and over, "I must quit smoking." And we know how many people say that but don't do anything about it.

The second way to become less difficult and be seen as less difficult involves a completely different mindset. It's one that should be familiar to you by now. You need to focus on your behavior. Your behavior is how people learn about you; it's what they base their impressions on. It's ultimately how they judge you. So it only makes sense to focus on your behavior because that's what determines whether people see you as a great person, a slightly difficult person, or a pain in the butt.

The other reason to look at behavior is that you may not be able to remake your personality, but you can change your behavior little piece by little piece. That *does* work, and it's less overwhelming. You can improve slowly by focusing on a few behaviors at a time and changing them. Then you choose a few more difficult behaviors and change those.

Besides, you may be a great person inside but have some difficult quirks that ruin the image you project to the people around you.

If you're going to change to less-difficult behaviors, you need to know what you need to stop doing and what you need to start doing, and that's what we're going to talk about.

How People Come to See You as Difficult

Generally, people come to see you as difficult as a result of one or both of the following. You do something really, really bad, like hollering or throwing things around your office or being really aggressive. Occasionally, one bad incident can color the perception of those around you, and it can do so permanently.

The second way is far more gradual. People around you don't wake up some morning and suddenly realize how much of a pain you really are. It's a slow process that happens over time. It's perception by a thousand little paper cuts. For most difficult people it's a case of having too many small difficult quirks. Over time the people they interact with see them as more and more difficult.

So what kinds of difficult quirks affect these perceptions and might make you appear difficult? It's simple. We can divide up your behavior (what you do) into two somewhat smaller chunks: your actions and words.

People draw conclusions about you based on what you do or the actions you take. For example, your boss might look at whether you complete your work on time. Your employees might look at whether you buy great presents for them at holiday season time (OK, that's not a great example). Here's another one. Do you evaluate your staff's performance in a way that appears fair? Do you assign workloads fairly?

Those are your actions. Ever hear the saying, "Actions speak louder than words?" Well, while there is truth in that statement, it's far more complicated than that.

The second chunk of your behavior is your *words*. It's what you say. It's how you say it. It's how often you communicate. Now, you might be a bit confused about what falls into the words category and what falls into the action category, but don't worry about it. Because here's the critical piece: While your actions are important and your words are important, it's the matchup between the two that is absolutely critical. When they don't match, people you work with will see you as untrustworthy.

Are You Trustworthy?

Let me explain the trust thing. One of the hallmarks of difficult people is they aren't trusted by others. Because we want to make this more about behavior, what does it mean to be trusted?

It's not that complicated. People will trust you when your words and behaviors are consistent over time and match each other—that is, they are congruent.

This Won't Work!

Ignoring your small difficult habits and quirks doesn't work. If you're seen as difficult by those around you, it's probably the accumulation of difficult habits and wee behaviors over time that cause that perception.

From the Manager's Desk

Yes, your actions are important. Your words are important. But when your actions and your words do *not* match, you're setting yourself up for misery. People need to see that you mean what you say, do what you say, and say what you mean.

So there are two parts. If you say things and change your mind a lot or behave unpredictably over time (being pleasant one day and unpleasant another day), people don't know what to expect from you or what to believe about you. That's the consistency part. It's almost better to be consistently unpleasant, because at least people will know what to expect.

Employee Handbook

The **congruency** part involves this question: Do your words and your deeds match? Also as important is whether the way you communicate (body language, tone of voice) matches the words you use. Do your actions and words give the exact same message?

The *congruency* part involves this question: Does what you say and what you do match? Do your actions and words give the exact same message?

If the answer is yes and they match consistently, then the people around you will see you as trustworthy, safe, and less difficult. If they don't match, you will be seen with suspicion and mistrust. You will be perceived as difficult.

Let's look at some examples.

Georgette is a rather optimistic manager. She sees the glass as half full, not half empty. So when people come to her with problems, she tends to make all kinds of promises, whether it concerns a promotion, a raise, or some kind of work issue. She really means well, and she believes what she says. But unfortunately, as time goes on, her employees start to react to her in negative ways.

Insider Secrets

Human beings naturally seek a degree of certainty and consistency in their relations with others. Whenever there is uncertainty and unpredictability in relationships, people will feel uncomfortable and perceive the unpredictable person as difficult.

Why? Because Georgette often promises things she can't deliver. And after awhile people catch on. Georgette is no monster, but that's neither here nor there.

What Georgette needs to do is change her behavior so that her words and promises are more congruent with the results or actions she creates. She doesn't need to change her personality or become some clinically depressed, cynical person. All she needs to do is see the problem of incongruity between words and action and bring the two in line.

Here's another example.

Throughout the year John, a manager, communicates about the performance of his subordinates. He's actually good at it and tries to praise his employees whenever possible and focus on the positives. That works really well until John has to do the formal written performance appraisals. At the individual meetings, John finds all sorts of negative things to talk about, and these get entered into the formal personnel file. Maybe it's because someone told him that not everyone can be evaluated quite so high. Who knows why? However, the bottom line is that his words and actions are inconsistent over time. Through the year he talks positive. Then bang—at the end of the year the other shoe drops.

> **From the Manager's Desk**
>
> A lot of the time, incongruent or inconsistent behavior comes from the best of intentions. You want to help. You want to make life easier. So you aren't always realistic in what you say. You aren't always realistic in what you can achieve. But you need to get in the habit of being more realistic, or you won't be trusted.

How is John going to be perceived by his staff? As someone not worthy of trust? As a tricky SOB? As a difficult person?

One final example that's somewhat different.

> Maury is not really good at expressing his feelings to people. He's OK with positive feelings, although most people wouldn't consider Maury as a "gushin' kinda guy." Where he's really bad is when he's angry or frustrated. He's learned to avoid the verbal expression of anger and frustration. Not a bad word comes out of his mouth even when he's really angry.

The bad part is that his words and his body language are completely out of whack. While he can control what he says, he just isn't so good at controlling how he says it or how he looks when he says it. In other words, his tone of voice and physical appearance make it clear to anyone but a computer that he's angry. Red face, tense muscles, choked tone of voice—nobody is fooled by the verbal control.

This is an incongruence or mismatch between what he says and how he says it. When there is mismatch between the two, what do you think people believe? The words or the appearance and body language? It's the body language. So people *know* when Maury is angry. They see his denial of being angry as problematic when everyone on the planet except Maury knows it. That worries people. How can you trust a guy who never admits to being angry? How can you work out problems because you don't know where things stand. So this mismatch of words and body language makes Maury appear difficult and just a little dangerous.

Insider Secrets

People who have trouble expressing anger, who deny it when they're angry but then send nonverbal messages that they are mad, are usually referred to as **passive-aggressive**. It's very common. The problem is that passive-aggressive people don't fool anyone and are seen as difficult and dangerous because their behaviors are incongruent.

Wanna Be More Consistent and Congruent?

Every manager can benefit from becoming more consistent and more congruent. No question. I can't stress how important this is. OK, so how do you do it? We'll look at some specific things you can do (or not do).

Change How You Promise or Commit

Unachievable promises and commitments are a huge problem for many managers. When the boss says to jump 16 feet in the air, you say, "Sure, I can do that," but in reality you can't. So eventually you have to go back and tell the boss you've failed. That's inconsistent. Your boss starts to see you as unreliable even though your intentions were the best.

It's a similar situation with employees. Here's a true story.

> Director Joe had a receptionist, Joan, who wanted to learn some new things in the area of desktop publishing. She was bored with her job. Joe promised her that she could attend some training courses on the subject and over time she would take over the desktop publishing responsibilities for the organization. Joe kept his promise about the training, which was good. He was being consistent in his actions and matched his words with his actions.

However, Joan didn't get the opportunity to use her new skills on the job. The reality was that nobody could take over her receptionist duties, so Joe had to stall, delay, and then finally tell Joan that her involvement in desktop publishing wouldn't be happening in the foreseeable future.

What happened? Joan saw her boss as a liar. Eventually, she turned into a problem employee and finally had to be let go. She felt manipulated. Everyone lost. Joe lost a good, dedicated employee (or at least that's what she was before this all happened). Joan lost her job.

From the Manager's Desk

Before you make a promise or commitment, ask yourself whether it's a realistic one and what is really needed to make it happen. Be realistic so you don't make promises you can't keep.

Did Joe lie intentionally? No. What happened was he really did want Joan to get the opportunity, but he just didn't think it through. He overcommitted.

So, here's the deal. Slow down your promises and commitments to people. While you may be eager to please at the moment, always keep in mind that if you fail to keep a commitment, you are much worse off then if you had made a realistic commitment and kept it. Think before you commit.

Review Your Decision Making

People make decisions in various ways. Some are quick and fast. Some take more time to weigh the pros and cons before deciding. Others can't make decisions at all and get stuck. Generally the best decision-making process is one that's in the middle. What does this have to do with being difficult and trustworthy?

It's simple. It goes back to the idea of consistency and how a lack of consistency causes people to see you as difficult, unpredictable, and untrustworthy. The more often you change a decision you've made, the less credibility you have. And if you avoid making decisions, the same fate can occur. People expect managers to make decisions. That's what they're there for. If you diddle around, procrastinate, and avoid the responsibility, you will be perceived as weak and ineffective.

So, look at your decision-making track record. Do you often have to reverse a decision? Why? What were the circumstances? Was it because you made a quick decision? Perhaps you didn't consider or know all the facts and issues?

Let's not go nuts about this. Every manager makes decisions that need to be reversed. Things change. Circumstances change. And you need to remain flexible to respond to those changes. So, use your head. If you *have* to change a decision, then do so. But here's the trick.

From the Manager's Desk

Not everyone is good at making decisions. Fortunately, you can learn to make decisions in a more logical and rational way. Consider taking one of the many courses on decision making or read a book or two on the subject.

This Won't Work!

You know the deal. A manager reads the latest best-selling management book or goes to a training course. She returns to work and tries to use what she's learned without digesting it and without understanding it. Three months later, she's doing something completely different yet again. Don't do this. Don't get pulled into management fadism.

Provided you don't do it too often, when you need to change a decision you've made, explain to all the parties involved why this decision reversal is necessary. Lay out the new circumstances. Explain your reasoning. Don't just make a decision on Tuesday and make the opposite decision the next Monday without explaining.

When you provide an explanation, people will be more likely to attribute the reversal to the change in circumstances. They are less likely to chalk it up to your bumbling or weakness, or to consider you a difficult person.

What About Your Demeanor and Management Approach?

When you're easygoing one day and really touchy the next, people will see you as difficult because you're unpredictable. When you're a democratic manager one month and an autocratic dictator the next, it drives people crazy.

Your employees need to know what to expect from you. The more unpredictable or inconsistent you are in your management approach, the more you alienate those who work for you.

Your job, then, is to become more consistent in both your demeanor and your management approach. That doesn't mean you have to always feel happy, but it does mean you need to be more consistent in your behavior. If you're prone to barking one day and purring the next, you'd better stop doing that. It might be better to bark all the time than switch back and forth by the minute. At least people will know what to expect!

Work to behave in consistent, predictable ways, regardless of your mood. That's one characteristic of professional behavior—that regardless of how you feel, you perform your job in an even-handed, consistent way.

In terms of your management approach, you need to adopt a consistent way of managing that doesn't change from day to day or month to month. That's not always easy, particularly if you're new to management. After all, we'd expect you to change over time and develop your own management philosophy. It's OK to change and grow and alter your management behavior. What you need to avoid is the ping-ponging back and forth—the democratic manager one week and the autocratic one the next and then back again.

How do you become more consistent? By having a clear idea about how you want to manage—a philosophy about management. How do you get one of these? By reading, digesting, going to training, and being exposed to new ideas.

But above all, avoid going to a course or reading a book and trying to implement all these new ideas the next day. Think about new ideas before you apply them. One of the biggest reasons managers flip-flop in their manager behavior is they get caught in the flavor-of-the-month management fad. Don't do that.

How to Become More Congruent

There's that word again: congruent. It means that your words and your body language send the same message. Let's use an example to help you see how you can become more congruent in your communication and actions.

Here's the situation.

> Jeff manages with what he calls an open-door policy. Every chance he gets, he tells his staff that if they have problems, have suggestions to make, or need to talk to him for whatever reason, to come see him. The door is, so to speak, always open, according to Jeff.

> But Jeff is going nuts. Despite his best efforts to encourage employees to come talk, they don't. Not only are people hesitant to make decisions, but they aren't giving him the information he needs to keep current. Things are going astray, and nobody tells him. And it's getting worse. The less people talk to Jeff, the more frustrated he gets. The more frustrated he gets, the angrier he appears. And he thinks there must be something wrong with his staff.

> He can't figure it out.

From the Manager's Desk

If you find your staff not taking your invitations seriously, look to see whether your words and your actions aren't matching up. Or, ask your employees for feedback.

What's really happening is that Jeff's got bad congruency. When people come to his office to talk, they sees Jeff hunched over his computer laboriously typing something or other. That's not a big deal. But when someone knocks on the door, Jeff either completely ignores him or her, or just grunts something. On a good day Jeff asks the person to come in, but doesn't even look up, sometimes for as long as five minutes.

His employees have discovered that it's bloody painful and uncomfortable to come talk to Jeff. There may be an open door, but there doesn't seem to be an open mind or even a positive reception. When there is a clash between what a person says and what a person does, people believe the actions and/or the body language.

So they stop going. They stop interrupting. And they begin to wonder about the genuineness of Jeff's invitation.

What should Jeff have done? Rather than get frustrated and blame employees for cutting him out of the loop, he should have asked for feedback. It's the obvious thing. If Jeff really wanted to fix the problem, all he had to do was ask whether there were things he was doing that made it difficult for people to come to him. Then he could address those behaviors.

Perhaps he could change what he says and put aside some specific office hours to talk with employees. Or he could modify his interpersonal behavior so it becomes more inviting and hospitable.

So if you find that people don't seem to believe what you say, your first action should be to determine why they aren't taking your words seriously. And the only way you can do that is to get feedback from people. If you talk about wanting people to be involved and make suggestions and they don't, find out why. Maybe they don't offer their ideas because you don't handle them well.

After you have identified the problem, you can fix it. And fixing it involves making your words and actions more congruent in the eyes of your employees or the people around you.

The Least You Need to Know

➤ Both your words and your actions affect how people see you.

➤ The more consistent you are over time, the more trustworthy you will appear.

➤ The match between what you say and what you do is absolutely critical.

➤ Work at improving your decision making to avoid having to reverse decisions.

➤ Avoid being pushed and pulled by management fads. Don't implement new ideas until you really understand them.

Chapter 25

Getting Less Difficult—The Words, Ma'am, Just the Words

In This Chapter

➤ Why do some people start trouble wherever they go?

➤ The difference between confrontational language and cooperative language

➤ Working with people, not ordering them around

➤ Being infallible is a bad thing

➤ How to avoid making people defensive

In the last chapter we talked about the importance of your words and your deeds. In particular we stressed that you're less likely to be seen as difficult if your words and deeds match up, if you're consistent in your demeanor and your management style, and if your words and body language are congruent.

What we haven't talked about is the actual words issue. Did you know that there are a lot of common phrases that actually will be perceived as difficult or conflict provoking? And that there are ways to replace those words and phrases with language that tends to build cooperation and relationships? It's true. In this chapter you'll learn the difference between confrontational and cooperative language, and you'll learn exactly how to replace confrontational language with cooperative language.

What's Your Style?

Have you ever noticed that some people go through life as if a black cloud of conflict follows them everywhere? Stick the person almost anywhere and conflict erupts,

This Won't Work!

Don't assume that because you aren't a radical conflict-starter, you never contribute to conflict or poor relationships. We all do on occasion. Everyone can benefit by looking at how they communicate.

whether it's with strangers, employees ... whomever. We call those people conflict-starters. They're pretty common. I hope you aren't one, but there's a little bit of the conflict-starter in each of us. So even if you aren't a full-fledged member of the club, you need to know this stuff.

Then there's the opposite. There are some people who seem to be almost free of conflict. They seem to exude harmony and get along with everyone. It's actually hard to start an argument with such people, and they just don't seem to provoke anyone. There aren't a lot of these people around, but there's enough so we can learn from them. We call these people conflict-preventers.

Don't assume that these relatively conflict-free people are wimpy or weak or lack courage. It's just the opposite. These are strong people. Yes, sometimes they have a particular personality that helps them prevent conflict, but there's a lot more—they actually communicate differently with people.

What sets apart the conflict-starter and the conflict-preventer? Conflict-preventers use different phrasings and words than those used by conflict-starters. What happens is that while conflict-starters create conflict with the poor use of language, conflict-preventers do the opposite. A conflict-starter can start a bonfire where there is almost no fuel. A preventer can put the fire out even if there's a lot of fuel. How?

I've labeled the two kinds of language used by these types of people as cooperative language and confrontational language.

Employee Handbook

Cooperative communication techniques tend to help other people see us as on the same side as they are. These simple techniques help prevent unnecessary conflict and are great for defusing conflict when it occurs.

Cooperative Language

The idea behind cooperative communication is that there are certain ways of expressing ourselves that encourage people to listen, hear, and work with us in cooperative ways. *Cooperative communication* techniques tend to help other people see us as on the same side as they are.

Confrontational Language

Conflict-provoking communication, or what I call *confrontational language,* tends to encourage others to see us as belonging on the other side. People who use these word patterns are viewed as being

➤ annoying.

➤ polarizing.

➤ demeaning or patronizing.

➤ uninterested in other people.

➤ self-centered.

➤ blame oriented.

And it's all a result of the language used. Conflict-starters aren't necessarily bad people. Often they lack language skills to prevent and defuse conflict. Quite simply, they use language badly.

What are the odds that you use confrontational language? Almost 100 percent. The use of confrontational language is a part of being human. We all do it, and in fact that means that chances are we can all stop doing it if we learn better ways to communicate. When we stop using confrontational language, we start getting along better with those around us. We appear less difficult. We end up more respected, and people want to work with us, not against us.

So, here's the deal. If you want to reduce how difficult you appear to be, you can do that by changing how you use language. We are going to teach you how to do that, but first you have to understand a bit of psychology.

What's Their Problem?

You need to understand what kinds of things set people off. Once you know the triggers that start conflict, you can work to eliminate the specific language and words associated with them. So let's start.

Lack of Listening/Understanding

One of the primary reasons people talk to others is a desire or need to be understood and to feel accepted. We all want to feel listened to. We prefer that people agree with us, but our primary desire is to be understood.

Employee Handbook

Confrontational language
tends to encourage others to see us as on the other side. This kind of language creates unnecessary and destructive conflict or can cause existing small conflicts to turn into forest fires.

From the Manager's Desk

Apart from appearing attentive, one way to tell the other person you are listening and understand is to use reflective listening. Reflect back what you heard this way: "If I understand what you're saying, you would like more time to do this job, is that right?"

When two people talk and one perceives that the other is not making an effort to understand, frustration and anger often result. The person feeling misunderstood is likely to escalate his or her efforts, increasing the intensity of the discussion. This kind of conversation can be a relationship killer. So one thing you need to do to become less difficult is start listening and demonstrating your understanding of another person.

"Less-than" Communication

We know that any language or action that somehow demeans or suggests one person is *"less than"* another person tends to trigger an emotional reaction. Many of the specific characteristics of confrontational language relate to this idea of comparing someone to someone else or putting someone down.

Employee's Handbook

"Less-than" communication refers to any comments or questions that hint that the other person is stupid, or otherwise less than yourself or other people. They are almost always about the person. Comments about behavior are better.

What's interesting is that we needn't be outright abusive to set somebody off. Our language contains hundreds, perhaps thousands of ways to suggest to someone they are unworthy, less than, or insignificant. It's pretty obvious that saying "You're a pea-brained idiot whose arms drag on the ground" is meant to be demeaning or insulting. What most people don't realize is that everyday language used by all of us can convey that message in subtle ways.

For example, what reaction wells up inside you when someone says "Whatever!" in response to something you said? Is it a good, friendly response? Or do you want to bite off that person's head?

The reason people act so emotionally to this rather trivial word is that it sends a message or even a set of nasty messages. It says, "You aren't important enough for me to bother listening to you." It says, "What you say is so trivial, and so are you right now." Here's another example. Someone says to you,

> "If you were really a loyal employee, you would work the overtime we're asking you to put in."

Doesn't that drive you nuts? Why? Because indirectly it says that the boss sees you as a disloyal person. Maybe the boss doesn't really *mean* that, but that's how it tends to be interpreted.

If you want to become less difficult, you need to learn to reduce the use of any language that suggests a person is less than or unworthy or trivial.

That doesn't mean you can't comment on work or even provide criticism now and then. You can. In fact, you may have an obligation to do so. What it does mean is that you have to make sure your comments pertain to behavior and not personality traits. That's the way to stay out of trouble.

Communicating Mistrust

Probably for reasons linked to the "less-than" thing earlier, people have a great deal of difficulty with language that suggests they are untrustworthy or unreliable.

This one is interesting because even when people are clearly unreliable in the workplace, pointing that out to them is likely to start a shooting war if you use the wrong kind of language.

Imagine you work with Sam. Sam isn't terribly good at time management or keeping his commitments. Let's assume you're working on a project together. If he is late with his part, you won't be able to do your part, and you'll catch heat from the higher-ups.

So you approach Sam, in good faith, hoping to remind him of the importance of getting the work done on time. You say:

"Sam, just so I know, you *will* get this done on time, won't you?"

This Won't Work!

Beware the accidental brush-off. Saying "whatever" to someone is a brush-off. So is not paying attention to the person, reading the newspaper while someone is talking. Be particularly alert if you are distracted. That's when accidental brush-offs are most likely to occur.

Insider Secrets

One of the real challenges is to work to improve someone's performance when they need it without giving them the impression you don't trust them or have confidence in them. Try your best to be gentle about it, and be helpful. But sometimes a poor performer is going to get upset regardless of how well you communicate with him or her. Guess it just goes with the territory.

How do you think Sam will react? Probably not very well, because you're sending the message that you don't trust him or you have little confidence in him. Nobody is fooled by the question. You didn't really want to get an answer. You wanted to send a message, and it got received. And it starts fires you don't need.

Can you think of a better way, a more cooperative way? Here's one.

> "Sam, I know the senior VP really wants to get this done on time, and we're going to look bad if we're late. Can we set up a way of tracking the project so we're sure we can get it in on time?"

Now isn't that better? Of course it is. And it's all in the words and phrasing.

Violation of Conversation Rules

This one's easy. Cultures have different rules of conduct for conversations. In North America, generally you're expected to take turns speaking, wait your turn, avoid bellowing, and so on. Your responses should tie in to what the other person said. If you interrupt, scratch your private parts, or read the newspaper when someone is speaking to you, you'll create bad feelings. Of course, if you live in New York, the scratching and interrupting is normal, but go figure (just a little joke).

So you need to conform to the general rules of courtesy that apply in your workplace, in your geographical location, and in your country.

From the Manager's Desk

Different cultures and even different geographic areas have somewhat different ideas of what constitutes civil communication. It's a challenge to know what those rules are. It's good to try to learn, particularly when you have a very diverse workplace. Sometimes it's worth asking.

Blatant Generalizations

Blatant generalizations are essentially overstatements or exaggerations, and usually contain words like "always," "never," and "every time." The major reason generalizations mobilize resistance and cause people's messages to go unheard is that they are almost always wrong. After all, what in life really occurs every time, each and every time? Not much in the area of human affairs and behavior.

When a speaker uses generalizations or overstatements, listeners tend to look for ways to attack the "always" position or poke holes in the argument. While they're doing that, they aren't listening anymore as they prepare to present their counterargument.

Generalizations are really bad when aimed at a particular person. For example, saying, "You know, every time I talk to you, you argue with me," is quite likely to start an argument about whether that's true. It really annoys people.

Power/Status-Based Communication

Power-based or *status-based communication* refers to communication that relies on the power or status of the speaker to pressure or convince the other person. For example, a person with an advanced degree (like a Ph.D.) might mention their degree to try to intimidate someone into accepting what they have to say. A similar statement would be: "I'm the boss around here and we're going to do it my way." No reasons are given, it's arbitrary sounding, and comes across as, well, bossy.

Insider Secrets

You may be the boss, but that doesn't mean you should be bossy or pushy or use your power all the time. A manager who relies on power to get work done ends up working too hard to keep the troops in line. When the manager is away, the employees tend to slack off without the "threat" of the manager around.

Another type of power-based communication is ordering people around and telling them they must do this, or they have to do that. Most adults hate this with a passion, even if it does come from the boss.

You need to tell someone what he or she has to do but you don't want to sound unreasonable or that you are using your power. Can you figure out how to do that so the person still understands?

Replacing Confrontational Language with Cooperative Language

What phrases and words do you need to stop using, and what can you replace them with? Let's begin with the power/status-based communication.

Move from Power to Cooperation

We want to move away from power- or status-based conversations and giving orders to a more cooperative, we're-on-the-same-side use of language. First, here are some examples of the things we don't want to say:

1. You *have* to do this by Monday.

2. I'm the boss, and it's my way or the highway.

3. What you need to do is file this under "mail."

From the Manager's Desk

It's the more competent, more confident, and better managers who use cooperative language rather than ordering people around. If you rely on orders and commands and power, you might want to see whether you need to develop your management skills through reading and training.

Let's change the first one. We're going to expand it, soften it, and change it from a *you* statement and an order to an *I* statement that sounds better. But it will still be understood.

> "I really need this on my desk by ten on Monday because it has to go upstairs right away. If you have any concerns about having it ready by then, let me know, and we'll see what we can do."

Employees understand this to mean it must get done on time, but it's communicated in a let's-work-together way.

How about the second one? There are times when managers need to make decisions. Heck, someone has to do it. But the important part is to not sound like Attila the Hun when you communicate it. What's a better way? How about this?

> "We've tried to come to some agreement but haven't succeeded. Because we need a decision right now and I'm the one responsible for the decision, this is the way we'll go for now."

Isn't that a better way to talk? No throwing your weight around. No rubbing a person's face in your power.

And let's look at the third. Rather than telling a person what they need to do (particularly when you haven't been asked), you can use a question form to soften the effect. For example:

> "My guess is it makes sense to file this under 'mail,' but if you have a better idea, let me know, so I know where to look."

Are you getting the idea here? Almost anything can be softened so it sounds cooperative. Cooperative phrasing still gets the job done. And when you start moving away from confrontational language you start being seen as a really great manager who isn't difficult at all.

Get Rid of the Mistrust Stuff

Whether you trust a person or not, it's not a good thing to throw that mistrust or lack of confidence in someone's face. In fact, to do so often creates a self-fulfilling prophecy. People tend to live up to (or down to) what others expect from them. So we want to eliminate most of the mistrust statements. But we still may need to address issues related to reliability, so we need to replace mistrust statements with something else.

Insider Secrets

It's a strange human quirk. The more you show your mistrust of someone, the less they like you, and the less they trust you, even though the facts are clearly behind you. Being right doesn't guarantee cooperation, but cooperative language really does help.

Here's the ticket. We will use more helpful task-oriented phrasings. It's no guarantee a person won't start to bristle, but it's better than banging them on the head. Here are some mistrust statements:

➤ I'll be back in an hour to make sure you've kept your promise.

➤ Because you aren't very good at finishing on time, I want you to report your progress to me every day.

Let's change the first one from confrontational mistrust to a cooperative request. You could say:

"This is a challenging task you have. Perhaps I'll drop by in an hour to see whether there is anything I can do to help, because we really need to get this done."

We can deal with the second one in a similar way. We'll move from insulting someone to offering help.

"Because the VP is on my back to get this done on time, I'd like to be in on what you're doing. Maybe I can help out if something comes up. How about if we meet briefly every morning for a status check?"

Here, we've moved the emphasis from the employee to the idea that we are working together. The manager offers help. And rather than order the person around, the manager phrases the status check as a question.

It's not that hard, is it? But it does take thinking.

Shed Blatant Generalizations

You just have to get rid of these; I order you to. You always use them! No wait. Let me rephrase. Perhaps you'll find that if you eliminate blatant generalizations, you will end up having fewer arguments. People may find you less difficult and easier to communicate with.

From the Manager's Desk

The use of qualifier words softens statements. *Qualifiers* are words like "perhaps," "sometimes," "it's possible," "it might be," and "it could be." They make it appear that you're reasonable and open to comment. They are the opposite of blatant generalizations.

Yes, that's it. It's true. This is a really easy one. Banish the words "always," "never," "every time," and similar absolute words to the same place where bad words go. You don't use the F word or the S word or any other of the seven words you can't say out loud. Neither is it going to help you if you use these absolute words.

There is one exception. When there is something of significant importance that *must* be done, then you can use these words to emphasize the importance. For example, it's OK to say:

"If you see a fire in progress you must always pull the fire alarm and exit the building immediately."

That's a fine thing to say. You can't say, "You might sometimes perhaps consider leaving the building," can you? They must. Just don't overuse these kinds of absolutes.

Lose Phrases that Cause Defensiveness

Some wordings and phrases cause people to feel defensive or intimidated. And while using them may give your ego a nice boost, they don't tend to build good relationships. If you have a communication style that tends to make people uncomfortable, they will see you as difficult and become more difficult themselves. What are some examples of phrases that are pretty much guaranteed to cause defensiveness?

➤ Why in the world would you say that?

➤ What makes you think that ...?

➤ How in the world did you come to that conclusion?

What to replace them with? Let's do the first one. The problem with this is the "why in the world" part. It implies the other person is stupid or nuts or something. One way of making it better is to say, "Why would you say that?" But that is still intimidating to at least some people. So here's an even better one.

> "I might be missing something here because I'm not sure I understand what you are saying. Could you explain a bit more for me?"

How about the second one? Instead of "what makes you think that …?" you can soften it this way:

> "I'm sure you have some good reasons to take that position. It would really help me if you could tell me what they are so I can understand better."

See the difference? We're going to get the same information by being cooperative sounding. In fact, we're probably going to get better information by doing so, because the person is likely to feel less threatened and speak more honestly because of it.

This Won't Work!

If someone says something dumb or odd, blaming them for it isn't likely to clarify what they meant or help them understand why it was dumb. Neither is trying to intimidate them or humiliate them.

More Fixing Up

That's a good start so far, but we have more language fix-up techniques for you. We'll start with a common complaint many employees have. Their bosses never seem to realize they aren't infallible.

Infallibility Breeds Contempt

Infallibility comments are questions or statements that sound as if the speaker believes he or she couldn't possibly be wrong. When people sense that a speaker is high and mighty or believes in his or her own infallibility, there is a tendency to try and bring that person down a peg. People stop listening and gather the resources needed to attack this "perfect" person.

You want to come across as confident but not perfect or infallible. Here are a couple of examples from an infallible-sounding person:

➤ I never make mistakes like that.

➤ I couldn't possibly have misplaced that report. You must have lost it.

➤ I've read all the literature on this; have you?

So how can we change the first one? Simple. Admit to being fallible. Change it to:

> "I'm pretty sure I didn't make a mistake, but maybe I should go back and check so we can figure out what happened."

Insider Secrets

Confident managers don't feel the need to appear perfect. Most of the best managers I've ever met have no difficulty admitting when they've made a mistake and don't try to come off as perfect—which is one reason they are good managers. Being open to the possibility they may be wrong, they learn constantly and improve constantly. And they win over their staff, because nobody likes someone who appears arrogant or "has all the right answers."

That's less likely to cause additional argument or make the speaker sound like an arrogant twit. It's a good way to say it, even if you are absolutely sure you didn't make an error (but, hmmm, are you really absolutely sure?).

We can fix up the second example by sticking to the facts and focusing on problem solving.

> "I don't believe I misplaced the report. Maybe we can backtrack. I recall leaving it on your desk on Monday. Do you remember seeing it there? If not, maybe someone's borrowed it without letting us know."

Notice that apart from avoiding the infallibility problem, it also allows the other person to save face, if in fact he or she has misplaced it.

Hints for Improving at Cooperative Communication

Because most of us have never been taught the ins and outs of language, all of us have some language habits that are less cooperative than they might be. Hopefully by now, you've realized that for every way of putting things in a confrontational way, there is a way of putting things in a cooperative way. And by doing so you get better results, and are seen as more helpful and less difficult.

Let's end this chapter with some suggestions so you continue to get better. First, moving to eliminate the confrontational language you use takes some time and attention, but it's not impossible. It takes perseverance and paying attention to what you're saying, particularly at the beginning. After a while you get into new and better language habits, and the better words will come out more automatically. But at the beginning, you need to pay attention to how and what you say.

Second, if you want to communicate more cooperatively, try to change your language in all settings, including at work and at home. Cooperative communication techniques work almost anywhere. It's hard to change habits in one place while talking differently in another.

From the Manager's Desk

The key to changing how you communicate is to do it little by little. It isn't difficult but it requires attention and perseverance. It's going to take time to change communication habits you've been using for decades. Remind yourself daily.

Finally, when working to change the words and phrases you use, do so little by little. For example, start with one type of confrontational language (say, power-based phrases). Decide that for the next six weeks you're going to work on reducing them and replacing them with more cooperative options. Do that. Succeed at that. When you have succeeded, try another area. And keep working at it.

Good luck!

The Least You Need to Know

➤ You want to be a conflict-preventer, not a conflict-starter.

➤ Confrontational language makes it seem as though you and the other person are on opposite sides.

➤ Cooperative language makes it seem as though you and the other person are on the same side (and that's good).

➤ You can replace confrontational ways of communicating with cooperative ones.

➤ To become less difficult and more cooperative sounding takes attention and perseverance, but it isn't impossible.

Glossary

A-1 executive decision   A decision that you make as a manager with formal power and authority.

abuse and personal attacks   Behaviors designed to demean, belittle, harass, or insult another person. They can be "in your face" and include things like swearing, yelling, threatening, or intimidating, or they can be a bit more subtle, where the attacks are implied.

Alternate Dispute Resolution (ADR)   Techniques by which parties in a conflict can try to resolve their differences informally, including mediation and arbitration. Also known as *Alternative Dispute Resolution*.

arbitration   A process where a third party gets the facts of the issue from each party, then makes a binding decision on behalf of both parties and the organization.

assertive limit setting   Setting limits for a person's behavior and setting out the consequences if that behavior continues.

attention deficit disorder   The term used to describe children (and now adults) who have low attention spans, are generally above average in intelligence, tend to be impulsive and disorganized, and are generally difficult to manage (ADD for short).

back-channel communication   Communicating about someone behind his or her back. It ranges from gossip to intentional defamation, from fairly harmless to very dangerous. Back-channel communication can erode the sense of trust in the workplace and encourage employees to take sides, which can destroy team spirit.

backroom politicking   A technique some venomous people use to erode your support internally through the use of back-channel communication, often with others in the company at the same level or the levels above you.

backstabber   A person who maliciously gossips about others.

blaming mind-set   A way of thinking that finds someone at fault, rather than focusing on preventing the problem from occurring.

boss cultivation   The long-term process of helping the boss get to know you and develop respect for your contributions, integrity, and character.

collaborative approach   An approach often called a win-win situation because the parties look for and achieve a solution that may exceed the expectations of both of the parties. They work towards that by defining the problem, negotiating, and generally working together towards a set of stated common goals.

compromise   Resolution of a conflict in which neither of the parties will get all of what they want, but both will get something of what they want. In compromise mode, the two parties are still working in adversarial mode.

conciliatory gestures   Things said that indicate movement of position to a more cooperative stance. They include apologizing, taking responsibility, expressing positive feelings, and similar expressions.

congruency   The match between a person's words and actions that determines the degree to which that person is considered trustworthy.

consistency   The predictability of a person's words and actions over time that determines the degree to which that person is considered trustworthy.

confrontational language   Conflict-provoking communication; language that tends to encourage others to see us as on the other side.

conversation rules   Code of conduct for conversations generally accepted as appropriate and followed by people in a specific culture or geographic area, governing such matters as participation, interaction, language, volume, and topics.

cooperative language   Conflict-preventing communication; language that tends to help other people see us as on the same side as themselves.

credit-stealing boss   A boss who usually takes credit for work done by those working for him or her and places the blame on staff when things go wrong.

cueing   Focusing a person's attention on some relevant and important results of his or her own behavior.

difficult person   Someone whom you or others do not like to interact with, due to stubbornness, abusiveness, or other difficult behavior. Difficult people get in the way of getting work done, and cause stress for others.

difficult-person vicious cycle   The situation that develops when two or more people consider each other to be difficult and then react negatively, causing an unpleasant interaction to grow progressively more difficult, as behavior becomes worse on both or all sides.

emotional feedback   Information about the emotional reactions of others toward the person or his or her behavior.

empathy responses   Things you can say that show that you understand the emotions of the person you are talking to.

factual feedback   Information about the results or outcomes of the person's behavior that is based on factual observations (what you see or hear or touch, for example).

feedback   Information about the effects of one's actions on others or on achieving results. It comes from outside the person, either from other people or naturally in the process of doing a task.

formal authority tools   Things you can do because you're in management, giving you more power and authority as a result. Examples might include taking disciplinary action, laying down the law, and using performance-management techniques.

garden-variety difficult person   Someone whose behavior you consider difficult, but not in ways that are intentionally harmful, although the results may be quite destructive.

guerrilla attacks   Attacks that occur behind your back, often among other employees.

indicators of violence   Signs that a person has the potential to be violent. These are possible clues, not evidence. Even experts are not very good at predicting workplace violence. The most reliable indicators will cause more prediction errors than prediction hits.

infallibility comments   Questions or statements that sound as if the speaker believes he or she couldn't possibly be wrong. Such comments generally cause others to stop listening and start attacking.

initial approach   The bedrock or foundation of creating a win-win situation; the first contact made by the manager towards the employee to present the option of working together and to get a commitment to do so.

insubordination   Deliberate refusal to do specific job tasks or reasonably alter job-related behavior.

interactivity   The degree to which two people can interact in real time.

less-than communication   Comments or questions that hint that the other person is stupid or otherwise less than the person speaking or others. "Less-than" communication is almost always about the person; it's better to focus on behavior.

managing conflict   A process used to minimize the negative aspects and effects of the conflict and maximize the positive aspects and effects.

mediation   A process in which a third party works with two people who are in conflict or cannot settle an issue themselves and brings them together to negotiate their own solution in a nonadversarial, noncoercive way.

no-fault Teflon co-worker   A person who is never responsible when things go wrong; it's always the fault of someone else or some other part of the organization. On the other hand, Teflon people have no problem accepting praise.

norms   Rules of conduct used by group members to guide their behavior. They can be explicit (formally written) or informal.

nutso boss   A boss who has certain characteristics and/or personal issues that cause him or her to treat other people in destructive, unpleasant ways. The nutso boss can't change because the reasons he or she acts badly are personality-related.

ongoing performance communication   A two-way process to track process, identify any barriers to performance, and provide feedback to employees.

outright sabotage   Attempts to interfere with the work of another person or the reputation and perceptions associated with the targeted person.

passive-aggressive   Term used to describe a person who has trouble expressing anger and denies it when he or she is angry, but then sends nonverbal messages that convey that anger.

performance management   An ongoing communication process, undertaken in partnership between an employee and his or her immediate supervisor, that involves establishing clear expectations and understandings about work results and work behavior.

performance planning   An annual (or more frequent) discussion between the manager and each individual employee to discuss his or her job responsibilities, goals, and any other expectations the manager has for his or her employees.

performance review   A meeting between employee and manager usually used to discuss how the employee has done over the past year (sometimes more often).

personality conflict   A term too often used to describe a problem with a difficult person. People who use this label are giving up control and giving up on the situation. We don't have difficulties with someone because of his or her personality; it's because of his or her behavior and your reactions.

personalized conflict   Conflict that has become focused on the other person's behavior, difficulty, personality, style, or other things that are not directly linked to a disagreement about business or task issues. The parties entertain a dislike and lack of respect for the other person.

problem-solving mind-set   An attitude of focusing on the present and the future, and focusing on solving problems, not finding fault.

progressive discipline   A series of steps that involve progressively firmer warnings and sanctions coupled with providing opportunities for the employee to address unacceptable behavior.

qualifier   A word or a phrase used to soften a statement, such as "perhaps," "sometimes," "it's possible," "it might be," or "it could be." Qualifiers suggest that you're reasonable and open to input from others.

reflective listening   A technique a person can use to show that he or she is listening attentively and to ensure accurate understanding. The person might reflect back what he or she heard like this: "If I understand what you're saying, then you would like more time to do this job, is that right?"

reinforcement   An event that follows after a behavior and that increases the probability that the behavior will be repeated. Non-psychologists usually equate reinforcement with reward.

resource hog   A person who is so focused on his or her own work unit that others suffer. Not team players or systems thinkers, resource hogs often do what they do because they really want to do a good job, but their focus is too narrow.

returning responsibility   Communicating to the employee that he or she is expected to be an active participant in problem solving.

self-talk   What we say to ourselves, in our heads. Self-talk reminds us how we should react and behave in various situations.

substantive conflict   Conflict that occurs as a result of a real (or apparent) disagreement about how things should be done, who should do it, or similar areas. Its roots are based in the premise that two well-meaning people can sincerely disagree about something.

ultimatum   A last resort for dealing with difficult people; a power play in which a person is gambling on his or her value to the organization. Because an ultimatum is basically a threat, people tend to take it personally and that generally works against the person delivering the ultimatum. Never issue an ultimatum unless you are prepared to leave immediately.

unreasonably demanding boss   A boss who, through cluelessness or inefficiency, makes impossible demands to get work done in an unrealistic time frame.

venomous difficult person   A person who behaves in destructive ways with the intent of causing damage to others around him or her.

victim mentality   A state of mind, often a feeling of helplessness, that ends up attracting difficult people and behaviors. Adopting a victim mentality makes things worse.

whistle-blower   A person who attempts to inform others about illegal or dangerous practices occurring in his or her workplace.

win-win   The term used when both parties to a problem or disagreement construct a solution that is good for everyone involved—in other words, nobody loses.

work-killer colleagues   Colleagues whose difficult behaviors interfere with your ability to get work done. They aren't just annoying; they lower productivity throughout a company.

Additional Resources

Websites

The following Internet Web sites are devoted to managing difficult people, verbal abuse, or other topics related to this book.

Work911 Supersite (Robert Bacal), www.work911.com

Huge site containing many articles on various aspects of managing difficult people, including topics like performance management, dealing with verbal abuse, and communication tips. This is the author's main site.

Mediation Training Institute International (Dan Dana),
www.mediationworks.com

Probably the best site on mediation, Dan was our resource for the chapter on mediation in this book.

World Verbal Self-Defense League (Dr. Suzette Haden Elgin),
www.worldvsdleague.com

Noted author of a number of excellent books on dealing with verbal abuse and difficult people (Verbal Self-Defense Series), Dr. Elgin now has a Web page.

Internet E-Mail Discussion Lists

E-mail discussion lists are great for getting help fast, and sharing information with others. All you need is the ability to use e-mail. For most lists you need to "subscribe" by sending an e-mail to a particular address. We've given the instructions for each discussion list.

For more information on these and other lists, go to www.work911.com/lists.html

Dealing With Difficult People Discussion List

Set up for readers of this book, and others interested in the topic. Get help with your specific difficult person, and help others. To join, send an e-mail to

difficultpeople-subscribe@egroups.com

Performance Management & Appraisal Discussion List

Here is the list to join if you want to learn more about these subjects. Experts galore to help, and someone will have an answer to your performance management or appraisal question. To join, send an e-mail to

perfmgt-subscribe@egroups.com

Workplace Communication Discussion List

For the discussion of all aspects of communication at work, and keep in mind that good communication is at the core of dealing effectively with difficult people. Small list, not too many messages. To join, send an e-mail to

workcomm-subscribe@egroups.com

Conflict At Work Discussion List

For discussion of all aspects of conflict at work, the good, the bad, and the ugly. Some great people participate in this group, ready to offer help. To join, send an e-mail to

workcon-subscribe@egroups.com

Books

Elgin, Suzette Haden, *How to Disagree Without Being Disagreeable: Getting Your Point Across With the Gentle Art of Verbal Self-Defense*, John Wiley & Sons, 1997.

Suzette is a noted psycholinguist, sci-fi writer, and originator of the term "verbal self-defense." This is the twelfth book in the Gentle Art of Verbal Self-Defense Series. All of her books are useful.

Fisher, Roger; William Ury; and Bruce Patton, (Editor). *Getting to Yes: Negotiating Agreement Without Giving In.* Penguin USA, 1991.

Fisher and Ury are among the acknowledged experts on negotiation. This book is part of their work and one of the most popular books at Amazon.com. Low-priced and readable. If you can read only one book on negotiation, read this one or another by the same authors.

Ury, William. *Getting Past No: Negotiating Your Way from Confrontation to Cooperation.* Bantam Doubleday, 1993.

Another great little book on negotiating.

Levine, Stewart. *Getting to Resolution: Turning Conflict into Collaboration.* Berrett-Koehler Pub; 1998.

Gives readers a set of tools for resolving personal and business conflicts.

Thompson, Dr. George; and Jerry B. Jenkins. *Verbal Judo: The Gentle Art of Persuasion.* Quill; 1994.

Dr. Thompson has a doctorate in English and has worked as a law enforcement officer. His books are readable in plain language. While his work is ideal for law enforcement, I recommend this book for everyone. If these techniques can work in law enforcement, they can work anywhere!

Index

A

A-1 executive decisions, 98
abusive attacks, venomous people, 133-135
actions, perception of others based on your actions, 303
ADD (attention deficit disorder), 40
addressing own reactions of annoying co-workers, 234-236
ADHD (attention deficit hyperactive disorder), 40
agreements (mediations), 124
alternative tips for dealing with difficult bosses, 191
annoying co-workers
  addressing own reactions, 234-236
  changing self perceptions, 236
    self-talks, 236-238
appeals, 203
  boss's boss, 203-204
  human resources, 204
appraisals, performance reviews, 108-109
arbitrations, 124
  process, 125
  versus mediations, 126
assertive limit settings (personal attacks), 93-94
assessments, consequences of difficult bosses, 196-197
attacks
  guerrilla, 24-25
  management, 24
  personal, 92
    assertive limit settings, 93-94
    privately, 93
    public attacks, 94

attention deficit disorder. *See* ADD
attention deficit hyperactive disorder. *See* ADHD
authority tools, 71-72
  appropriate usages, 73-74
  overusage of powers, 72-73
authority underminer co-workers, 245-246
avoiding conflict management, 254-255

B

back door approaches, credit-stealing bosses, 213
back-channel
  behaviors, 26
  gossip (behavioral management), 94
    behavior modeling, 95
    group pressure mobilizations, 95
    skill building, 96
backroom politicking, 138
backstabbing co-workers, 243-245
bad conflicts, 252-253
behavioral changes
  managers, 301
    altering personality, 301
    mind-set, 302
  workplace violence, 176-177
behavioral management
  back-channel gossip, 94
    behavior modeling, 95
    group pressure mobilizations, 95
    skill building, 96
  complainers, 89
    beginning processes, 90
    empathy responses, 91

returning responsibilities, 91-92
  meeting disrupters, 97-98
  naysayers, 98-99
  performance management, 102
    data collections, 107-108
    documentations, 107
    group issues, 110-112
    misconceptions, 103-104
    ongoing performance communications, 106-107
    performance planning, 104-105
    productivity issues, 109-110
    reviews, 108-109
    venomous people, 141
    win-win situations, 144-153
  work and responsibility avoiders, 96-97
behaviors
  blaming, 21-22
  chronic versus occasional difficult behaviors, 26-27
  focusing vs. labeling, 19-20
  garden-variety difficult people, 68
  managers
    listening mind-sets, 59
    lowest common denominators, 57-58
    slowing of speech, 58-59
    time-outs, 59
  manipulation techniques
    back-channel behaviors, 26
    direct work related, 24
    guerrilla attacks, 24-25

interpersonal behaviors, 25

management attacks, 24

rewards of difficult behaviors, 37
center of attention, 38-39
reaction from others, 39
sense of control, 37-38

self evaluation indicators, 292-294

tools for dealing with difficult employees
formal authority tools, 71-74
interpersonal tools, 70-71
prevention tools, 74-76

understanding, 31-32
biological factors, 39
emotional states, 35-36
lack of social skills, 34-35
learned behaviors, 33

benefits of self evaluations, 291-292

biological factors, 39
ADD, 40
ADHD, 40

blaming
difficult people, 21-22
mind-sets, 55-57

blatant generalizations (conflict triggers), 316

bosses, 184. *See also* managers
conflict
resolutions, approach process, 267-269
consequences of difficult bosses, 195
assessment, 196-197
personal considerations, 198-199
credit-stealing, 209
tips to dealing with behaviors, 210-213
cultivation of relationships, 263
principles, 264-266
egomaniacs, 185
illegal activities, 221-222
communication process, 226-227

gray-area illegal acts, 227-229
options to dealing with activities, 223-226
policy violations, 229
rumor vs. facts, 222-223
jelly-fished out bosses, 184
nice addicts, 186
paranoid bosses, 185
substance abusers, 185
tip for dealing with difficut bosses, 186-194, 199-208
appeals, 203-204
conduct business publicly, 189
connections within company, 187-188
documentation of interactions, 189
learning what drives your bosses, 192
linking goals to bosses problems, 192
living with it, 207-208
low profiles, 189
negotiating a solution, 206-207
pitches, 193-194
productive mind-sets, 190-191
quitting, 199-203
sabotages, 205-206
unreasonable demanding bosses, 214-217
breakthroughs (mediation process), 122

C

center of attention (reward of difficult behavior), 38-39
characteristics
garden-variety difficult people, 68
venomous difficult people, 130-131
chronic versus occasional difficult behaviors, 26-27
collaborative approaches, conflict management, 259-261
collecting data (performance management), 107-108

commitments
avoiding unachievable commitments, 306-307
win-win situations, 152
communication
performance, 106-107
process, dealing with bosses illegal activities, 226-227
communication methods, 276
differences
formality, 278
interactivity, 277
speed of communications, 276
spontaneity, 278
e-mail, 281-282
lost e-mails, 283
privacy issues, 284
reflection of feelings, 283
usage tips, 284-285
face-to-face, 278-279
written, 280-281
communication styles, 311
conflict triggers, 313
blatant generalizations, 316
demeaning comments, 314
lack of listening, 313
mistrust, 315
power-based communications, 317
violation of conversation conduct, 316
confrontational, 312-313
replacing with cooperative communications, 317-322
cooperative, 312-313
improving, 322-323
company
channels, dealing with bosses illegal activities, 224
initiatives (workplace violence), 177-178
policy violations (bosses), 229
ramifications of difficult people's actions, 7-8

complainers (behavioral management), 89
  beginning processes, 90
  empathy responses, 91
  returning responsibilities, 91-92
compromises (conflict management), 257
conducting business publicly, 189
conflict resolutions, 116
  arbitrations, 124
    process, 125
    vs. mediations, 126
  mediations, 117
    decision process, 118-120
    facilitation of discussions, 121-124
    logistics, 121
    preliminary meetings, 120-121
    suitability questions, 118
conflicts, 249
  bad, 252-253
  co-workers
    boss involvement, 267-269
    help sources, 270-272
  good, 251-252
  management options, 254
    avoidance, 254-255
    collaborative approaches, 259-261
    compromises, 257
    denials, 254-255
    giving in, 256
    power-based approaches, 258
  personalized, 250-251
  starters vs. preventers, communication styles, 311-313
  substantive, 250
  triggers, 313
    blatant generalizations, 316
    demeaning comments, 314-315
    lack of listening, 313
    mistrust, 315-316

power-based communications, 317
status-based communications, 317
violation of conversation conduct, 316
ugly, 253
confrontation
  avoidance (choosing victimhood), 13-14
  results of adding fuel to the fire, 11-12
  languages, replacing with cooperative communications, 313-322
    eliminating blatant generalizations, 320
    eliminating defensive statements, 320-321
    eliminating infallibilities, 321-322
    mistrust elimination, 319
    removing power-based communications, 317-318
  versus cooperation, 312-313
congruency (managers), 306-310
  decision-making, 307-308
  management approach and demeanor, 308-309
  perception of others, 304-306
  promises and commitments, 306-307
consequences
  difficult bosses, 195
    assessments, 196-197
    personal considerations, 198-199
  garden-variety difficult people, 69-70
consistency (managers), 306-310
  decision-making, 307-308
  management approach and demeanor, 308-309
  perception of others, 304-306

  promises and commitments, 306-307
constructiveness, 59-60
contracts
  explicit, 157
  implicit, 157
control issues, rewards of difficult behaviors, 37-38
cooperative communications
  improving, 322-323
  versus confrontational, 312-313
corporate
  initiatives (workplace violence), 177-178
  policy violations (bosses), 229
co-workers
  annoying and frustrating behaviors
    addressing own reactions, 234-236
    changing self perceptions, 236-238
  conflicts
    boss involvement, 266-270
    help sources, 270-272
  ramifications of difficult people's actions, 5-7
  work-killers, 238
    authority underminers, 245-246
    backstabbers, 243-245
    insensitive co-workers, 241-242
    no-fault co-workers, 243
    resource hogs, 239-241
    turf warriors, 246
credit-stealing bosses, tips to dealing with behaviors, 209-213
  back door approaches, 213
  meetings, 211-212
  objective thinking, 210-211
  ultimatums, 213
cueing, 84
customers, ramifications of difficult people's actions, 5-7

D

data collections, performance managements, 107-108
decision-making, making timely decisions, 307-308
defensiveness (confrontational language), 320-321
demanding bosses, tips for dealing with behaviors, 214-217
  educating, 214-215
  organization of roles, 217
  pitches, 216
  ultimatums, 217
demeaning comments (conflict triggers), 314
demeanor (managers), 308-309
denials (conflict management), 254-255
difficult people, 4
  avoiding becoming a victim, 10
  behavioral management
    back-channel gossip, 94
    complainers, 89
    meeting disrupters, 97-98
    naysayers, 98-99
    performance, 102
    venomous people, 141
    work and responsibility avoiders, 96-97
  chronic versus occasional, 26-27
  conflict management options, 254
    avoidance, 254-255
    collaborative approaches, 259-261
    compromises, 257
    denials, 254-255
    giving in, 256
    power-based approaches, 258
  costs to co-workers and customers, 5-7
  costs to managers, 4-5
    loss of time, 4
    physical and mental health, 4

costs to the organization, 7-8
inaction, 10-11
labeling, versus focusing on behaviors, 18-20
manipulation techniques, 23
  back-channel behaviors, 26
  direct work-related behaviors, 24
  guerrilla attacks, 24-25
  interpersonal behaviors, 25
  management attacks, 24
performance management, 102
  data collections, 107-108
  documentations, 107
  group issues, 110-112
  misconceptions, 103-104
  ongoing performance communications, 106-107
  performance planning, 104-105
  productivity issues, 109-110
  reviews, 108-109
results of confrontation, 11-12
rewards of behaviors, 37
  center of attention, 38-39
  reaction from others, 39
  sense of control, 37-38
understanding behaviors, 31-32
  biological factors, 39
  emotional states, 35-36
  lack of social skills, 34-35
  learned behaviors, 33
value, 8
  insightful thoughts, 8-9
  provoke others to look closer at themselves, 10
direct feedback, 82
disbelief (choosing victimhood), 13

disciplinary issues
  legalities, 158-160
  progressive discipline, 160
    final warnings, 162
    oral warnings, 160-161
    terminations, 162
    written warnings, 161
dismissals
  progressive disciplines, 162
  violent behaviors
    employees, 169-170
    preventative measures, 170-174
documentations
  dealing with difficult bosses, 189
  performance management, 107

E

e-mail communications, 281-282
  lost e-mails, 283
  privacy issues, 284
  relection of feelings, 283
  usage tips, 284-285
educating demanding bosses, 214-215
egomaniac bosses, 185
emotional
  feedback, 79-81
  states, 35-36
empathy responses (managing complainers), 91
explicit contracts, 157

F

face-to-face communications, 278-279
facilitation of mediations, 121
  breakthroughs, 122
  framing agreements, 124
  roles of mediators, 122-123
facilitative feedback, 82-83
factual feedback, 79-81
federal laws, 157
feedback, 78-79
  emotional, 79-81
  factual, 79-81

guidelines for giving, 85
    framing, 87
    overload avoidance, 86
    positive and negative
        balances, 86
    recipient controls, 85
    specifics, 86
informal, self evaluations,
    294-297
sources, 81
strategies, 81
    direct, 82
    facilitative, 82-83
    tasks, 84
"fight or flight" phenomenon
    (choosing victimhood), 15
final warnings (progressive
    discipline), 162
firing employees
    progressive disciplines, 162
    violent behaviors
        employees, 169-170
        preventative measures,
            170-174
follow-ups, win-win situa-
    tions, 152-153
formal authority tools, 71-72
    appropriate usages, 73-74
    overusage of powers, 72-73
framing
    agreements (mediations),
        124
    providing feedback, 87
frustrating co-workers
    addressing own reactions,
        234-236
    changing self perceptions,
        self-talks, 236-238

G

garden-variety difficult peo-
    ple, 68
    behaviors, 68
    consequences of behaviors,
        69-70
giving in (conflict manage-
    ment), 256
good conflicts, 251-252
gossip (back-channel)
    behavior modeling, 95

group pressure mobiliza-
    tions, 95
    skill building, 96
gray-area illegal acts, 227-229
groundwork for quitting jobs,
    200-201
group pressure mobilzations
    (back-channel gossip), 95
guerrilla attacks, 24-25
guidelines for providing feed-
    back, 85
    framing, 87
    overload avoidance, 86
    positive and negative bal-
        ances, 86
    recipient controls, 85
    specifics, 86

H

help sources (co-worker con-
    flicts), 270-272
human resources, appeals,
    204

I

illegal activites, bosses,
    221-222
    communication process,
        226-227
    company channels, 224
    gray-area illegal acts, 227,
        229
    ignoring, 223-224
    law enforcement agencies,
        226
    policy violations, 229
    rumor vs. facts, 222-223
implicit contracts, 157
inaction, 10-11
indicators
    self evaluations, 292-294
    workplace violence, 175
        behavioral changes,
            176-177
        obsessions, 176
        personal indicators, 175
infallibilities (confrontational
    language), 321-322
informal feedback, self evalua-
    tions, 294-297

initial approaches (win-win
    situations), 147-149
insensitive co-workers,
    241-242
insubordinations, 136
interactivity of communica-
    tion methods, 277
interpersonal
    behaviors of difficult peo-
        ple, 25
    tools, 70-71
interpretations (laws), 158
intervention avoidance
    (choosing victimhood),
    14-15

J-L

jelly-fished out bosses, 184

labeling difficult people,
    18-19
    versus focusing on behav-
        iors, 19-20
lack of social skills, 34-35
languages (communication
    styles), 312-323
    conflict triggers, 313
        blatant generalizations,
            316
        demeaning comments,
            314
        lack of listening, 313
        mistrust, 315
        power-based communi-
            cations, 317
        violation of conversa-
            tion conduct, 316
    confrontational, 312-313
        replacing with coopera-
            tive communications,
            317-322
    cooperative, 312-313
        improving, 322-323
law-enforcement agencies,
    illegal activities of bosses,
    226
laws, 156
    disciplinary issues, 158-160
        progressive disciplines,
            160-162
    environmental safety
        issues, 163-164

explicit contracts, 157
federal, 157
implicit contracts, 157
interpretations, 158
local, 156
sexual harrassment,
163-164
learned behaviors, 33
less-than communications
(conflict triggers), 314
lies, venomous people tactics,
139-140
listening mind-sets (man-
agers), 59
local laws, 156
logistics (mediations), 121
low profiles, dealing with
difficult bosses, 189
lowest common denomina-
tors, 57-58

M

management
conflicts, 254
avoidance, 254-255
collaborative
approaches, 259-261
compromises, 257
denials, 254-255
giving in, 256
power-based
approaches, 258
understanding behaviors
emotional states, 35
lack of social skills,
34-35
learned behaviors, 33
workplace violence prevention, 178-179
managers. *See also* bosses
appropriate behaviors
avoidance of lowest
common denomina-
tors, 57-58
listening mind-sets, 59
slowing of speech, 58-59
time-outs, 59
attacks, 24
guerrilla attacks, 24-25
personal, 92

behavioral management
back-channel gossip,
94-96
complainers, 89-92
meeting disrupters,
97-98
naysayers, 98-99
venomous people,
141-153
work and responsibility
avoiders, 96-97
changing behaviors, 301
altering personality, 301
mind-set, 302
communication styles
conflict triggers, 313
confrontational,
312-313
cooperative, 312-313
conflict resolution, 116
arbitrations, 124-126
mediations, 117-124
confrontation, 11-12
constructiveness, 59-60
employee perception, 302
actions, 303
congruency, 304-310
trustworthiness, 303-304
words, 303
feedbacks, 78
direct, 82
emotional, 79-80
facilitative, 82
factual, 79
guidelines for giving,
85-87
task, 84
illegal activities
disciplinary actions,
158-162
law enforcement agency,
226
laws, 156-158
options to dealing with
activities, 223
unsafe work environ-
ments, 163
inaction, 10-11
mind-sets, 54-55
blaming, 55-57
problem-solving, 55-57
nutso bosses, 184

performance management,
102
data collections,
107-108
documentations, 107
group issues, 110-112
misconceptions,
103-104
ongoing performance
communications,
106-107
performance planning,
104-105
productivity issues,
109-110
reviews, 108-109
personal attacks, 92
assertive limit settings,
93-94
privately, 93
public attacks, 94
ramifications of difficult
people's actions, 4-5
loss of time, 4
physical and mental
health, 4
responsibilities, 48
mediations, 50
productivity, 48
staff welfare, 49
self assessment of behav-
iors, 45-46, 289-294
behavioral indicators,
292-294
benefits, 291-292
changing behaviors,
47-48
informal feedback,
294-297
performance reviews,
297-299
reactions from others,
46-47
self-interests, 50-51
self-talks, 61
negative, 61-62
positive, 62-63
tools for dealing with
employee behaviors
formal authority tools,
71-74

interpersonal tools, 70-71
prevention tools, 74-76
victim mentality, 10-12
avoiding intervention, 14-15
confrontation avoidance, 13-14
disbelief, 13
"fight or flight" phenomenon, 15
necessity of action, 15
violence in the workplace, 168-169
predictability, 174-176
preventative measures, 177-179
terminations, 169-173
manipulation techniques
difficult people, 23
back-channel behaviors, 26
direct work-related behaviors, 24
guerrilla attacks, 24-25
interpersonal behaviors, 25
management attacks, 24
venomous difficult people, 133
abuse and personal attacks, 133-135
backroom politicking, 138
lies, 139-140
outright sabotages, 136-137
mediations, 50, 117
decision process, 118-120
facilitation of discussions, 121
breakthroughs, 122
framing agreements, 124
roles of mediators, 122-123
logistics, 121
preliminary meetings, 120-121
suitability questions, 118
versus arbitrations, 126
meeting disrupters (behavioral management), 97-98

meeting phase (win-win situations), 150-152
meetings, 211-212
credit-stealing bosses, 212
mediations, 120-121
methods of communication, 276
differences
formality, 278
interactivity, 277
speed of communications, 276
spontaneity, 278
e-mail, 281-282
lost e-mails, 283
privacy issues, 284
reflection of feelings, 283
usage tips, 284-285
face-to-face, 278-279
written, 280-281
mind-sets, 54-55
blaming, 55-57
listening, 59
problem-solving, 55-57
productivity, 190
alternatives, 191
expectations, 191
focus on work, 190
misconceptions (performance management), 103-104
mistrust (conflict triggers), 315
modeling of behaviors, back-channel gossip, 95

N

naysayers (behavioral management), 98-99
negative self-talks, 61-62
negotiating with difficult bosses, 206-208
nice addict bosses, 186
no-fault co-workers, 243
norms, 74-75
self policing, 75-76
nutso bosses, 184

O

objective thinking, dealing with credit-stealing bosses, 210-211
obsessions (workplace violence), 176
occasional versus chronic difficult behaviors, 26-27
ongoing performance communications, 106-107
options for dealing with difficult bosses, 199
appeals, 203-204
living with it, 207-208
negotiating a solution, 206-207
quitting, 199-203
sabotages, 205-206
oral warnings, progressive disciplines, 160-161
organizations
channels, dealing with bosses illegal activities, 224
initiatives (workplace violence), 177-178
policy violations (bosses), 229
ramifications of difficult people's actions, 7-8
outright sabotages, 136-137
overloads, feedback, 86

P

paranoid bosses, 185
passive-aggressive persons, 306
performance management, 102
data collections, 107-108
documentations, 107
group issues, 110-112
misconceptions, 103-104
ongoing performance communications, 106-107
performance planning, 104-105
productivity issues, 109-110

reviews, 108-109
performance planning,
  104-105
performance reviews
  appraisals, 108-109
  self evaluations, 297-299
personal attacks, 92
  assertive limit settings,
    93-94
  privately, 93
  public attacks, 94
  toward managers, 43-45
  venomous people, 133-135
personal indicators (workplace violence), 175
personality changes (man-
  agers), 301
personalized conflicts,
  250-253
pitches, 193
  dealing with demanding
    bosses, 216
  tips, 193-194
policy violations, bosses, 229
politicking, 138
positive self-talks, 62-63
power-based
  approaches (conflict man-
    agement), 258
  communications (conflict
    triggers), 317
predictability (workplace violence), 174
preliminary meetings (mediations), 120-121
preventative measures
  violent terminations,
    170-174
  workplace violence,
    172-177
    corporate initiatives,
      177-178
    management initiatives,
      178-179
principles, boss cultivation,
  264-266
privacy issues, e-mail communications, 284
private attacks, 93
problem-solving mind-sets,
  55-57

productive mind-sets, tips for
  dealing with difficult bosses,
  190
  alternatives, 191
  expectations, 191
  focus on work, 190
productivity
  managers responsibilities,
    48
  performance management,
    109-110
  tips for dealing with diffi-
    cult bosses, 190
    alternatives, 191
    expectations, 191
    focus on work, 190
progressive discipline steps,
  160
  final warnings, 162
  oral warnings, 160-161
  terminations, 162
  written warnings, 161
promises, avoiding unachievable promises, 306-307
public attacks, 94

Q-R

quitting jobs, 199-200
  groundwork, 200-201
  ultimatums, 202-203

ramifications (difficult
  people's actions)
  co-workers and customers,
    5-7
  managers, 4-5
    loss of time, 4
    physical and mental
      health, 4
    organization, 7-8
recipients (feedback), control
  of feedback, 85
relationships with bossess,
  cultivation principles,
  263-266
resolution of conflicts, 116
  arbitrations, 124
    process, 125
    versus mediations, 126
  mediations, 117
    decision process,
      118-120

facilitation of discus-
  sions, 121-124
logistics, 121
preliminary meetings,
  120-121
suitability questions,
  118
versus arbitrations, 126
resource hogs, 239-241
responsibilities (managers), 48
  mediations, 50
  productivity, 48
  staff welfare, 49
responsibility avoiders
  (behavioral management),
  96-97
returning responsibilities
  (management of complainers), 91-92
reviews, performance,
  108-109
rewards of difficult behaviors,
  37
  center of attention, 38-39
  reaction from others, 39
  sense of control, 37-38
roles, mediators, 122-123

S

sabotages, 136-137
  bosses, 205-206
safety issues of workplace,
  legalities, 163-164
self evaluations (managers),
  45-46, 289-294
  behavioral indicators,
    292-294
  benefits, 291-292
  changing behaviors, 301
    altering personality, 301
    mind-set, 302
  informal feedback, 294-297
  performance reviews,
    297-299
  reactions from others,
    46-47
    changing behaviors,
      47-48
  recognizing how others
    perceive you, 302
    actions, 303

congruency, 304-310
trustworthiness, 303-304
words, 303
self perceptions, annoying co-
workers
addressing self reactions,
236
changing perceptions, 236,
238
self policing norms, 75-76
self-interests (managers),
50-51
self-talks, 61
changing perceptions of
annoying co-workers,
236-238
negative, 61-62
positive, 62-63
sense of control (reward of
difficult behaviors), 37-38
sexual harrassment, legalities,
163-164
slowing of speech, managers,
58-59
social skills, 34-35
solution phase (win-win situations), 152
sources of feedback, 81
speech (managers), 58-59
speed (communication methods), 276
spontaneity (communication
methods), 278
staff welfare, managers
responsibilities, 49
status-based communications
(conflict triggers), 317
steps of progressive discipline
final warnings, 162
oral warnings, 160-161
terminations, 162
written warnings, 161
strategies (feedback), 81
direct, 82
facilitative, 82-83
tasks, 84
styles of communication
conflict triggers, 313
blatant generalizations,
316
demeaning comments,
314
lack of listening, 313

mistrust, 315
power-based communi-
cations, 317
violation of conversa-
tion conduct, 316
confrontational, 312-313
replacing with coopera-
tive communications,
317-322
cooperative, 312-313
improving, 322-323
substance abuse bosses, 185
substantive conflicts, 250

T

task feedback, 84
techniques (interacting with
difficult bosses), 191
learning what drives your
bosses, 192
linking goals to bosses
problems, 192
pitches, 193-194
techniques (manipulation)
difficult people, 23
back-channel behaviors,
26
direct work-related
behaviors, 24
guerrilla attacks, 24-25
interpersonal behaviors,
25
management attacks, 24
venomous difficult people,
133
abuse and personal
attacks, 133-135
backroom politicking,
138
lies, 139-140
outright sabotages,
136-137
terminations
progressive disciplines, 162
violent behaviors
employees, 169-170
preventative measures,
170-174
time-outs, managers, 59
tips for dealing with difficult
bosses, 186

conducting business pub-
licly, 189
connections within com-
pany, 187-188
credit stealing bosses
back door approaches,
213
meetings, 211-212
objective thinking,
210-211
ultimatums, 213
demanding bosses
educating, 214-215
organization of roles,
217
pitches, 216
ultimatums, 217
documentation of interac-
tions, 189
low profiles, 189
productive mind-sets, 190
alternatives, 191
expectations, 191
focus on work, 190
tools
formal authority, 71-72
appropriate usages,
73-74
overusage of powers,
72-73
interpersonal, 70-71
prevention, 74
creating norms, 74-76
triggers (conflicts), 313
blatant generalizations,
316
demeaning comments,
314-315
lack of listening, 313
mistrust, 315-316
power-based communica-
tions, 317
status-based communica-
tions, 317
violation of conversation
conduct, 316
trustworthiness (managers),
perception of others,
303-304
turf warriors, 246

U

ugly conflicts, 253
ultimatums, 202-203
  credit-stealing bosses, 213
  demanding bosses, 217
understanding behaviors,
  31-32
  biological factors, 39
  emotional states, 35-36
  lack of social skills, 34-35
  learned behaviors, 33
unreasonable demanding
  bosses, 214
  educating, 214-215
  organization of roles, 217
  pitches, 216
  ultimatums, 217

V

value (difficult persons), 8
  insightful thoughts, 8-9
  provoke others to look
    closer at themselves, 10
venomous difficult people
  behavioral management,
    141
  characteristics, 130-131
  manipulation techniques,
    133
    abuse and personal
      attacks, 133-135
    backroom politicking,
      138
    lies, 139-140
    outright sabotages,
      136-137
  win-win situations, 144
    advantages, 144-146
    commitments, 152
    disadvantages, 146
    follow-ups, 152-153
    initial approaches,
      147-149
    meeting phase, 150-152
    solution phase, 152
    suitability questions,
      147

victim mentality, 10-12
  avoiding intervention,
    14-15
  confrontation avoidance,
    13-14
  disbelief, 13
  "fight or flight" phenome-
    non, 15
  necessity of action, 15
violence in the workplace,
  168-169
  indicators, 175
    behavioral changes,
      176-177
    obsessions, 176
    personal, 175
    workplace behaviors,
      176
  predictability, 174
  preventative measures,
    169-177
    corporate initiatives,
      177-178
    management initiatives,
      178-179
    termination related,
      169-170

W-Z

warnings (progressive discipline)
  final, 162
  oral, 160
  written, 161
whistle-blowers, 159
win-win situations, 144
  advantages, 144-146
  commitments, 152
  disadvantages, 146
  follow-ups, 152-153
  initial approaches, 147-149
  meeting phases, 150-152
  solution phase, 152
  suitability questions, 147
work avoiders (behavioral
  management), 96-97
work-killer co-workers, 238
  authority underminers,
    245-246
  backstabbers, 243-245

insensitive co-workers,
  241-242
no-fault co-workers, 243
resource hogs, 239-241
turf warriors, 246
workplace violence, 168-169
  indicators, 175
    behavioral changes,
      176-177
    obsessions, 176
    personal indicators, 175
    workplace behaviors,
      176
  predictability, 174
  preventative measures,
    169-177
    corporate initiatives,
      177-178
    management initiatives,
      178-179
    termination related vio-
      lence, 169-170
written communications,
  280-281
written warnings (progressive
  disciplines), 161

yielding (conflict management), 256